The Tiger Moth Story

by

ALAN BRAMSON

and

NEVILLE BIRCH

With a Preface
by
Sir Alan J. Cobham, K.B.E., A.F.C.

D0914782

AIR REVIEW LIMITED
LETCHWORTH
HERTS ENGLAND

By the same authors:
Flight Briefing for Pilots (Vols. I, II, III and IV)
A Guide to Aircraft Ownership

U.S.A. Library of Congress Catalog Card No. 79 – 141822

SBN 902853 00 7

Printed in Great Britain by
The Sidney Press Limited
Bedford, England

DH 82 Tiger Moth K2579, one of the original batch ordered by the Air Ministry that went to 3 F.T.S., R.A.F. Grantham.

G-EBKT, the prototype DH 60 Cirrus Moth, may perhaps be regarded as the first really practical light aeroplane.

Preface

BY SIR ALAN J. COBHAM, K.B.E., A.F.C.

The Tiger Moth can be put in that rare category of aircraft which have lived through perhaps half the life of aviation. There are a number of these wonderful aeroplanes, such as the Avro 504K which was in active use from 1912 to about 1930; the DC 3 came into being around 1935 and is still going strong; the Avro Anson which came into service in 1935 is still being used; and there is the Tiger Moth which started life in the early thirties and is still flying in considerable numbers. This famous aeroplane has gone on year after year being used all over the world, predominantly as a training aircraft. There are many reasons for its success —one would suggest the low initial purchase price, its supreme reliability and above all it is a good aeroplane in which to train a pilot to fly. In the early years of aviation we all suffered from the fear of engine failure, but the coming of the Gipsy engine was the beginning of motors that made it possible for a pilot who was not a mechanic to fly a Moth single-handed across the world, knowing that he had a reasonable chance of getting to his destination without the engine breaking down.

Many readers will be surprised to learn that although nearly nine thousand Tiger Moths were produced, no book has ever been devoted to its remarkably varied life. Perhaps this is because it has gone on quietly over the years doing its job without fuss or bother. Not all of its duties were without hazard, particularly its operational flying, and much of the information in the pages that follow has resulted from fresh lines of historical research. Many of the stories will be new even to those who pride themselves as knowledgeable on the subject of the Tiger Moth, but it is the very casual way of its coming into being that is so fascinating.

Of all its exploits, and there seems to be no end to their variety, the Tiger Moth's greatest role is undoubtedly that of a trainer. It is therefore appropriate that the writers of this story should be joint authors of the official civil flying training manuals.

This book relates the story of the Tiger Moth's birth, youth, military service and return to civil life, and in so doing it will conjure up for many pleasant reminiscences, not the least of which is the sound of the wind in the wires, at the same time paying a fitting tribute to this remarkable aeroplane.

Authors' Foreword

It wasn't the prettiest aeroplane of its day and in some respects its construction could be considered almost crude. Many would claim that it doesn't handle as well as some other aeroplanes of similiar vintage, that it is cold and draughty even by open cockpit standards, and above all has the unflattering habit of magnifying whatever minor faults its pilot may possess in his flying technique. Yet notwithstanding this somewhat bleak assessment of its characteristics, the Tiger Moth was to endear itself to countless thousands of pilots from every nation imaginable and far outlive its contemporaries and other light trainers of more modern design. For although more than thirty years have elapsed since its inception, the Tiger Moth is with us today, crop spraying in New Zealand, barnstorming at air displays all over the world, and nursing the inexperienced pupil pilot during his first faltering hours of solo flight with the many Aero Clubs that still offer the 'Tiger' to their members.

That the Tiger Moth should have become one of the immortal names in aviation is made the more surprising when it is realized that few if any epic flights have been made on the type. Perhaps it is the old story of the 'son of the famous father', etc., for it almost seems as though the Tiger has been content to rest on the laurels of its forefathers, the famous Cirrus and Gipsy Moths which at one time broke every record and accomplished the incredible in long distance 'plane flying. No, the Tiger Moth's achievement is one of service in the main with a little of the spectacular thrown in here and there.

What makes a successful aeroplane? The answer is not easy to define but we would say that in common with a work of art or a highly regarded motor-car each ingredient contributes something of importance. Undoubtedly circumstances play their part and many an otherwise good aeroplane has failed to hit the jackpot by having committed the cardinal error of appearing on the scene at the wrong time in history.

There have been many admirable books devoted to the more glamorous aeroplanes of the past. In its own way the Tiger has, in our opinion, a rightful place amongst the greatest. In telling its story we have delved into a period when flying in this country was at its most colourful, and we hope that many readers able to remember those days will recapture the magic atmosphere of the pre-war Aero Club, the great travelling Air Displays of Sir Alan Cobham and the later wartime Grading Schools and Elementary Flying Training Schools. That some 8,800 Tigers were built gives us 8,800 good reasons for writing this book.

A.E.B.
N.H.B.

Contents

To our wives
Miriam and Patricia
whose patience, encouragement and
practical assistance have made so
vital a contribution to this book

Illustrations

In the preparation of the Log of Tiger Moths registered in 1970, the
Publishers have gratefully received information and assistance from owners,
organisations large and small, and from many enthusiastic individuals world-
wide. All this information has been carefully checked and recorded to bring
the Log up to date, and where possible to provide the original service number
or manufacturer's number of each machine. Despite the help received, this
has been no easy task, for even while going to press, reports are still coming in
of ownership changes and registration transfers. No claim is made that the
Log is complete regarding ALL Tiger Moths still in existence, and in this
light the Publishers ask for details of all machines not included. This information will be printed on an insert slip, which will be sent free of charge to all
purchasers of The Tiger Moth Story in due course.

Acknowledgements

Additional to our own first-hand experience of the Tiger Moth we have had the good fortune to amass a wealth of factual information from a great number of contributors living in many parts of the world who have written us letters, some passages from which are quoted in this book. We should like to express our gratitude to these contributors without whose help a book such as this could not have been written. In most cases it has been possible to include their names in the relevant parts of the text, but in addition our sincere thanks go to Sir Geoffrey de Havilland and the directors of the de Havilland division of Hawker Siddeley for their encouragement and for making available the files of the de Havilland Gazette. We greatly value the assistance we have received from C. Martin Sharp and Wing Commander C. A. Pike, O.B.E., A.F.C., F. S. C. Plumb of de Havilland Aircraft of Canada Ltd., E. J. Hunt and R. W. Jamieson of Hawker Siddeley International New Zealand Ltd., and Major Hereward de Havilland, Miss E. Popko and Mr. L. M. Gardiner of Hawker de Havilland Ltd. Australia.

In our search for Queen Bee information we have been materially assisted by Sir George Gardner, C.B., C.B.E., D.Sc., F.R.Ae.S., G. Harding of Air Ministry Archives and Wing Commander N. Capper, A.F.C.

We are indebted to Major-General Christie, C. in C.

ACKNOWLEDGEMENTS

Royal Norwegian Air Force, Squadron Leader G. Reid, D.F.C., Wing Commander G. E. Lowdell, D.F.M., H. P. Maskell, W. A. Webb, W. E. A. Cullum, C. F. Franks, B. Robertson, L. Hunt, Arthur E. Hagg, Hubert Broad, R. W. Cantello and Wing Commander 'Henry' Hall.

Our call for assistance was adequately met by Mrs. M. E. Phillipps, A. E. O. Pierce and D. C. Bateman of the Air Ministry Air Historical Branch and C. C. H. Cole, Information Division of the Air Ministry.

We thank Air Britain for their good offices, in particular Peter W. Moss for permission to use information from Vol. II of his Impressments Log and J. Bagley, B.Sc., for assistance with registrations and other information. Other contributions have emanated from Malcolm D. N. Fisher, C. Nepean Bishop, K. Hamnet, O.B.E., J. G. Baus of Sabena, A. Deverell of Rollason Aircraft and Engines Ltd., Captain J. Crewdson, F.R. Met.S., A.R.Ae.S. of Film Aviation Services Ltd., J. H. Blake of the Royal Aero Club, Squadron Leader J. E. Doran-Webb and R. Prizeman, D.C.Ae., A.M.I.Mech.E., A.F.R.Ae.S.

Our gratitude to Sir Alan Cobham, K.B.E., A.F.C., for writing the foreword. We also extend our thanks to those fortunate owners of Tiger Moths still flying, who have kindly provided photographs of their aircraft and thus enabled us to give additional coverage of the subject.

Finally, our sincere thanks to the Directors and Editorial staff of Air Review Ltd and their associates who, between them, have compiled the "LOG" of every Tiger Moth known (to the best of their ability) to have a current C of A as at the end of September 1970. (To the owner of any Tiger Moth omitted from the list we tender our apologies). We greatly appreciate also, their efforts in arranging for updated information we have provided, to be included at the end of most of the chapters in this third, and considerably enlarged edition.

1. The Family Tree

It was one of those sunny days which create such an impression that years later we complain that our summers are not as pleasant as they used to be. Such is the behaviour of human memory that we tend to minimize the discomforts of the past and highlight experiences such as those glorious summer days of years ago. Yet this one was real enough and, thus encouraged, a number of us were picknicking on the lawn outside one of the well-known flying clubs in the Home Counties. Every now and then a visiting aircraft would arrive or a local 'plane depart to another club. An Airedale landed and taxied up to the club followed by a sleek fighter-like Comanche painted in some exotic colour-scheme of doubtful taste but undisputed brilliance. Suddenly our attention was diverted by a sound alien amongst the modern light 'planes. It was the unmistakable 'pop, pop, pop' of a throttled back Gipsy engine, and sure enough a Tiger Moth swept in to land but a few yards away from the line of parked aircraft.

It was just another visiting Tiger so far as the younger club members were concerned, but to those connected with flying and old enough to remember the year 1931 it represented something quite different. Like vintage motor-cars, famous elderly aeroplanes have a habit of bringing back memories, and as the little Tiger parked between a diminutive Turbulent and the sleek Comanche one couldn't help but notice the pensive look of those who would never see forty again. Some thought of the hotted-up versions so skilfully flown by the spirited Tiger Club and the many Tigers, some good and others not so good, still in every day use at clubs all over the world, whilst others recalled their immediate post-war years with the R.A.F.V.R. One of the gathering thought back to the 1939–45 period and wondered what had happened to Dizzy Bearsby and Dusty Miller and all the others at Shellingford and similar Elementary Flying Schools. Then there were the pre-war days at Brooklands—Geoffrey Tyson and his superb performances on the Tiger at Sir Alan Cobham's Air Displays —and Hubert Broad who flew the first-ever Tiger Moth.

One or two of the members had by now walked over to greet the visiting pilot who was extracting himself from the rear cockpit. How old was this Tiger? Was it made by de Havillands or Morris Motors? Did it see service in this country or was it stationed in Australia or Southern Rhodesia? Perhaps it was an old pre-war club machine. . . . If only it could talk! But it is as well that it could not because it would recall hard years at the hands of pupil pilots in two shades of blue and others in khaki, followed by a still longer period of hammering at a flying club. It would instance the day that X dropped it from the height of a hangar whilst practising landings—treatment that would wreck a less robust aeroplane.

But to be really familiar with the sequence of events that gave us the evergreen Tiger, recalling our pleasant reminiscences on the club lawn is not enough; we shall have to put the clock back again and review the early nineteen twenties, or perhaps even earlier times.

There is an old saying to the effect that, were it not for unreasonable men, nothing would ever be accomplished in this world of ours. Perhaps it is nearer the truth to say that those who are in the forefront of progress often push their own security to the background. And so it was with the young Geoffrey de Havilland. With little or no knowledge of aerodynamics and only half-promises of financial assistance he gave up a steady position with an acceptable future and turned his thoughts to the building of his No. 1 Biplane. Like the Wright Brothers he was soon to realize that the success of the project depended to a large extent on finding a suitable engine, and his training as an engineer enabled him to design his own aero engine, which he then had built by the old Iris Car Company. It seems that his grandfather was not only understanding but uncommonly far-sighted, for the old gentleman advanced £500 to Geoffrey de Havilland so that he might relinquish his job with a reputable firm of automobile engineers and set about building an aeroplane— this in the days when they were looked upon as new-fangled contraptions only fit for madmen to meddle with.

The frail machine was assembled in a small shed near Newbury, Berkshire, and in May 1909 its first flight resulted in a brief hop, whereupon it broke up and was wrecked beyond repair. Fortunately de Havilland was uninjured, save for a damaged wrist occasioned when he signalled his well-being from the wreckage and collected a sharp blow from the still rotating propeller. It is indicative of the courage of the man that he chose this time, when his fortunes were at a low ebb, to get married.

Looking back it is perhaps not surprising that so many of the early attempts to fly should have ended in failure, for there were no flying schools in existence and, indeed, hardly any previous experience of flight to call upon. The designer had to teach himself to pilot by trial and error. A famous pioneer aviator of those days, the late Otto Lilienthal, would often say, 'To design a flying machine is nothing; to build is something; to test it is everything.' These words were certainly true, for little was known at the time about stability and most of the early wire-and-stick machines were capricious in the extreme.

If de Havilland was undaunted by his early failure, grandfather at least matched him in spirit, for on hearing of the setback he announced that since he intended leaving his grandson £1,000 he might as well have the other £500.

Backed by this additional money, Geoffrey de Havilland designed and built Biplane No. 2, and his tenacity was rewarded by a successful first flight on 10th September 1910. Indeed, his achievements soon came to the notice of the authorities when the Government bought his aeroplane for £400 and gave him a job as an aircraft designer at Farnborough.

A brief period in the Royal Flying Corps during the early days of the Great War led to his being seconded to the Aircraft Manufacturing Co. Ltd. at Hendon where he produced some of the most successful designs of that period. It is not generally realized that during World War I a very considerable part of the American Air Force was equipped with an aeroplane of his design, the DH 4, and that many of the 4,800 built in the U.S.A. were in use until 1929.

With the winding down of production that inevitably followed the Armistice, the Aircraft Manufacturing Company rapidly ceased its activities. His reputation as a brilliant aircraft designer and the combined qualities of quiet confidence and far-sightedness that have always distinguished Geoffrey de Havilland enabled him to raise £20,000 and form the de Havilland Aircraft Company Ltd. at Stag Lane aerodrome, Edgware, an old airfield that had been the home of a flying school for some years.

Activity was confined to 'civilianizing' old wartime aeroplanes, and many of the early passenger services were flown with somewhat grotesque-looking converted DH 4's. Life at Stag Lane was very hand to mouth in those days with work coming through the shops in dribs and drabs. Private aeroplanes and private pilots were practically non-existent, and anyone wealthy enough to consider an aeroplane for his own use would have little or no ready-made market at his disposal, so that it was very much like buying a new suit—the aeroplane was tailor-made for the customer. It was just such a transaction that was to have the most profound effect on the destiny of the still young de Havilland Company. A wealthy sporting pilot by the name of Alan S. Butler

The prototype DH 51, de Havilland's first attempt at breaking into the private aeroplane market.

The DH 53 Humming Bird. Painted in the original blue and silver colour-scheme with the name in French as it appeared at the Brussels Aero Show of 1923, the diminutive Humming Bird makes its first take-off at Hatfield in the hands of Chris Capper after being rebuilt in 1960.

Many of the personalities connected with the early days of the Tiger Moth are shown in this photograph taken in September 1960. *Left to right*: Sir Geoffrey de Havilland, W. E. Nixon, F. T. Hearle, C. C. Walker, Sir Alan Cobham, A. E. Hagg and Captain Hubert Broad. The wooden hut behind the Humming Bird was the de Havilland Aircraft Company's Head Office at Stag Lane in 1920, and is now preserved as a museum.

The Family Tree

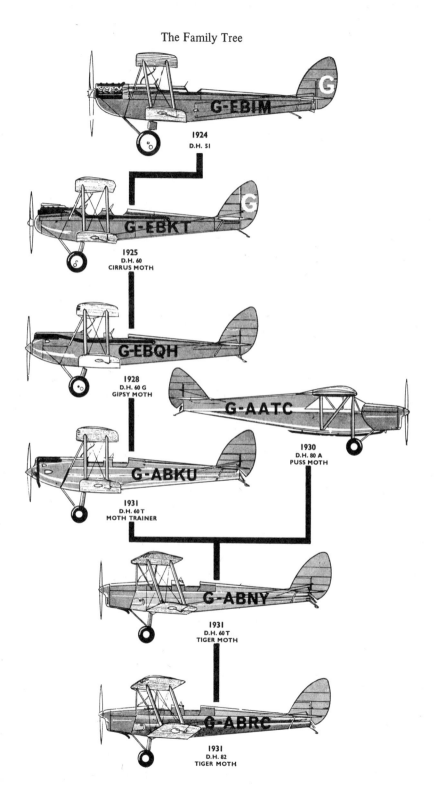

G-EBIM

1924
D.H. 51

G-EBKT

1925
D.H. 60
CIRRUS MOTH

G-EBQH

1928
D.H. 60 G
GIPSY MOTH

G-AATC

1930
D.H. 80 A
PUSS MOTH

G-ABKU

1931
D.H. 60 T
MOTH TRAINER

G-ABNY

1931
D.H. 60 T
TIGER MOTH

G-ABRC

1931
D.H. 82
TIGER MOTH

approached de Havillands with an inquiry for a private touring aeroplane. A design was prepared and the result emerged as the DH 37, a handsome-looking biplane that was fitted with a Rolls Royce Falcon engine of 275 h.p. Butler took delivery of his aeroplane and became one of the first private owners in the country. So pleased was he with his new mount that he inquired, quite casually, if de Havillands would like any additional finance since he was prepared to invest in the Company. It was an opportune request, for the enterprise was faced with the need to purchase the freehold of Stag Lane aerodrome—the offer was readily accepted.

The DH 37 as bought by Butler was a typical 'small' aeroplane of the period, with its massive engine originating from the Great War. In effect the aeroplane was as large and powerful as the R.A.F. fighters of the day, and as such hardly likely to do much to popularize flying in the eyes of the general public.

Many minds were turned to the engaging thought of providing an aeroplane inexpensive to buy and run, so that the man-in-the-street could contemplate private ownership. With this object in view the Lympne Trials were arranged in 1923, and de Havillands rose to the occasion with the DH 53 Humming Bird, a tiny single-seater aeroplane powered by a Douglas motor-cycle engine. The Air Ministry placed a small order for the type and used it for communication duties. Later one took part in some rather frightening experiments when it was suspended underneath an airship and released in flight, later to re-attach itself to the mother ship. Nevertheless de Havillands had little faith in the Humming Bird as a serious means of transport, nor for that matter could they see it as the answer to their quest for 'everyman's aeroplane'.

Somewhat reluctantly a certain Mr. Alan Cobham agreed to fly one over to the Continent so that it might take its place on the de Havilland stand at an aeronautical exhibition in company with a notice to the effect that it had actually flown the Channel!

With so little power, fuel and in consequence range was strictly limited and it was necessary to refuel the diminutive machine at Lympne airport before leaving the coast. From all accounts Cobham was somewhat embarrassed at having to ask the petrol crew to fill his two-gallon fuel tank; but worse was to come, for, battling against a headwind on the return journey, the Humming Bird was overtaken by, of all things, a Belgian goods-train. On landing back at Stag Lane Cobham is said to have expressed his opinion of the aeroplane in somewhat forthright terms, no doubt adding weight to the lack of affection de Havillands had for this product of the Lympne Trials.

In the following year a competition was arranged by the Air Ministry for two-seater designs with engines limited to a maximum capacity of 1,150 c.c. Such an engine is little bigger than that to be found in a modern miniature car, and it should be remembered that in 1924 engines were developing less power for a given size than they do now. Many of the modern materials that we now take for granted were non-existent at the time, so that, whereas to the modern designer weight must be saved in the interest of added range or pay-load, during the 1924 competition a few pounds here and there, using an engine of such low power as that stipulated by the Air Ministry, could actually mean the difference between flying and remaining on the ground. Because of these problems and remembering the not very satisfactory outcome of the Lympne Trials, de Havilland himself decided not to take part in the Air Ministry competition but to devote his energies to a design which was the company's first serious attempt to build an inexpensive aeroplane suitable for private ownership and with practical touring capabilities.

In many ways the aeroplane may be regarded as the great-grandfather of the Tiger Moth. Certainly the DH 51, as it was called, was unmistakably Moth-like in appearance, and it was to set the fashion in small aeroplanes for many years to come.

Some ingenious features were incorporated in the DH 51.

It was a conventional enough looking biplane in its original form with two bays, although later machines had the wing-span reduced by five feet and single pairs of inter-plane struts. The fuselage was plywood covered and two cockpits were arranged, the rear one with a single seat for the pilot. Two passengers could be accommodated tandem fashion in the larger front cockpit, and it was possible to make the opening smaller by pulling back the windscreen which was attached to a sliding portion of the fuselage top decking. In this way draughts were minimized when only one passenger was carried. A Tiger Moth-type, spring-loaded trimmer was used.

Determined efforts were made to keep down the price of the aeroplane so that it might appeal to a large section of the public. Vast quantities of war surplus aero engines were on the market at the time, and de Havillands were able to purchase a number of R.A.F. 1a engines at the incredible price of 14/6 each! The R.A.F. 1a developed 90 h.p. and was an air-cooled V8 engine. On the prototype it drove an enormous four-bladed propeller 8 ft. 9 in. in diameter. In these days when the V8 engine is considered as something of an achievement in motor-cars, it is perhaps surprising to realize that such engines existed in aeroplanes during the 1914–18 War.

Although the engine had been designed and built by the Royal Aircraft Establishment, the authorities confined the DH 51 to flying within the vicinity of Stag Lane Aerodrome because by this time dual ignition was considered necessary for civil aeroplanes and the R.A.F. 1a was not possessed of this refinement. Rather than face the cost of modifying the engine and obtaining type approval, de Havillands re-engined the DH 51 with an Airdisco motor of 120 h.p. which was in reality a much improved version of the war-time 80 h.p. Renault design. If the Airdisco engine vastly enhanced the performance of the DH 51, it shattered de Havillands vision of an inexpensive private aeroplane. Disappointing as this must have been to the manufacturers, the aeroplane deserves its place in aeronautical history as the link between the heavy military-type biplane of the nineteen twenties and the private light 'plane of today.

The first Airdisco-engined DH 51 took part in the 1925 Kings Cup Race, although fog prevented the course being completed. Later it was to be the first aeroplane to land on the cliff-top at John O'Groats. A later version known as the DH 51a even sported automatic camber-changing flaps —a very advanced refinement in those days.

The fifth and last of the DH 51 aeroplanes to be built was purchased by a Mr. Carberry of Mombasa, and was named 'Miss Kenya'. To this day it may be seen in immaculate condition, flying with a current C. of A. from Wilson Field, Nairobi, with the registration VP-KAA. As such it is believed to be the oldest de Havilland aeroplane still flying—the great-grandfather of all the Moths!

Looking back there is little doubt that were it not for the difficulties that arose with the authorities over the use of war surplus engines at 14/6 a time, many more DH 51's would have been sold and the resultant chain of events may have led to an aeroplane quite different from the Tiger Moth.

By now de Havillands had reached the conclusion that, whilst the little Humming Bird had been too small to be practical, the DH 51 with the 120 h.p. Airdisco engine represented the other extreme and was too large for the private owner. Nevertheless the experience gained from these two designs was to prove invaluable to Geoffrey de Havilland and his colleagues, enabling them to draw up a clear set of requirements for the ideal private aeroplane. They commenced the design with these thoughts in mind:

1. The engine must not weigh more than 350 lbs. and it should develop 60 h.p.
2. It must be a two-seater with dual control.
3. There must be a space for week-end luggage.
4. It must be easy to fly and capable of operating from relatively small fields.
5. It must have a genuine 80 m.p.h. cruising speed.
6. It must carry sufficient fuel for three hours flying.

7. The wings must fold to facilitate hangarage in small sheds and towing behind a car.
8. It must be inexpensive both in first and running costs.

A problem that had existed since the earliest attempts to fly was immediately apparent to the de Havilland Company—there was no suitable engine in existence.

Before relating the fascinating sequence of events that led to the development of what was possibly the first ever light aeroplane engine, the name of Frank Halford must be introduced, a man who was to play a most important part in the development of the de Havilland enterprise and without whose activities this story may never have been told.

As a young man Major Halford graduated from Nottingham University. He learned to fly with the Bristol Aeroplane School at Brooklands and in the far away days of 1912 became one of their Assistant Flying Instructors. Shortly afterwards he joined the Aeronautical Inspection Department at the Air Ministry as Engine Examiner, and it was in this capacity that he amassed the valuable knowledge that was to place him amongst the foremost of the world's aero engine designers.

On the outbreak of the First World War in 1914 he went to France as a sergeant in the R.F.C. and was commissioned the following year. Such was his reputation that in 1916 he was returned home to design new engines. His first engine unit, the famous 230 h.p. 'B.H.P.', eventually developed into the Siddeley Puma, which was fitted to thousands of DH 4s and DH 9s.

He worked with the eminent Ricardo, maestro of the internal-combustion engine, and together they produced the first inverted motor. It was Halford who modified the original wartime Renault engine and raised its power from 80 to 120 h.p. In its improved form it was manufactured during the Great War by the Aircraft Disposal Company when it was known as the Airdisco engine. This was the motor that powered the DH 51.

At the time of the Armistice Major Halford was assistant in charge of engine production at the Air Ministry. He spent the next two and a half years marketing Ricardo patents in America.

In 1923 Halford started on his own as a free-lance engine designer. His premises in North Kensington are usually described as 'humble' and his one and only assistant, Mr. John L. P. Brodie, M.I.A.E., remained with him until his (Halford's) death in 1955.

During the years that followed the setting up of his own drawing office Halford designed engines for Napier, the Aircraft Disposal Company, de Havillands and numerous motor-cycle and car firms. As his staff increased and larger premises became necessary, he moved his office, first to Croydon Airport and then to Windsor House in Victoria Street. In 1929 he made camp at 9 Golden Square and eventually had to take three floors in the building to cope with the demands on his talents. By 1938 there were something in excess of 15,000 engines of his design in service.

Frank Halford eventually joined de Havillands as head of their engine division and continued to produce successful designs such as the Goblin and Ghost turbo-jets. His death in 1955 was a grievous loss to British aviation.

It was to his old friend Frank Halford that Geoffrey de Havilland turned with a request that he should help produce a 60 h.p. engine for the new private aeroplane venture. The discussion was well stage-managed by de Havilland who had arranged for half a V8 Airdisco engine to be stripped and set out on the table during their talk. De Havilland's idea was both logical and practical. No time was available to design a completely new engine from scratch, so why not use four of the eight cylinders from an existing well-proved design? The price could be kept down by using good quality motor components for such parts as the carburettor and magnetos (fitted to most cars in those days). At first Halford was not at all convinced that half an Airdisco would make one light aero engine and in any case he was heavily committed to other projects, including a new 1½-litre engine for Aston Martin cars. Eventually he agreed to design the new engine using Airdisco cylinders, pistons, valves, etc., on a new crankcase, and the Aircraft Disposal Company accepted an order for a limited number of engines.

Given the name 'Cirrus' the new engine was an immediate success. Oil was carried in the crankcase car-engine fashion and it developed its required 60 h.p. on ordinary motor fuel.

While the Cirrus engine was being developed, work progressed steadily on the new aeroplane which had been given the design number DH 60. What a famous number it was to become! In many ways, with its plywood box fuselage and straight unstaggered wings, it was a scaled-down version of the DH 51. Simplicity was the theme throughout the design and there were no separate metal engine-mountings, the motor being bolted direct to the top longerons in the front of the aeroplane. There were two separate cockpits for pilot and passenger, and the front one had a large luggage shelf. Fuel was carried in a fifteen-gallon tank of airfoil shape that was supported by the centre section struts, an arrangement that is retained in the Tiger Moth. For the first time de Havillands used an undercarriage with telescopic struts containing rubber under compression—a big advance over the crude elastic cords that were wrapped round the axles of so many aeroplanes of the period. New ideas went into the design as it progressed on the drawing boards. Bad aileron controls plagued many of the early aeroplanes. When a pilot wishes to alter course he initiates the turn by banking in the required direction. In the process the down-going aileron increases its angle of attack through the air and sets up increased resistance that tends to hold back the raised wing and retard the turn. By rearranging the geometry of the control linkage de Havillands were able to make this aileron depress very slightly whilst the one on the other wing moved up through a much greater angle, so increasing the drag on the inside of the turn where it was needed. This ingeniously simple device, the Differential Aileron, was patented by de Havillands and incorporated for the first time in the new DH 60. It has been used in countless designs all over the world ever since.

With the exception of metal tube tips, the wings were almost entirely of wooden construction and, when folded, lay within the span of the 9 ft. 8 in. tailplane. The spring-loaded trimmer as used on the DH 51 was fitted to the DH 60, and the ignition was controlled by enormous brass domestic-type switches that were in vogue during the 'twenties.

Geoffrey de Havilland was a keen entomologist, an interest he holds to this day, so it is perhaps not surprising that the graceful little DH 60 with its new engine should have been named the Cirrus Moth.

On Sunday afternoon, 22nd February 1925, the great moment arrived when G-EBKT, the prototype Cirrus Moth, emerged from the works at Stag Lane carrying factory number 168.

De Havilland himself did the first test flight and landed back at the airfield enthralled with the delightful handling qualities of the little biplane. G-EBKT had exceeded all expectations and at last the true private 'plane had arrived!

From that moment events moved with almost bewildering speed. The then Director of Civil Aviation, Sir Sefton Brancker, was so enthusiastic about the economics of the Cirrus Moth that he founded five Air Ministry subsidized flying clubs and ordered ninety Moths for the purpose, a staggering number considering that private or sporting flying was more or less non-existent in 1925. One of the first eight production machines, G-EBLV, was ferried to the Lancashire Aero Club by A. J. (now Sir Alan) Cobham. It is now maintained in perfect flying condition at Hatfield aerodrome by the de Havilland Company.

So great was the success of the clubs that prospective members were being turned away every day. The capabilities of the little aeroplane were soon being demonstrated enthusiastically by some of the most famous pilots of the day, and in 1925 Cobham flew the prototype Cirrus Moth

500 miles non-stop to Zurich and returned home after lunch! The following year Hubert Broad, another significant figure in the story, won the King's Cup in a Cirrus Moth at 92.5 m.p.h.—a performance to be repeated in 1927 by Wally Hope. Records were being broken every day, and it was not long before the DH 60 was invincible all over the world; Moth service depots sprang up at such foreign airports as Tempelhof (Berlin); there were the famous Moth Lock-up Garages at Stag Lane aerodrome. Private flying had arrived with a vengeance.

It was not long before Moths were being assembled in Canada, where they did valiant work on floats spotting forest fires. Cobham took one by sea to America in 1926 with a view to production in the U.S.A., and later the Moth Aircraft Corporation of America was formed for the purpose. Regrettably the project was killed by the depression.

Early production aircraft had clear doped wings, but later silver was adopted as the standard finish. The exhaust pipe was moved from the right- to the left-hand side of the nose, and a horn balanced rudder introduced to improve the handling of this control. The luggage shelf was removed from the front and replaced by a separate locker behind the rear cockpit.

In 1927 a new model appeared with a slightly greater span and a reduced gap between the wings. The engine was lowered slightly to improve the pilot's view, and this version was known as the Cirrus II Moth. The engine was up-rated to the point where it delivered 105 h.p. when it was renamed the Cirrus Hermes, and later Moths fitted with this motor were given the type number DH 60X.

A few Moths had Armstrong Siddeley Genet engines, a small radial of 75 h.p., and the R.A.F. Central Flying School gave brilliant displays with the type (Genet Moth) at the Hendon display of 1927. Amongst distinguished owners to use the Moth was the U.S. Naval Attaché in London who had one at his disposal.

As time went on various improvements continued to be incorporated, and the later versions of the Moth had a split-axle undercarriage like a Tiger Moth, and Handley Page automatic slats.

It is generally conceded that the Moth, in its various forms, was responsible for laying the foundations of de Havillands success, and it is interesting to look at the growth of that Company over the period in question. In 1924 the Company employed less than 300 people and its capital was under £49,000. Within five years it grew into a £400,000 public company with a pay-roll of 1,500 people, turning out sixteen light 'planes a week. In 1926 Cirrus Moth production totalled fifty machines, with 117 being completed in the following year when there were forty-two private Moth owners. Nineteen twenty-eight saw another 336 Moths on the register, and by then they traversed the skies of such widely separated countries as Australia, the Irish Free State, Canada, Chile, Africa and the United States of America.

How much did it cost to own and operate a Moth in 1927? The little Cirrus engine used four and a half gallons of fuel per hour—rather thirsty by modern standards for a mere 60 h.p. Nevertheless petrol was only 1/2½d. per gallon in those days so that, assuming the private owner did 250 hours flying in twelve months, his annual bill for fuel and oil would be in the region of £80. It used to cost £5 for a top overhaul on the engine, and a Certificate of Airworthiness overhaul would amount to £20 with another five guineas for the issue of the Certificate. Replacement parts were cheap enough, so that a year's maintenance would total less than £45. Hangarage and landing fees would account for up to £1 a week, although some airfields would charge only 2/6d. for a landing and overnight hangarage provided the wings were folded. Insurance was rather heavy at £100, unless the owner was an experienced pilot when the rate diminished accordingly. Allowing another £10 for such sundry items as motoring maps, Royal Aero Club subscriptions and 5/- for the pilot's licence, the total cost of 250 hours flying was brought to £228, or about 3¼d. per mile for pilot and passenger. Of course one must remember that earnings were very much lower in 1927 than they are now and these figures should be viewed against the value of the pound as it was then, with many of the popular family cars selling on the right side of £200 new.

People in all walks of life became interested in sporting aviation and it was the fashion of the day to refer to every light 'plane as a 'Moth' even if it was a different type of aeroplane entirely; such was the popularity of the little biplane that its name became a household word. There had for many years been another 'Moth', a range of machinery manufactured by John Morton & Co. Ltd. of Wolverhampton. Fortunately that old-established company agreed to de Havillands registering the word 'Moth', and it became their (de Havillands') trade mark for light aeroplanes.

With every justification de Havillands were proud of the impact the Moth was making on the imagination of the general public, and this interesting report appeared in the de Havilland Gazette of April 1927:

A London Store Selling Moths

It is of singular interest that the first sale of an aeroplane from a London Shop occurred early this month. Much interest was aroused when William Whiteley Ltd., the well-known London emporium, decided to include the Moth among the 'lines' handled by their motor department. Under their enterprising policy their customers are offered Moths either for cash or by a convenient system of deferred terms.

Their first exhibition machine, which was attractively displayed in a central position on the ground floor of the big store, was sold within ten days of its first appearance there, and this prompt sale, coupled with the volume of inquiries with which their motor department has been bombarded, has decided them to take a second machine as soon as one can be prepared.

The purchaser of their first Moth, smartly finished in dark red, was Mr. L. G. Richardson, an officer of the Fleet Air Arm, who intends to use his machine purely for pleasure travel.

Our readers may be interested to hear that Messrs. White-leys can offer almost immediate delivery of further Moths on the following alternative terms:

Cash Price   £730

Or £230 cash deposit and 12 monthly payments of £47. 0. 0
Or 18 monthly payments of £32. 5. 0
Or 24 monthly payments of £24. 15. 0

Other automobile traders are also handling Moth sales, and two big provincial car distributors are now exhibiting machines. Down in Bournemouth the local Moth agents are Motor Macs Ltd., where a Moth is exhibited in spacious showrooms and inquirers are attended by qualified salesmen under an ex-R.A.F. pilot. At Liverpool the well-known Lancashire and Cheshire automobile distributors, the Voss Motor Car Co. Ltd., are displaying a Moth in their galleries on the ground floor of the famous Adelphi Hotel. Although they are not showing an actual Moth at present, Messrs. S. T. Lea's showrooms at 41 New Bond Street have become known as the 'Aeroplane Shop' and prospective buyers can there obtain the fullest information about private flying.

In these days of ever-increasing prices it is worthy of note that when the Cirrus Moth was first introduced in 1926 it cost £830. In 1927 its price was reduced to £730 and the following year a new Moth could be bought for as little as £650.

There are many young pilots today who have never experienced the joys of an open cockpit on a hot summer's afternoon, or the taut, compact feeling one gets when flying a small biplane, since most flying schools now train their pupils on cabin monoplanes, in some cases with tricycle undercarriages that almost land themselves. To describe the Moth from the pilot's point of view this chapter concludes with an article that was written long ago, in 1927:

The 'Moth' Machine
by Capt. Geoffrey de Havilland, O.B.E., A.F.C., F.R.Ae.S.

These notes on flying a Moth may possibly be of interest to the private owner. I am writing chiefly from the private owner's point of view and with the idea that he or she may wish to know something more about the machine; and if he or she happens to be a beginner the notes on flying may be of use.

I took delivery of my machine G-EBNO last summer; it was fitted with the first Mark II Cirrus engine, and the first flight exceeded all expectations of performance as compared with the Mark I engine.

There are people who get much pleasure in adjusting, oiling, fitting and cleaning odd accessories for comfort or efficiency to their cars. I can spend hours in this way, and owning a light aircraft at once gave a new interest in this direction. Every owner of car, motor-cycle or aeroplane has individual tastes and ideas, and the embodiment of these ideas often means improvement, as well as being interesting work. You cannot, of course, make big alterations and it is best not to try altering any structural part, and in any case it should not be necessary. As regards strength, the Moth has a very high factor of safety. Its breaking load in the air is the equivalent weight of 50 (fifty!) people (fortunately you cannot get them all in), and if a front or rear flying wire were to fracture (this has not occurred in 800,000 miles of Moth flying), the load is taken via the incidence wires between the outer struts to the remaining flying wire. Duplication is carried out in this way wherever necessary, including the controls, and, therefore, it is carrying matters too far to suggest a duplicated control failing; but if this extraordinary event happened, say, to the rudder, it would be easily possible to keep directional control by throttling down the engine, in order to eliminate propeller torque and slip, and controlling on the ailerons. This can be tried at any time by detaching the spring on the left side of the rudder bar, which should, normally, be adjusted to take all the load off the feet when cruising. It will be found that by throttling and taking the feet off the rudder bar the machine can be landed with precision by the use of ailerons alone. And, vice versa, the rudder can be used to control the machine laterally.

Fire in the air is not possible because the tank is placed in the centre section of the top wings and is therefore entirely isolated from the engine. If you were able to ignite the petrol issuing from a hole in the tank, it would be extinguished at once, due to the speed of the machine through the air, and for the same reason petrol would stream out in a straight line and would not fall into or onto the cockpits or fuselage.

I have mentioned these few points relating to safety because many people do not realize how safe civil flying has become; to my mind it is certainly safer than modern motoring.

There are a few hints worth considering which bear on safety and comfort in flying. Cultivate the use of the air speed indicator and you will fly safely. In all modern D.H. machines there is a notice giving stalling, climbing and gliding speeds, and this information should never be overlooked. Climb at the speed given on the cockpit notice and always glide in by air speed. Instruments very seldom go wrong, but an excellent practice is to stall gently at a safe height and check the indicator reading with the speed shown on the plate.

When cruising try to run at a speed round about normal cruising revolutions where the engine is smoothest; all car and aeroplane engines have periods where vibration is more or less apparent. The trimming lever should be so placed that no elevator load is felt on the hand; the machine will then fly 'hands off' for some time. Always adjust rudder pedals to suit your length, so that you can sit comfortably; this is all the more important on a long flight.

Some remarks on cross-country flying may be of use to those who are starting. In the first place, height makes for safety—it is generally advisable to fly not under 1,000 ft. unless the ground is exceptionally good. In the event of a landing being necessary, height enables you to choose a suitable ground. The first consideration in the choice of a landing ground is the approach. Do not choose a field with trees on the approach side; a relatively small field with a low hedge is far better. Taking an average height of trees as 50 ft., you would require four times the length of ground compared with that bounded by a low hedge. It is hardly necessary to mention that the wind direction relative to the machine should be committed to memory when starting every flight. For normal wind conditions and a low boundary

hedge, the distance required for the landing run is approx.
270 yds.—that is to say the minimum length of field measured
from the hedge should be 300 yds. It is assumed that the
boundary will be crossed at about 55 m.p.h.

A good compass is almost essential for comfortable flying
across country. There are two points worth mentioning about
compass flying. In clouds or bad fog the compass dial may
start to rotate—or may appear to rotate. When this happens
it is as well to realize that the machine is rotating around
the compass card which is, of course, approximately stationary. Owing to having no visible ground point, you may not
at first appreciate this fact; but it often happens that when
the ground and horizon cannot be seen the pilot involun-
tarily rudders to right or left, and hence the compass dance.
Being ready for this phenomenon is practically its cure, and
practice will enable you to fly steadily in clouds.

The other matter is a more complex one, because it is
chiefly psychological. You may be flying on a compass course
over unknown country and you will suddenly feel that the
compass is not leading you right and that you must go to
port or starboard, as the case may be. It is astonishing how
many experienced pilots have found this tendency to dis-
believe or compromise with the compass. When you are
stricken with this disbelief in the compass, it may range from
north being south to only a few degrees of deviation, but,
whatever the amount, it is essential to remember that a good
compass is more likely to be correct than your temporary
sense of direction.

In these complex days of Instrument Ratings, the reference near the top of this page, to
flying 'in clouds or bad fog' using little more than the compass and a determination to ignore instinct
may seem unbelievably naive but pilots went flying in cloud long before the appearance of comprehensive flight panels. It is not that modern man has lost some inbred instinct of balance but merely
a case of 'you never miss what you've never had' and to the light aeroplane pilot of 1927 the
Cirrus Moth was the last word.

The inadequacies of the little Humming Bird led to the
building of the DH 51 and the shortcomings of this much
larger aeroplane pointed the way to the Cirrus Moth.
Before we can trace the path that eventually led to the
Tiger Moth, we must introduce the Gipsy engine, as
famous in its own right as the Moth, for its evolution is an
integral part of the Tiger Moth story.

Service fore-runner of the Tiger Moth; one of a batch of thirty D.H.60M Gipsy Moths used by the R.A.F. for communications duties in the early 'thirties.

Flying Testbed for the Gipsy I engine. The DH 71 Tiger Moth.

The legendary Gipsy Moth. Three machines of Australian National Airways; that nearest the camera is the wooden DH60G while the two far machines are DH60M's with fabric-covered metal fuselages

2. Birth of the Tiger

The success of the Moth was such that supplies of war surplus Airdisco engine parts were becoming difficult. Always mindful of their original intention to manufacture 'everyman's aeroplane' de Havillands approached the Aircraft Disposal Company (who were making the Cirrus engines for the Moth) in the hope that the price of the motor could be lowered. Discussions between the two firms soon revealed that, business-wise, the Cirrus engine was not a very attractive proposition for the Air Disposal Company and there was no hope of reducing its price.

The Moth project was of course entirely dependent upon the supply of Cirrus engines, and the dangers of the situation were only too clear to Geoffrey de Havilland. However friendly the Air Disposal Company may be, what would result if they were to find it impossible to continue making the Cirrus engine? With the Moth programme gathering momentum such a situation was unthinkable. A decision had to be made and it was one that would either make or break de Havillands. They would build their own light aero engine and it would be specially designed for the purpose, down to the last nut and bolt. It was of course logical that Frank Halford should be retained to create the new engine, but the project was not a straightforward matter of designing the parts and going into production. By now the Moth was universally accepted as a thoroughly reliable

21

means of transport, and any engine that went into it would have to be equally reliable.

Piston engines are complex and in some ways crude pieces of machinery with their many reciprocating parts and valves that snap shut under the influence of powerful springs. A new piston engine rarely works well from the moment the first one is assembled, and much test, modification and development work is the usual order of things before production can be considered. You can test an engine on the bench day in and day out, but there is no real substitute for airborne experience, and the way de Havillands set about obtaining this is typical of the practical approach that company has always adopted to its engineering problems. They would build a racer and the first engines would be run at 135 h.p. in up-rated form so that experience could be gained in the air under the most arduous conditions. When they had the engine performing really well in racing trim it would be de-rated to about 100 h.p. and then the Moth would have a thoroughly reliable motor that had served its apprenticeship in a racing monoplane. Two examples of the racer were made in the greatest secrecy under the designation DH 71 and, although the name Tiger Moth was chosen, the design bore no resemblance to the aeroplane that forms the subject of this book, and to avoid confusion from now on we shall refer to them as DH 71's.

The de Havilland design team set about creating the smallest possible cockpit around their test pilot Hubert Broad, and the aeroplane emerged as an incredibly sleek racer without a superfluous inch of frontal area. Two sets of wings were made, 22 ft. 6 in. span for touring and 19 ft. span for racing purposes.

A unique feature, years ahead of its time, was the simple rigid undercarriage designed to reduce drag. Landing and taxiing shocks were absorbed by internally sprung wheels, an arrangement that was to find favour with the Gloster Gladiator and the Westland Lysander some years later. Both machines were entered for the 1927 King's Cup Air Race by Sir Charles and Lady Wakefield. From all accounts they were something of a handful to fly until one or two changes were made in the design, and this is what Hubert Broad had to say on the subject at the time:

What is she like to fly? is always the very first question asked by pilots about any new type of aeroplane. It has a particular significance in connection with the Tiger Moth [DH 71], which is not only a new type but an entirely different species of aeroplane from anything yet produced.

My first impression of the machine in the air can be reproduced by anyone who cares to stand on a garden roller on one foot with his eyes shut. The causes were obvious: first, a nasty bumpy day, and secondly, too high gearing of the controls on a super-sensitive machine. Since the original flights all controls have been geared down by approximately 40 per cent., and with this alteration the feeling of instability has entirely disappeared. The original flights were also made with wings of considerably smaller area than those fitted for the King's Cup Race.

The lower gearing, although allowing more movement of the stick and rudder bar, has made the controls even lighter in operation, together with a lessened total movement of all control services. The cure is, of course, variable gearing; low gear for small movements and the gear increasing rapidly as the controls reach their maximum movement. The fitting of this to the Tiger Moth will be extremely interesting, and is just one of the instances of the tremendous use of this machine as a research aeroplane. The take off and behaviour in the air is perfectly straightforward. The machine has no vices. The actual landing is not difficult, the only feature likely to worry anyone flying the machine for the first time is the very flat glide, or rather the time taken to lose speed when landing, even though the flight path of the machine is very flat. This, of course, is a feature of all aeroplanes of low resistance—it is like stopping a car with no brakes. Also, after flying at high speed it takes quite an effort of will to bring the speed down to 100 m.p.h. and realize that you are nowhere near the stalling speed.

At the beginning I had some misgiving about the undercarriage. With the exception, however, of one tin-tack through a tyre, no trouble whatever has been experienced.

Stag Lane is not the smoothest of aerodromes, and the landings have not always been of the best.

The view is distinctly good, and there is no necessity to wear goggles at any time. Provided the mica screens are kept clean and unscratched, it is quite easy to fly across country without putting one's head outside the office. The screens are, of course, slightly splayed out to provide for a forward view.

Cross country on a fine day is a real joy. It seems only necessary to point the nose of the machine, well throttled down, to some town, and wait till it turns up. After passing Leicester, on the way to Nottingham, I looked out for Loughborough on the left front, and failed to see it. Having no compass, the idea ocurred to me that I had swung off my course, until out of the tail of my eye I spotted the town I was looking for, behind me, and Nottingham just ahead. The actual time taken from point to point is little over half that taken by a normal aeroplane, and at first it takes some time to adjust one's ideas to the actual difference in time for distance.

In conclusion, I would say that the Tiger Moth [DH 71] is not Everyman's aeroplane. It has been produced with the sole object of high speed research at moderate cost, and I have no doubt that the experience we are already gaining from it will be reflected in later products from Stag Lane.*

Whilst the design team and craftsmen at Stag Lane prepared the two DH 71 racing monoplanes, Halford's drawings were gradually translated, part by part, into the new engines. As producers of airframes, de Havillands had no suitable machinery for the new venture, and in order to purchase this additional capital had to be raised.

Once more Frank Halford excelled himself. His new engine had a capacity of 5.23 litres and a compression ratio of 5.5. On the bench it returned 135 h.p. at 2,650 r.p.m. and weighed 300 lbs., only 14 lbs. more than the original 60 h.p. Cirrus engine.

Geoffrey de Havilland had always admired a particular species of moth called the Gipsy, and it was decided to give the name to Halford's new engine so that when it

*See additional note at end of chapter, page 39.

replaced the Cirrus motor the new DH 60 would be known as the Gipsy Moth. But much remained to be done before the Gipsy engine was considered worthy of the famous Moth aeroplane, and after a period of bench testing the prototypes were fitted into the DH 71 monoplanes, one of which had already flown powered by a Cirrus II.

Bert Groombridge, the works manager at Stag Lane, supervised the building and equipping of the new engine shop, and within sixteen weeks it was in production turning out the de-rated 100 h.p. version of the Gipsy destined to be the forerunner of a long line of engines that were to be installed in countless types of aircraft from manufacturers of every nationality.

Hubert Broad continued to hammer the racing version of the Gipsy in the DH 71 monoplane, breaking the Class III (Light aeroplane category) record for the 100 km. closed circuit at 186.47 m.p.h. on 24th August 1927.

The first production Gipsy I was delivered from the new engine works on 20th June 1928. It was not the Gipsy engine that we have all come to recognize, for during its early life the cylinders and valve gear were above the crankcase in the 'upright' position. The first Gipsy I went into G-EBQH, a standard Moth airframe, and by the end of 1928 they were coming out of the engine shops at the rate of twenty per week. By now Hubert Broad had amassed a considerable amount of experience with the racing version of the engine, and the lessons learned from the DH 71 project were of the utmost benefit to the production Gipsy I which soon established quite unprecedented standards of reliability. Under Government supervision a Gipsy I was sealed and flown for 600 hours without other than routine maintenance. At the end of the test period which involved 51,000 miles of flying over nine months, power had only dropped by one and half per cent. and the cost of replacement parts amounted to £7 2s. 11d!

We have dwelt on the Gipsy I engine at some length because its role in our story is just as important as the Moth itself. If the Moth had been successful with its original engine the Gipsy I was to provide the necessary shot in the arm to make it a world beater against the best that could be offered anywhere. How refreshing it is to look back to those days when this country was the Mecca of sporting flying.

Manufacturing licences were granted in France and Norway and by 1929 the Gipsy Moth, at £650, was in such demand that de Havillands were making three a day. Eighty-five per cent. of British private aeroplanes were Moths at that time, and the Prince of Wales was an enthusiastic owner. By the end of 1929 there were 220 Moths flying in Canada.

Although the Cirrus Moth claims the distinction of sparking off the light aeroplane movement, the Gipsy-engined version can be said to have carried on the good work without compromise. Many foreign governments used it as a military trainer, and other foreign operators of the time are too numerous to mention. All over the world Gipsy Moths were winning competitions, breaking records and walking away with air races. In America an intrepid lady pilot by name of Ingalls set up a novel record by doing 344 loops in succession. Francis Chichester flew one to Australia in 1929. Recently he has made two solo return crossings of the Atlantic in a small sailing boat—named *Gipsy Moth III*. The depression came and killed the projected American Moth enterprise, but these difficult years saw many record flights.

Perhaps the one that most captured public imagination was that of Amy Johnson who in May 1930 made the first solo flight by a woman to Australia using G-AAAH, a not very new Moth named 'Jason' which she had purchased for a song. During that year John Grierson, later Sales Manager (Executive Aircraft) of the de Havilland Aircraft Company Ltd., flew a Gipsy Moth to Lahore, Baghdad and Moscow. Several years later he made another outstanding flight to Iceland in a Gipsy Moth fitted with Blackburn floats.

By the end of 1930 there were some 1,800 Moths of all marks in existence, but a number of these already showed signs of becoming Tiger Moths for, with the rigorous conditions that prevail in undeveloped countries in mind, de Havillands decided to make a version of the Gipsy Moth with a fabric-covered welded steel tube fuselage in place of the familiar wooden structure. The DH 6oM, or Metal Moth as it was often called, first appeared in 1928 and, although it was much stronger than the original design, the steel fuselage weighed only 62 lb. more than the wooden version of the Gipsy Moth which, incidentally, continued in production until 1934. To this day a few are to be seen flying in Australia, New Zealand, the U.S.A. and one or two European countries.

Metal Moths soon found favour in Canada where a large sliding canopy was fitted to keep out the extreme cold. So equipped they flew the first Air Mail to Newfoundland.

Whilst the Moth grew up things of importance were happening to the Gipsy engine. Development of both Moth airframe and Gipsy engine continued, sometimes together in one aeroplane but occasionally in parallel with one another. The engine was enlarged slightly and became the Gipsy II. It developed 120 h.p., a significant increase in power over the original engine (in standard form), and later versions of the Metal Moth were fitted with it.

In 1931 the Metal Moth moved a step nearer to becoming a Tiger Moth, in the form of the DH 6oT or Moth Trainer. In effect this was a military trainer version of the Metal Moth. The exhaust pipe was moved forward and doors were fitted to each side of both cockpits to improve entry and exit. Additionally, the rear flying wires, always something of a menace when getting into the front cockpit, were moved forward from their old points of attachment above the rear spars of the lower wings to a new position adjacent to where the front flying wires anchored themselves (just above the front spars). The wings were strengthened to cater for the increased all-up weight that resulted from such military items as 20 lb. practice bombs, a camera gun, radio, etc. Many look upon the Moth Trainer as the immediate forerunner of the Tiger Moth. It was certainly closely related although it still had the upright Gipsy II engine—but it is at this point that parallel development of the motor occurred in a different airframe.

Early in 1929 de Havillands were considering the possibility of an inverted version of the Gipsy engine. As far back as 1917 Halford and Ricardo had experimented with a supercharged, inverted, six-cylinder engine which delivered 260 h.p., so that the idea was not particularly new. The prime thought behind turning the Gipsy engine upside down with cylinders below the crankcase emanated from a desire to improve the pilot's view ahead. With an upright engine such as the Cirrus or Gipsy I the cylinders and valve gear tend to obscure the pilot's vision along the nose of the aircraft, and whilst the engine position was lowered in some later Moths there is a limit to how much this can be done. The propeller must clear the ground safely as the aeroplane runs along with its tail up during the take-off, and lowering the engine means lengthening the undercarriage to provide the necessary gap. In any case from a purely aerodynamic point of view the designer must arrange that the thrust from the propeller is in the right place relative to the complete aeroplane. The inverted engine provided the practical answer to all three problems; improved view for the pilot, adequate clearance between propeller and ground and a thrust line in the correct position for stability.

A Gipsy II was modified to run inverted when it became the Gipsy III giving the same 120 h.p. as its predecessor. The experimental engine powered the DH 80, a high-wing monoplane which made its initial flight on 9th September 1929. In its developed form it became the famous Puss Moth and the motor used was the inverted Gipsy III, the first production engine being delivered early in May 1930. In 1932 the Gipsy III had its capacity increased to produce 130 h.p. The Gipsy Major had arrived—the most famous light aero engine ever to be produced. Thousands are still in service all over the world and such is its standard of reliability that this little engine is allowed to run for 1,500 hours between major overhauls. In the days of the Gipsy I 400 hours was considered good.

The Gipsy Major went into the wooden version of the DH 60 and became the very attractive Moth Major, the fastest of the biplane Moth series, but before reverting to the pre-Tiger Moth days of 1931 it is interesting to compare the de Havilland-inspired engines associated with the Moth series. They are listed in chronological order:

Development of Moth Engines

	Litres	Weight lbs.	Max. b.h.p.
Cirrus I	4.05	286	65
Cirrus II	4.94	256	80
Gipsy (racing)	5.23	300	135
Gipsy I	5.23	300	98
Gipsy II	5.71	298	120
Gipsy III (inverted)	5.71	305	120
Gipsy Major I	6.12	305	130

Returning to the situation as it existed during the early part of 1931, two of the designs already introduced in this chapter were in production at de Havillands and each was to contribute some of its characteristics to the Tiger Moth; the Moth Trainer gave its fabric-covered steel tube fuselage, and the DH 80 Puss Moth with its inverted Gipsy III engine provided the now familiar lines of the engine cowling with the propeller mounted just a few inches below the top of the nose. With the advantages that result from such an installation it was inevitable that the inverted Gipsy III should be fitted to the metal Moth Trainer, and this particular version may be regarded as the truth forerunner of the Tiger Moth.

In common with all the DH 60 series the inverted-engined Moth Trainer had straight unstaggered wings, that is to say when seen from above the mainplanes were not raked backwards and the top wing was positioned directly above the lower one. This arrangement, which had remained basically unchanged since the first Cirrus Moth, had the disadvantage that it placed the fuel tank directly above the front cockpit, leaving only 24 ins. or so between its undersurface and the top of the fuselage. For this reason the Moth Trainer never found favour with our Air Ministry although the Governments of Sweden, Egypt, Iraq and Brazil used the earlier version as a service trainer. At least one went to China.

As a nation we perhaps tend to decry most official decisions as a matter of principle, but it is interesting to consider the Air Ministry's objection on this occasion, partly as it was based upon sound reasoning but mainly because it was to determine the shape of the Tiger Moth. It was not easy for a civilian passenger to clamber into the front cockpit of a Moth, and R.A.F. personnel found access even more difficult for it should be remembered that, whereas civilian pilots rarely don parachutes, service flying instructors and their pupils always do. The R.A.F. reasoned that what amounted to nothing more than an acrobatic struggle getting into the front cockpit could be a matter of life or death should the instructor have to leave the aircraft in an emergency. Nevertheless they were sufficiently interested in the Moth Trainer to ask de Havillands if something could be done to improve the accessibility of the front cockpit. Arthur E. Hagg was chief designer at the time and with the help of F. T. Hearle a Moth Trainer was dismantled in a small shed and the components used to make a full scale mock up. Various wing arrangements were tried, and Hagg recalls that the centre section struts supporting the fuel tank were more or less welded up on the job.

The entire project seems to have been carried through on an *ad hoc* basis, and it is almost unbelievable but nevertheless true to say that the Tiger Moth, perhaps the most successful biplane trainer of all times, was evolved without drawings. Just how hit and miss were the methods used are best described by the original engineer responsible for producing the prototype, Mr. F. C. Plumb, now with the de Havilland Aircraft of Canada Ltd.:

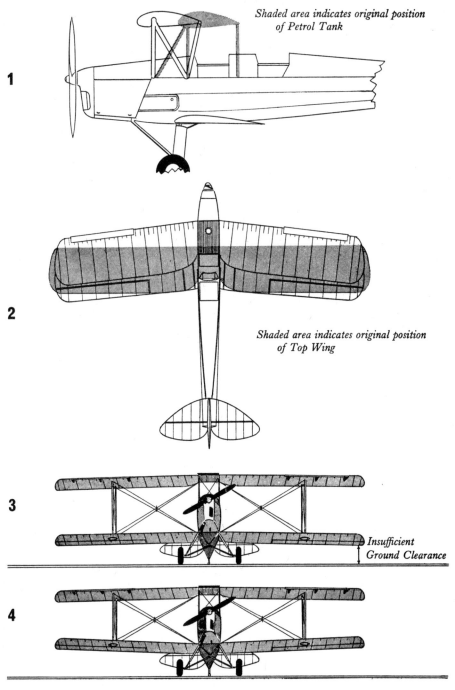

*Shaded area indicates original position
of Petrol Tank*

*Shaded area indicates original position
of Top Wing*

*Insufficient
Ground Clearance*

Transformation from Metal Moth to Tiger Moth in three stages

1. Tank moved clear of front cockpit
2&3. Wings swept back to preserve balance
4. Bottom wings raised to increase ground clearance

The major limitation to the use of the DH 60T (Moth Trainer) as a training aircraft was the location of the fuel tank in the centre section of the top wing. It was very difficult for occupants of the front cockpit to make an emergency exit by parachute as the only way this could be effected was by clambering out of the cockpit onto the lower wing in a crouched position and then crawling between the rear set of rigging wires before being able to leave the aircraft.

My first knowledge of the Tiger Moth project was an intimation that I would be responsible for producing the prototype aircraft and that Mr. W. D. Hunter would be the Project Engineer in charge of design. I have no doubt that by this time considerable thought had already been given to the project by Sir Geoffrey* and members of his engineering staff.

Mr. Hunter told me that initially they wished to move the centre section forward of the front cockpit entrance to permit unimpeded exit from it. The amount of forward movement was not known and the easiest way to determine this was to rig up the centre section with temporary struts until it was sufficiently clear of the cockpit.

Plumb's account of the proceedings is, after all these years, in close accord with Hagg's recent disclosures. It seems that initially the fuel tank which acted as the centre section on a Moth was moved forward 18 ins., but after Hubert Broad and de Havilland himself had examined the new arrangements it was decided to move it forward another 4 ins. Since the upper wing was attached to the centre section this too moved forward, placing the lift from the wings too far ahead of the aircraft's centre of gravity. To bring the aeroplane into balance again it was necessary to sweep back the wings.

Moth wings were constructed mostly of wood, the main load being carried on a front and rear spar. These were of solid timber lightened by spindling out some of the wood from places not likely to cause structural weakness. To achieve sweepback it was necessary to shorten the rear spars on each of the four wings, and these had to be specially

* Geoffrey de Havilland was knighted in 1944.

made without the spindling at the wing root. Three sets of rear spars were tried before the engineers were able to re-establish the aircraft's centre of gravity in relation to lift. Here again trial and error were used to find the correct amount of sweepback, and this is how Plumb describes the experiments that took place in the little shed on the old Stag Lane airfield.

> After some discussion between Mr. Hunter and myself it was decided to try moving the wings back 9 ins. at the inter-plane struts from the original position. When the rear spars in all four wings had been shortened the aircraft was temporarily rigged and the centre of gravity position checked. It was then found that 9 ins. was not enough sweepback and rather than remove and refit new rear spars to all four wings it was decided to swing back the upper wings an additional 2 ins. and check the effect of this on the C.G. This was sufficient to re-establish the centre of gravity range—hence the difference in sweepback between the upper and lower wings.

The only material difference between the standard Moth Trainer and the aeroplane that resulted from Mr. Plumb's attention was the position of the wings and their sweep-back, so it is perhaps understandable that the first eight aeroplanes manufactured to these standards were still refer-red to as examples of the DH 60T although the name Tiger Moth was added for the first time. These eight machines bearing the registrations G-ABNC, G-ABNI, G-ABNJ, G-ABNK, G-ABNL, G-ABNM, G-ABNY and G-ABPH can best be considered as the missing link between the Moth Trainer with the inverted Gipsy III engine and the true Tiger Moth.

There was, however, a snag with these aeroplanes. The gap between the wings on the Moth series of biplanes was constant from tip to tip, and in order to maintain this relationship it was necessary to lengthen the inter-plane struts when the top mainplane was moved forward. Mr. Plumb recalls that, like most other things on the original example, the length of these struts was established on a trial and error basis. But when sweepback was added the tips of the lower wings were perilously close to the ground with the aeroplane in the tail-down position so that whilst taxiing over rough terrain or perhaps during the latter part of a landing it was all too easy to strike the ground with one of the lower wings tips. To overcome this fault one of the eight 'missing links' had its inter-plane struts shortened so lifting each lower wing at the tips. G-ABPH was chosen for the experiment and thus modified it was evaluated at Martlesham during September 1931. Its ground handling and general performance was compared with G-ABNJ, one of the other DH 60 Tiger Moths in original form, and the results were so encouraging that it was decided to adopt the improved version as the standard R.A.F. trainer.

A prototype was ordered against Air Ministry Specification 15/31 based upon the modified DH 60T. With the incorporation of stagger and sweepback and the addition of increased dihedral on the lower wings, the time had come to give the new trainer a designation of its own and G-ABRC, works number 1733, was the first to be made under the new type number—DH 82.

The Tiger Moth was born. There had been no complex calculations and no drawings; just a group of men in a little shed and a dismantled Moth Trainer. One can imagine a voice saying, 'It will have to go forward another four inches or he'll never get in with a parachute.' Yet from these almost Gilbert and Sullivan beginnings came the first of many thousands of little biplanes that were to become as famous as the Model 'T' Ford. Asked recently if in 1931 he or any of his colleagues realized that they had produced a masterpiece from the components of another aeroplane, Arthur Hagg replied, 'Although of course we knew there would be a demand for a small trainer with upward view for both occupants we little visualized the numbers that were eventually produced.'

October 26th 1931 saw G-ABRC on its first trip at the

hands of Hubert Broad—the first of countless thousands of flights under the most varied of circumstances that were to continue to the present day. The Tiger Moth's first pilot is himself a man of interest representing a generation of test pilots who gave so much to flying during what may be described as its adolescent period. Although he is now retired from active testing, he maintains a keen interest in sporting flying.

Hubert Broad had learned to fly on an old 35 Caudron at the Hall School, Hendon, during May 1915. No one had heard of dual control in those days and but a few years previously it had been the practice for flying schools to add the cost of repairs to the flying fees. Incidents were many and the insurance companies were not entirely sympathetically disposed towards aeroplanes. Pilots were considered as a race apart, an attitude which regrettably persists to a degree in Britain today.

Broad had spent a period immediately after the First World War joy riding in America but on 7th October 1921 he landed at Stag Lane aerodrome to have some work done on a Sopwith Camel which he was using at the time for exhibition flying in Wales. That landing was to influence his future profoundly because de Havillands asked if he would like to deliver a DH 9 for them, and he remained with the company as test pilot until his retirement. Around 1923 he was testing aeroplanes for Gloster, Handley Page, Saunders Roe and Parnall in addition to his work with de Havillands, and if speeds were low in those days, of hazards there were plenty. Farnborough has a good film of Broad going to the bottom of Felixstowe harbour on 20th September 1924 surrounded by a Gloster II seaplane that had been destined for the Schneider Trophy Races. A float had collapsed on landing and Broad attributes his survival to the fact that he was wearing neither parachute nor safety belt and was able to kick himself clear of the submerged and very cramped cockpit. At a time when more and more motorists are fitting safety belts to their cars it is perhaps not fashionable to suggest that there are circumstances when a harness can be a danger, although such incidents must be regarded as exceptions to the general rule. One of these rare occasions happened when Hubert Broad was testing the effectiveness of Handley Page slats on a Moth. The test—a rather hair-raising performance involved taking off, cutting the engine at a low height and then turning back through 180 degrees and landing on the airfield—was a procedure calculated to turn the modern flying instructor white in the shortest possible time. Broad misjudged on one occasion and sank into the hedge on the airfield boundary. Once more he was saved by not wearing a harness and although he was thrown forward injuring his face on the instrument panel he did at least avoid one of the rear mainspars that burst into the cockpit and shot across the seat he had been occupying but a fraction of a second before.

It is only in recent years that a solution was found to a problem, once regarded as insurmountable, commonly known as the Sound Barrier. Now the Heat Barrier is with us and no doubt with the introduction of new materials and techniques this too will be mastered. Progress in aviation is marked by many such barriers, some of them seemingly beyond the capabilities of man until a remedy is found, often of the simplest kind. Such a barrier was that known as Flutter, an unpleasant and highly dangerous condition of flight rather like the speed wobble experienced by some motor cyclists, in so far as both often occurred at a particular speed.

With lightness always high on the aircraft designer's list of priorities it is readily understandable that many of the earlier aeroplanes were reasonably strong but not rigid; the two factors being quite different. As the performance of aeroplanes increased, this lack of rigidity allowed certain parts, notably the control surfaces, to vibrate or flutter, and it was only a matter of seconds before the violent fluctuations broke up the aeroplane. In the flying fraternity of those days flutter was regarded with much the same respect as was the sound barrier a few years ago. The Gloster

DH60T Tiger Moth. One of the original prototypes on test at Martlesham Heath with its lower wing tips perilously close to the ground. Compare picture with the one below (actually an early DH 82a).

The first of the many. G-ABRC, the prototype DH 82 Tiger Moth, with its fabric-covered top fuselage.

First DH 82a to enter R.A.F. service showing the instrument hood pulled over the pupil's cockpit.

Grebe claimed a number of R.A.F. pilots because of Flutter problems until someone cured the fault by placing mass balance weights ahead of the hinge line of the affected control—it was as simple as that!

Hubert Broad recalls flying a Grebe at full throttle when the stick became a blurr and he 'felt as if someone was waving a sheet of *The Times* in my face'. Instinctively he closed the throttle, Flutter stopped immediately and he was able to land safely at Brockworth although the vibration had split the mainspars in the wings. September was a bad month for Broad in 1924. The Flutter incident occurred on the 15th to be followed five days later by the ducking in Felixstowe harbour.

Peaceful little aeroplane that it is, the Tiger Moth had its moments for Hubert Broad and at one time there was quite a collection of tools in his office that had been left in various aircraft, sometimes without causing trouble but not always so. A hammer once lodged below the fulcrum of the stick restricting its movement in the air until a determined tug broke the shaft. On another occasion a screwdriver left in the wing by a mechanic became entangled with a short length of chain operating one of the aileron differential mechanisms. With the ailerons locked in the banked position the aeroplane would only fly level during a flat turn made with full rudder in opposition to bank. Broad was unable to approach Stag Lane in the right direction during those frightening moments and eventually went into Hendon.

Routine tests proceeded to the point where the Tiger Moth was ready for its aerobatic trials. Handley Page slats were fitted as standard equipment and under normal flight conditions these were arranged to open automatically at a pre-determined angle of attack, so delaying the onset of the stall. This highly desirable function could be an embarrassment during aerobatics so that on the right-hand side of the rear cockpit a lever was provided to lock the slats in the closed position and a thin cable extended from the lever, up the right-hand centre section strut and into the top wings where it terminated at the linkage supporting the slats.

For some reason or other no slat control was fitted to the Tiger Moth used for aerobatic tests but the cable leading from the top wings was pulled tightly into the 'locked' position and then held by insulating tape to the rear centre section strut. The remainder of the wire that should have led to the locking lever in the rear cockpit was looped into a neat coil and fixed with more insulating tape to the inside of the front cockpit.

As he inspected the aircraft just before the test Hubert Broad questioned whether the slats were properly locked and gave the cable a tug. The length running up to the top wings held firm but he succeeded in dislodging the neatly coiled end which was now free to waft around the front cockpit. It so happens that when flown solo the rear seat of a Tiger Moth must be occupied and during the test Broad's first intimation that all was not well followed a slow roll when he found that the stick would move to the right but not to the left. Although the loose coil of wire was no more than an inch larger in diameter than the front stick it had nevertheless descended upon the front control with the precision of a hoop-la ring.

After all these years Plumb remembers 'a rather shaken test pilot complaining of locked aileron controls and then hurrying to the bar of the London Aeroplane Club for sedation'.

Notwithstanding these moments of drama, as testing went on it became apparent that here was a light aeroplane possessed of all the advantages of its illustrious forebears but with the added attraction that the instructor could get into and out of the front cockpit without having to go into training.

Aeroplane design is usually a matter of painstaking calculation and aerodynamic study followed by wind tunnel experiments. Then comes the details design stage and more drawings. Every precaution may have been taken and much thought put into the design, yet the prototype occasionally proves a disappointment to all concerned. It is sometimes the perverse nature of things that when one tries hardest the results are not up to expectation, whilst success can result from the most casual effort. This is not to suggest that Arthur Hagg and his engineers were not trying when they experimented with Moth components, but the fact remains that the Tiger Moth was a little bit of this and a bit of that with a few inches more here and a few less there. Never can such a successful aeroplane have had such inauspicious beginnings, but G-ABRC had met its Air Ministry requirements and the R.A.F. had a new trainer.

*It is interesting to compare the racing version of the DH 71, designed and built in 1927, with the Rollason Beta a little aeroplane of late 1960 vintage which emerged as the winner of a design competition for formula I racing aircraft. This competition, inspired by the Duke of Edinburgh and translated into reality by the veteran sporting pilot, Norman Jones is of particular interest because in many ways it recaptured some of the excitement and magic of the old light aeroplane trials which did so much to advance light aviation. A comparison of leading particulars for the two designs reveals a number of remarkable similarities. Admittedly the DH 71 had the advantage of an additional 35 h.p. but the Beta had 30 more years experience built into it.

Racing DH 71 (1927)		Rollason Beta (1969)
19' 0"	SPAN	20' 5"
18' 7"	LENGTH	16' 8"
7' 0"	HEIGHT	4' 10"
62½ sq. ft.	WING AREA	66 sq. ft.
619 lbs.	TARE WEIGHT	565 lbs.
905 lbs.	GROSS WEIGHT	875 lbs.
193 m.p.h.	MAX. SPEED	192 m.p.h.

In its day the DH 71 was faster than contemporary R.A.F. fighters and modifications to the controls had to be made because high operating speeds coupled with low gross weight made the little machine over sensitive and difficult to handle in rough weather. Regretfully nothing remains of the two machines built. In 1930 G-EBQV was shipped to Australia where it force-landed into a street killing Mr. David Smith the pilot. For many years G-EBRV the other DH 71 was on display at de Havillands Hatfield works. This only remaining example was on Oct. 3rd 1940 destroyed by a bomb from a Junkers 88.

3. The Colourful Thirties

The fact that de Havillands had been able to produce a small biplane with good access to both cockpits by no means ensured that the Tiger Moth would be ordered by the R.A.F., for there were other contenders in the field and some of these were very good aeroplanes indeed. There was the Blackburn Bluebird, a two-seater biplane which like the Moth series had originated as a wooden aeroplane. A later version had its structure translated into metal and was known as the Bluebird IV. G-AABV the prototype first flew at the beginning of 1929 and was therefore in the field some two and a half years prior to the Tiger Moth. A further development, the Blackburn B2, appeared in 1932 with metal panels covering the fuselage instead of the usual fabric, and this version found favour with some of the Reserve Schools. During the early stages of the war Blackburns operated B2 aircraft from the Elementary Flying Training School which was under their management at Brough near Hull. The Bluebird–B2 series had side-by-side seating in place of the usual tandem arrangement that found favour with the R.A.F. until recent years.

Then there was the Hawker Tomtit, a small biplane of metal construction that appeared on the scene during 1930. It performed very nicely on its 155 h.p. Armstrong Siddeley Mongoose radial engine and its rate of climb was quite outstanding for a light aeroplane. Small numbers were in fact used by the R.A.F. on training duties.

The Tiger Moth had yet another rival in the Robinson Redwing, an all wooden biplane which in common with the Blackburn Bluebird had side-by-side seating for the two occupants. In 1930 this attractive little aeroplane cost only £575 but its performance on an 88 h.p. Genet IIa engine placed it at a disadvantage as an R.A.F. trainer.

The emergence of the Tiger Moth coincided with the appearance of a serious rival from the Avro Company whose Avian had provided such competition for the de Havilland Moths during the preceding years. Avro's light biplane was rarely out of the newspapers at that time breaking one record after another. During the Great War the celebrated Avro 504 replaced one of de Havilland's designs, the DH 6, and had gone on to become the outstanding trainer of the period. It was therefore understandable that the Avro Company should endeavour to repeat their success and the new trainer emerged as the Tutor or Avro 621. It was somewhat larger and considerably heavier than the other aeroplanes under consideration by the Air Ministry. The 215 h.p. Armstrong Siddeley Lynx engine was chosen, nearly one hundred more horse power than the Gipsy III that was fitted to the early Tiger Moths, so that the Tutor was inevitably more expensive than its smaller contemporaries. A scaled-down version powered by the 135 h.p. Genet Major engine followed during 1931, and this design, the Avro 631, was given the name of 'Cadet'.

So these were the aeroplanes at the disposal of the Air Ministry when, as already stated in Chapter 2, the evaluation trials took place during the second half of 1931. In that chapter the sequence of events was given brief mention, but at this point in the story it is interesting to look back to the Martlesham trials in greater detail since this event was to set the stage for the Tiger Moths' future success.

In those days it was the practice to send new aircraft,

both military and civil, to the Aeroplane and Armament Experimental Establishment. This impressively named unit was in reality the old R.A.F. Testing Squadron, hitherto based at Upavon, by now removed to Martlesham Heath near Ipswich in order to allow more room for the ever-expanding Central Flying School.

When the Air Ministry invited tenders to meet a particular specification it was usual for a number of manufacturers to compete, and from the foregoing it will be realized that this particular occasion was no exception. Under the circumstances the comparative tests were conducted on a highly competitive basis, for so many factors were involved in addition to the more obvious ones of performance. Aeroplane A might be cheaper than aeroplane B which may in turn be more economical to operate than A because of easier servicing. Then again another aeroplane may be inexpensive in both first and operating costs but out of the running because of some undesirable flying characteristic.

Tests were in the hands of Flight Lieutenant Don Flemming and Flight Lieutenant C. B. Wincott (later Air Marshal Wincott, C.B.E.) in company with a young and newly commissioned R.A.F. officer named A. J. Pegg. In later years he was to become well known as 'Bill' Pegg, M.B.E., Chief Test Pilot for the Bristol Aeroplane Company. The mechanics at Martlesham often doubled as flight observers and one so involved at the time of the trials was Sergeant Alf Heskins. Whilst he is unable to recall any dramatic moments during the Comprehensive Military Tests he clearly remembers long periods of straight and level flying watching an infuriating instrument with a bubble that burst whenever the aeroplane climbed or descended more than twenty feet from its allotted height.

The first DH 60T Tiger Moth began its trials on 22nd August 1931. This was G-ABNJ with its aileron tips uncomfortably close to the ground. The test report on G-ABNJ dated 15th September had this to say under the following heading:

Summary of Type Requirements

There is little difference between this aircraft and Moth E3 reported on in M/465th [this was the DH 60T fitted with the Gipsy III engine but with the top wing directly above the front cockpit].

The sweepback has brought the lower wing-tips rather close to the ground but no difficulty arises from this provided the correct tyre pressure is maintained.

The report quotes the initial rate of climb as 700 ft. per minute and the maximum speed 107.5 m.p.h. at 2,000 ft., but perhaps the most important part of the document, certainly likely to influence the final choice, was that which appeared under the heading of 'Maintenance':

> In so far as maintenance by Service personnel is concerned this aircraft is excellent. The trials carried out on an earlier aircraft gave particularly good results (see Martlesham Heath report No. M/465b/Q1). Since that date many refinements have been incorporated, increasing the accessibility considerably. No trouble has been experienced during the tests at this unit.

Such an organization as the A and AEE could readily be excused if it developed a somewhat blase attitude towards aircraft so that this assessment was praise indeed coming as it did from people who had reached the stage where they were hardly likely to be easily impressed by a new aeroplane. The low wing tips was another matter and here the test report would seem to have treated G-ABNJ too generously. Experience proved that even when the tyre pressures were correct it was all too easy to run a wing tip along the ground, particularly during cross wind landings. Within a matter of weeks one of the original eight DH 60T Tiger Moths had its lower wings set at a more pronounced dihedral angle and its sweepback increased slightly. It seems likely that thus modified G-ABPH won the contract for de Havillands against all comers.

The Air Ministry placed an order for thirty-five machines

against specification T23/31 which was based upon
G-ABPH. By now the type was considered so dissimilar
to the Moth series that it became the DH 82. The R.A.F.
called it the Tiger Moth MK I. Minor refinements excepted,
these aeroplanes were very similar to the aeroplane we
recognize to this day as a Tiger Moth, the most noticeable
difference being the top of the fuselage behind the rear
cockpit. Unlike the well-known plywood top deck on the
'modern' Tiger, this was fabric covered. The engine was
the 120 h.p. Gipsy III as fitted in the Puss Moth, for the
130 h.p. Gipsy Major was yet to be made.

The Air Ministry numbered these thirty-five machines
K2567 to K2601 and allocated the first fifteen of them
(K2567 to K2581) to No. 3 Flying Training School R.A.F.
Grantham. To the pupils of this R.A.F.-manned flying
school must go the distinction of being the first to receive
their pilot training on Tiger Moths. It is doubtful if any
one of these cadet pilots (or for that matter their flying
instructors) could have visualized the untold thousands of
pupil pilots, military and civil, who would follow their
example or that the nineteen-sixties would see a continuing
stream of learners climbing out of Tigers after perhaps a
first solo or their qualifying cross-country flight.

One of the six pilots from 24 Squadron who ferried the
first R.A.F. Tiger Moths from Stag Lane to Grantham was
P. Heath (now Group Captain Heath, ret.). Apparently it
was a bitterly cold day and the pilots were forced to wait
for the weather to improve before flying to Grantham. In
an effort to keep them warm the ever hospitable de Havilland Company supplied the pilots with rum in generous
quantities, and the act of kindness resulted in Heath getting into trouble for crazy flying in his new Tiger Moth
before setting course. During this period the Flight Commander of 'A' Flight, 3 F.T.S. Grantham, was the now
retired Group Captain P. Holyroyd Smith, O.B.E. Hitherto
his pupils had done their training on the much liked
Hawker Tomtit. It was at a time when his latest entry of
cadet pilots had reached the critical pre-solo stage that

Heath and his colleagues arrived from Stag Lane with the first ten Tiger Moths to enter R.A.F. service.

'A' Flight was ordered to convert its pupils to the new machines, all protests from Holroyd Smith and requests that he might be allowed to postpone the conversion from Tomtit to Tiger until after first solo being refused by the Air Ministry, so that each pupil required a further three to four hours dual before being sent off on his own.

The new Tiger Moths were considered to be far more difficult to fly than the Tomtits, but very good trainers for this reason. Mr. C. S. Thom, then Sales Manager of de Havillands, flew up with Hubert Broad on many occasions to see how the R.A.F. were managing with their new trainers. Being a new and somewhat experimental type, the Air Ministry had ordered few if any spares. Unserviceability, therefore, was feared as the tail skids wore out, but these were delivered by Hubert Broad as required. The Gipsy III tended to overheat in a prolonged climb at too low an airspeed, a weakness that was later rectified when the improved Gipsy Major took its place in the Tiger Moth.

R.A.F. Grantham received its new Tiger Moths between November 1931 and February 1932. They had a mixed reception from the flying instructors and Wing Commander H. A. C. Stratton, A.F.C., describes his early impressions, 'The shaking and juddering whilst ticking over, the dreadful aileron control, the effort required to put up an inverted formation show at Hendon, the difficulty of operating in any sort of wind; no brakes and the tail skid tearing up great chunks of grass field!! Points for: *NO* trouble; very cheap to run and had a nice locker for instructor's suitcases when on week-ends.'

There will be many experienced pilots who would endorse those remarks, but equally they would be the first to admit their affection for the 'old Tiger'—and it is this very ability to worm its way into one's affection that seems to be the prime cause of its success despite one or two unvarnishable faults.

In May 1932 the Central Flying School, by now removed

45

from Upavon to Wittering, received six Tiger Moths from the Home Aircraft Depot at Henlow where they had been held since December 1931 (K2582 to K2587).

It was towards the end of 1932 that one of the original Grantham machines figured in an experiment at Martlesham Heath. An Avro Cadet had disintegrated whilst being dived by 'Bill' Pegg and the incident was traced to aileron flutter. Probably as a result of Pegg's report and of course those of other test pilots, the Air Ministry had become very sensitive about the possibility of flutter developing at high speed, and Tiger Moth K2578 was fitted with mass balance weights to the ailerons whereupon it was dived to 215 m.p.h. The test report says that 'considerable force is required to hold the aircraft in the dive', and at over 200 this is not difficult to believe.

The following year one of the Central Flying School machines (K2583) went to Martlesham Heath for further mass balance tests. On this occasion a rudder from an old Metal Moth (K1864) was fitted after $2\frac{1}{4}$ lbs. of lead had been added to the extremity of the horn balance. The test report noted no change in handling characteristics, and from the end of 1933 onwards all Service machines had mass balance on the rudder in addition to the ailerons.

The next five machines from the original Air Ministry order were fitted with floats. K2588, 2590 and 2591 were dispatched to Singapore during June 1934, whilst K2589 and 2592 were on their way to Hong Kong the following June.

The last of this batch of thirty-five Tiger Moths went to the Home Aircraft Depot, Henlow, the order being completed by January 1932, some fifteen months after the original DH 82 (G-ABRC) had made its first flight. Taking into account the test flying programme and the usual delays associated with a new product, this was by any standards a commendable achievement on the part of the Stag Lane factory.

Looking back it seems strange that some of these aircraft should have remained inactive for several years after leaving the factory, for the Home Aircraft Depot did not issue K2594 to 604 Squadron until December 1934 and the last eight remained in their possession until June 1935 when they were sent to R.A.F. Kenley. By that time the DH 82a had appeared, but more of this later.

When the Tiger Moth first appeared in 1931 there was a more or less immediate demand from the clubs whose activities were booming under the stimulus of a not unacceptable Government subsidy that had been in existence in one form or another for some years.

We now look upon the Tiger as a light 'plane ideally suited to a nip around the countryside on a hot summer's day, or a few moments hilarious aerobatics, but in the early 'thirties it commanded far more respect. When the first machines appeared they were treated with almost the same reverence as a new operational aeroplane, and production was confined to the R.A.F. and the many foreign governments who saw in the Tiger Moth the answer to their training needs.

During the period 1931–32 the de Havilland Company conducted a vigorous advertising campaign promoting the Tiger Moth. One double-page spread in particular that appeared in the 2nd March 1932 issue of *The Aeroplane* carried the headline, 'ONE MACHINE ADAPTABLE FOR EVERY BRANCH OF TRAINING'. There were five insert pictures depicting the aeroplane in its various roles and these were captioned, 'Flying', 'Fighting', 'Bombing', 'Photography' and 'Wireless'. The fighter version was shown as a single-seater with a camera-gun, whilst the bomber had four 20 lb. practice bombs under the fuselage. The caption said, 'Low converging bombing and high altitude sighting could be carried out.' The Photography version had a survey-type camera in the front cockpit which was to be operated by the Observer, or alternatively he could devote his attention to 'a wireless transmitting and receiving set'—VHF was yet to appear in aeroplanes.

Such versatility was not lost on the aviation authorities in other countries, and soon the great export success that had been de Havilland's when they introduced the original Moth was being repeated all over again.

Following on the Air Ministry contract for thirty-five machines, orders began to pour in so that large-scale production was immediately put in hand at Stag Lane. One DH 82 went to Hong Kong (VR-HAR), followed by four to the Swedish Air Force. Another four Tigers went on to the Swedish Civil Register (SE-ADE to SE-ADH), and works number 3116 was sold to the Nosowa Co. in Japan. The Persian Air Force placed a sizeable order for twenty machines, and this was followed by five to Brazil and three to China. Eleven were built for the Portuguese Air Force. Altogether 114 DH 82 Tiger Moths were produced in this country, the last five machines (Works Nos. 3170–4) going to the Danish Air Force. Licences were granted to A. B. Svensker Järnvagsverkstädena, Lindingö, of Stockholm, Sweden, who produced three (FV 597 to 599), and Haerens Flyvemaskinefabric, Kjeller, Norway. This company manufactured seventeen DH 82 Tiger Moths for the Royal Norwegian Air Force.*

The majority of the 114 machines produced by the de Havilland Company were destined to become military aeroplanes, either with the R.A.F. or the foreign air forces already mentioned. Eighteen did appear in civil markings, but fifteen of these had strong Service connections being used by the Elementary and Reserve Flying Schools (civilian managed units training R.A.F. pilots prior to their advancement to Service Flying Training Schools). Notwithstanding this almost exclusive confinement to Service needs G-ABTB was bought by Standard Telephones Ltd. for experiments in radio communications, whilst Sir Alan Cobham was able to purchase the prototype G-ABRC and G-ABUL for use during his world famous National Aviation Day Displays.

The flying clubs were to wait a long time for their Tiger Moths, for it was not until 1937 that the backlog of orders had been met to the point that the de Havilland Company was able to divert its attention from R.A.F. and foreign

*See additional note at end of chapter, page 59.

government orders. In the face of such heavy demand from official customers it was something of an achievement that Sir Alan Cobham was able to obtain two of the early Tiger Moths.

Cobham had for many years been closely connected with the de Havilland Company, testing some of their prototypes and using other of their aircraft for many of his record-breaking flights. In his case the question of breaking records was often secondary to the prime occupation of surveying possible air routes, a task to which he devoted his efforts with the most incredible energy. Sir Geoffrey de Havilland recalls that he can never remember Cobham taking more than ten minutes to eat a full cooked lunch, and often his midday meal was eaten whilst dashing to and fro from one aeroplane to another. Throughout these proceedings he somehow or other contrived to give his colleagues standing by a complete running commentary on what he was doing and where he was going. A brilliant flight during 1926, to Australia and back in a DH 50 fitted with floats, culminated in his landing on the Thames in front of the Houses of Parliament. On that occasion, before an enormous crowd cheering its approval, he received his well-deserved knighthood.

It was not, however, his personal connection alone that enabled him to jump the Tiger Moth queue so much as the great importance attached to the National Aviation Day Displays which he organized between 1932 and 1935. Although the country had been stirred by the heroic achievements of such pioneers as Jim Mollison, Bert Hinkler and Amy Johnson, in 1932 the public looked upon flying still very much as something for the birds. Yet British achievement in the air was without parallel anywhere in the world. British pilots were the first to fly the Atlantic by both airship and aeroplane, the first to fly to Australia and the Cape, holders of the world's height record (Cyril Uwins in a Vickers Vespa reached 43,976 feet on 16th September 1932), the world's long distance record (Cranwell to Walvis Bay, South Africa 5,340 miles non-stop by Fairey Monoplane on 6th February 1933), and the coveted world speed record was won in 1931 by Flight Lieutenant G. H. Stainforth in a Supermarine S6B Seaplane at the then fantastic speed of 407.5 m.p.h. Furthermore, during the 'thirties we were exporting more aeroplanes than any other nation, so it is perhaps surprising to realize that public attitude to flying at the time was one of polite but sceptical interest. Certainly it was the exception rather than the rule that anyone had actually flown—even as passenger. Sir Alan Cobham set about championing the cause of aviation for he firmly believed that an air-minded Britain would eventually lead to greater national prosperity and fuller employment.

These were the days of the Geneva disarmament conferences when a well-intended but misguided British Government had entered into unilateral disarmament—a move that was to put us at the mercy of a Hitler-roused Germany and all but leave us defenceless when the moment of truth arrived. The National Aviation Day Displays, in themselves a form of light and amusing entertainment, had a serious underlying principal: the need to arouse public interest in flying and make it aware of our dangerously weak position amongst the air forces of the world.

The days of the 'Cobham Air Circuses', as they were affectionately called, brought aviation in Britain into its most colourful phase, and by a combination of good publicity, sound business management and superb showmanship, thousands flocked to see these 'Circuses of the Air'. Over 300 towns were visited in one season, and for the first time vast sections of the public had the opportunity to fly for as little as 5/-. Such was the demand for these joy rides that when the display visited Ireland people continued to queue until after sunset, and flying continued into the night with nothing but the moon to light the field, whilst the aeroplanes landed and took off with their passengers.

It was part of Sir Alan Cobham's campaign to persuade local authorities to open municipal aerodromes, and because these were few in the early 'thirties suitable landing areas had to be found for the displays. In conjunction with his pilots and engineers Sir Alan and his organizers would select a likely town for the next display. When this was decided one of the pilots would fly over to find a large field. Such a field had to be chosen with care. It had to be within easy reach of the town, and be large enough to accommodate several thousand spectators and a stream of aircraft, including the lumbering Handley Page Clive. It was also advisable to choose a field away from hills—such vantage points used to detract from box-office receipts, and became known to the Cobham team as 'Aberdonian grandstands'. Then again the ground had to be hard enough to withstand the weight of aircraft and the surface smooth enough to permit landing and taking-off. Where possible, therefore, the reconnoitring pilot would land, inspect the field and find the owner, who was often the local farmer. A chat followed by a five-pound note and promises of free trips for the farmer and his family would usually clinch the deal.

Then the wheels would begin turning. Aircraft would fly in, the bigger ones carrying equipment, while the engineers' and pilots' families would be making their way to the field by road. Soon caravans would appear and marquees mushroom up. Large screens proclaiming this brand of petrol or that make of oil were erected, their primary function being to hide from those who did not want to pay all the activity on the ground, which is half the fun of a big air display. The box-office would be set up, public address system installed, catering laid on and all the usual 'offices' provided. Meanwhile the publicity side would be at full pressure putting up posters on vantage points and distributing leaflets in the pubs.

First light on the great day itself would see the engineers completing their final checks on the aircraft. It says much for these engineers and the organizers that, notwithstanding the highly spectacular nature of the demonstration flying, no serious accidents that could be attributed to the Cobham team occurred during the four years on tour.

Then came the first spectacle—the aerial counterpart

to the circus parade down the high street, but instead of clowns and elephants there was a mass formation, led by the great Handley Page airliner, a twin-engined biplane of massive proportions which was usually flown by Cobham himself. On either side of the airliner would fly two Tiger Moths which in turn were flanked by a pair of Avro 504s. Bringing up the rear would be another large biplane, the three-engined Airspeed Ferry, with a Gipsy Moth on either side, and the formation sometimes included an Autogiro. As this impressive fleet of aircraft swept overhead, traffic would stop and windows fly open to make way for craning necks and excited exchanges of conversation.

A fine day would see a steady stream of people wending their way to the field. The Mayor and other civic leaders would be flown during the morning, together with inn-keepers and others who had lent their support in one way or another, so that by midday all complimentary flights had been dealt with. And then the show was on. It would open with a grand formation fly past of all the aircraft, similar to the crowd raising one that had taken place that morning, but this time held low over the field in full view of the spectators. The next item featured the Tiger Moth, and the 1933 Souvenir Programme describes the routine as follows:

2. Premier Display of Advanced Aerobatics

This demonstration will be given on the 1933 de Havilland Tiger Moth, specially built for the advanced training of Royal Air Force pilots. The aim is to display the capabilities of a modern aeroplane and the liberties which can be taken with it. The pilot is renowned for his aerobatic skill and with such a machine as the Tiger Moth he gives an out-standing performance, which includes the most difficult flying manœuvres yet conceived. As each stunt is performed it will be explaind by Sir Alan Cobham through the loud-speakers.

During the first year of the Cobham Shows this particular part of the programme was carried out by Flight Lieutenant C. Turner-Hughes, a brilliant aerobatic pilot. Turner-Hughes repeated his performance twice on each day of the

The engines in the story: reading top to bottom, A.D.C. Cirrus, Gipsy I and Gipsy Major I.

Very important training characteristics of the Tiger Moth are unrestricted visibility all round and above from both cockpits, and ease of egress with a parachute from the front as well as back seat. This is made possible by especially deep doors and absence of flying wires or exhaust pipes in the vicinity of the front cockpit.

The Tiger Moth fulfils all primary, intermediate and advanced training requirements. It exhibits the characteristics of the high-powered, high-performance types in which pupils will ultimately fly, yet it is economical both in first cost and upkeep. For the training and exercise of fighting the Tiger Moth is equipped with a camera gun. As a two-seater observation or reconnaissance aircraft it carries wireless telegraphy apparatus and camera equipment. As a long-range light bomber a bomb rack is fitted carrying four 2o-lb. practise bombs.

TIGER MOTH

'AB-INITIO' . INTERMEDIATE . ADVANCED & AEROBATIC TRAINING

Fully illustrated Specification will be forwarded upon request.

THE DE HAVILLAND AIRCRAFT COMPANY LIMITED, STAG LANE AERODROME, EDGWARE, MIDDLESEX, ENGLAND
Associated Companies in Australia, Canada, India, and South Africa. Licensees, Selling and Service Agents throughout the World.

KINDLY MENTION "THE AEROPLANE" WHEN CORRESPONDING WITH ADVERTISERS.

Tiger Moth advertisement which appeared in *The Aeroplane*, 6 January 193 displays and his log book shows that he flew 780 hours during his association with the National Aviation Day Displays. A record of each aerobatic manœuvre was kept, and the 780 hours display flying consisted of 2,328 Loops, 2,190 Rolls, 567 Bunts, 522 Upward Rolls, 40 Inverted Falling Leaves and 5 Inverted Loops. In the course of his outstanding exhibition flying, 3,830 landings were made, but these figures are the more remarkable when it is remembered that he was with Cobham for only one year. During this time he spent no less than 170 hours upside-down in his Tiger.

Provided an aeroplane is robust enough it is not very difficult for a pilot to roll into the inverted position, but due to the fact that most engines rely upon a carburettor that owes its inheritance to the humble domestic W.C. cistern, no power is forthcoming once the inverted attitude is reached. An inverted glide follows with the aeroplane perfectly controllable and ready to return to normal flight whenever the pilot decides he has lost enough height hanging in his safety harness. From the spectators' point of view such a performance, although interesting for a short while, cannot compare with the sight of an aeroplane flying inverted under power doing turns and other manœuvres.

To enable the Tiger to fly upside down it was necessary to persuade the already inverted Gipsy III engine to work in the upright position of its ancestors, the earlier Gipsy I and II. For the purpose a separate auxiliary tank was installed on the floor of the front cockpit and this was pressurized at $2\frac{1}{2}$ lbs. p.s.i. by a small wind-driven air pump bolted to a fixed part of the undercarriage. An additional engine control in the cockpit brought the system into operation as required and made it possible for inverted flight to continue so long as there was sufficient petrol in the auxiliary tank. During the early stages of the Cobham Shows G-ABUL was modified for inverted flight.

For air displays the ability to execute aerobatic manœuvres is in itself not enough. If the crowd is to really enjoy the show positioning is all important, and Turner-

Hughes was very aware of this factor. The position of the sun must be taken into account or the audience may be unable to watch the aeroplane. Then the wind direction has to be considered, otherwise, in a slow roll for instance, the aeroplane may appear to be drifting off direction. Most of the manœuvres should be completed in front of, rather than above the crowd, not only for safety's sake but also because it is tiring for the spectators to have to look upwards for more than brief periods. There was however one item in his repertoire that Turner-Hughes considered should be executed right overhead. It was usually the finale and is best described by quoting from an article entitled 'Stunting and Showmanship' written by Turner-Hughes for the December 1933 issue of the now defunct pre-war magazine *Popular Flying*:

> Rolling into the normal position he climbs quickly, rolls into the inverted and, diving at the crowd, passes over their astonished heads at a height of between 100 and 150 ft. There's the thrill. They can see his face, his hands on the stick and his tie fluttering in the breeze, as he goes, but care must be taken not to over repeat this or the thrill is gone. The attitude of the public is inclined to be, 'If he does it so often and so low, it can't be terribly dangerous or difficult,' and the kick is gone.

It is revealing that Turner-Hughes did not look upon inverted flying near the ground as a dangerous manœuvre although he was concerned with what the crowd thought of his performance. Such was the sense of security generated by the robust little Tiger Moth that it was possible for a naturally cautious man such as Turner-Hughes to fly upside-down above a large crowd.

Turner-Hughes, or as he was known to his friends, 'Toc-H', left display flying in 1933 to become test pilot for Armstrong-Whitworth, and his place as star aerobatic pilot was taken by another brilliant performer—G. A. V. Tyson. Tyson too seemed able to coerce the Tiger Moth into any position, and in addition to the usual rolls and stall turns, used to loop around a length of bunting stretched between two posts arranged so that with the Tiger Moth standing on the ground there was only 4 ft. clearance between each wing tip and post and 6 ft. between the top wing and the bunting.

A later Tiger, G-ACEZ, was fitted with a 9 in. long arm projecting outwards from the tip of the bottom port wing. The arm terminated in a small hook and during the period 1934–6 Geoffrey Tyson picked a handkerchief from the ground on more than 800 occasions—a superb demonstration of the Tiger's controllability.

There were of course many items of varied interest during the National Aviation Day Displays. Parachute jumping could be seen either from the ground or as a passenger in one of the large multi-engined biplanes. There was an exciting air race around a tight closed circuit. Music was played over the public address system and relayed by 'wireless' to the pilot of an aircraft overhead who would make his machine 'give a display of syncopated flying in time to dance music'. Members of the public would be invited to step up to the microphone and request the pilot to carry out certain manœuvres—such was the novelty of radio communications in 1932. The short take-off and landing performance of the Autogiro followed, and then there was formation aerobatics, very much more difficult on low-powered aircraft than the immaculate sequences performed today by modern high-powered jets.

An old Avro 504 was used for a ' Display of Wing Walking' and during the show an invitation was extended to any ex-R.F.C. pilot who flew in World War I to try his hand again with one of the Cobham team as safety pilot. They even had a trapeze artist hanging from one aeroplane, going through the usual routine at 100 m.p.h., 700 ft. above the crowd.

Comedy played a big part in the Cobham Shows and the item entitled 'The Battle of the Flours' was described in the programme, 'This item shows the sad fate of a bridal party. Owing to the villainy of the chauffeur, who is greatly hated by his pilot friends, the honeymoon couple meet with disaster from the air.' In practice what happened was this: An ancient 'bull-nosed' Morris would lurch across the field whilst the commentator explained to the crowd that the irate parents had enlisted an aerial deterrent, whereupon the aircraft bombarded the couple with flour bombs delivered with devastating accuracy.

The National Aviation Day Displays made heavy demands on Sir Alan's team and it was not uncommon to see one or two of them fall asleep over their evening meal. Without doubt the skill and daring of Sir Alan's pilots fired the imagination of many young men and women at the time, who then pinched and scraped so that they might learn to fly at their local club. Many of these same young men were to become members of 'The Few' who defended the country during the dark days of 1940, whilst some of the girls joined the A.T.A. and did invaluable work ferrying all types of aircraft from factory to squadron. The Tiger Moth made its contribution by creating enthusiasm all over the country.

There was an occasion when a summons was issued against one of the pilots for low flying. Sir Alan himself appeared in court and with great dignity informed the bench that they had actually issued the summons to a 'professional' pilot, whereupon the case was promptly dismissed. It seems that in those days, whereas a prosecution might be contemplated against ordinary pilots, such a thing was unthinkable when it involved a professional.

These were the glorious golden days of sporting aviation, and the Tiger Moth's part in air displays is well stated by P. R. Allison, a member of the National Aviation Day Display team who is with Sir Alan Cobham to this day as Technical Services Manager of one of his companies, Flight Refuelling Ltd.: 'There was no doubt about it that the Tiger Moth, from the aircraft handling side and the flexibility of its engine, made an extremely good combination both for enjoyable normal flying and for a full aerobatic set-up.'

Inverted Tiger flying was not confined to the Cobham Air Displays, for in 1932 the R.A.F. Central Flying School formed a team around five modified DH 82 Tiger Moths and these gave a superb show of inverted formation flying at the Hendon display of that year. It is rarely the case that an aeroplane handles as well upside-down as it does in normal flight and the Tiger Moth is no exception, so that the C.F.S. team was hard put to give a really good show.

Following on their extensive advertising campaign, the de Havilland Company organized a sales tour which was in the hands of their test pilot, Hubert Broad. While he was flying the demonstration Tiger Moth inverted over Rio de Janeiro, his gold cigarette-case fell out of his pocket and disappeared somewhere into the middle of the city. This was a sad loss since it had been presented to him suitably inscribed by that grand Lady of flying, the Duchess of Bedford. Very much to his surprise the police delivered it to him at his hotel after apprehending the finder in the process of pawning it.

Clem Pike (later Wing Commander C. A. Pike, A.F.C.) took Tiger Moth G-ACJA out to Bucharest during August 1933 and, since his wife was with him as passenger, decided to combine pleasure with business and show her the most attractive parts of the Rhine. It was his intention on leaving Brussels to join the river at Coblenz but an oil pipe fracture made necessary a forced landing in Holland at a place called Wiljig. No one seemed very worried about such formalities as Customs, so without further ado Pike went into the village and got the pipe repaired. On his return to the aeroplane he was astonished to find his wife standing next to the Tiger and being photographed by every available camera while a local policeman held back the crowd with a drawn sword!

The Tiger Moth in the hands of Geoffrey Tyson was to make headline news on Wednesday 25th July 1934. The *News Chronicle* carried front-page pictures of Tyson flying inverted in his Tiger accompanied by a Gipsy Moth (allegedly flown by Sir Alan Cobham), and a banner headline proclaimed TWENTY-FIVE YEARS AFTER—THIS! The occasion was the twenty-fifth anniversary of Bleriot's heroic first flight across the Channel in 1909. Tyson made two attempts, for on the first occasion he followed the coast instead of crossing the Channel. The compass will not function when inverted and as conditions were hazy at the time it was then decided that Sir Alan would lead the way in his personal Airspeed Courier (not in the Gipsy Moth as suggested by the *News Chronicle*).

At approximately 11 a.m. they set off with Tyson inverted, followed by a number of Press reporters deporting themselves in a miniature armada of assorted aeroplanes. The actual crossing took sixteen minutes and a report in a Bristol newspaper (typical of others covering the event) outlined the facts and concluded:

> Flight Lieutenant Tyson after he landed near Lympne [on his return] said he could have gone on flying for another three or four minutes in an upside-down position.
>
> 'When I pulled the machine back to normal flying,' he said, 'I naturally felt the blood rushing back to my body. It was nothing more, and I experienced no great physical discomfort.'
>
> Flight Lieutenant Tyson is regarded as the greatest expert on upside-down flying in this country. It is estimated that during the course of a year he flies some 15,000 miles upside down.

Tyson remembers the time during one display when for some inexplicable reason the pin of his safety harness came out while he was inverted at 600 ft. Fortunately but a few days previously the original plain control column had been replaced by one of the spade-grip variety, and he was able to hang on to this although his action of self-preservation put the Tiger Moth into an inverted dive. With one hand on the stick and the other grasping the instrument panel, Tyson was able to recover in a screaming half loop which terminated at tree-top height in a valley near Tunbridge Wells—more or less below ground level!

Tyson eventually followed the example of his predecessor Turner-Hughes and became an experimental test pilot. After a short period with the Avro company he returned in 1937 to join Sir Alan Cobham's new enterprise, Flight Refuelling Ltd. His last prototype was the 140-ton Saunders-Roe Princess flying boat.

Happily both Turner-Hughes and Tyson have maintained their contact with aviation and may be seen on occasions judging international aerobatic competitions.

The last DH 82 to be produced carried works number 3174, and this particular Tiger Moth formed part of a batch of five machines for the Danish Air Force, bearing the Service marking S5 on joining that Air Force.

One hundred and fourteen aeroplanes of one type produced over two years is not a big number, particularly when the design is in the light aeroplane category, and one wonders how many of these early type Tigers would have been made in their original form had not certain improvements occurred in time to meet a demand created by rapidly changing world affairs. The Gipsy III engine performed well, but under the influence of Frank Halford it was soon to do even better in slightly enlarged form as the 130 h.p. Gipsy Major. With this improved engine and certain other modifications of a quite minor nature a new Tiger Moth appeared in 1934, the DH 82a.

*It is believed that the Tigers delivered to Persia were fitted with a single machine gun of Czechoslovakian origin. Certainly the prototype G-ABRC was in 1933 so fitted, the gun being mounted in the front cockpit and firing over the top of the engine cowling. An ammunition box held 200 rounds and the gun was aimed through a simple ring and bead. A trigger on the rear control stick controlled the gun via a Bowden cable, fire being interrupted as each propeller blade swept across the "line-of-fire", by a Pratt and Whitney synchronising gear, driven from the rear of the engine. The system was tested by temporarily attaching a large plywood disc behind the propeller which was pulled over during the initial trials by a very brave man thus firing the first shot.

Firing tests with the engine running, cut a small arc in the disc, well clear of the propeller blades and so proved synchronisation!

4. Growing Up

The first of the improved Tiger Moths was tested at Martlesham Heath during September 1934, where it appeared in civil markings as G-ACDA (works number 3175). Apart from the new Gipsy Major I engine the most radical change —one that immediately met the eye—was the smooth, curved, plywood fuselage top which replaced the original fabric-and-stringer arrangement. The earlier Tigers had deep hinged doors to the front cockpit which had made it necessary to step down the top longerons in that area. Later an alternative fuselage was offered to customers without the bigger doors, and this more straightforward structure was adopted for the improved aeroplane. Fuel capacity was increased from eighteen to nineteen gallons, the rear cockpit seat was no longer adjustable, but otherwise the aeroplane was almost identical to the original G-ABRC.

The test report gave Rate of Climb as 635 feet per minute —rather less than the earlier model although the cruising speed was some 5 m.p.h. better. Whilst the new Tiger was known as the DH 82a, de Havillands' biggest customer, the Royal Air Force, called it the Tiger Moth II and without delay placed an order for fifty machines to specification 26/33 giving them service numbers K4242 to K4291. All fifty machines were delivered to R.A.F. Kenley between November 1934 and January 1935 and later transferred to various R.A.F. Flying Training Schools, No. 24 Squadron

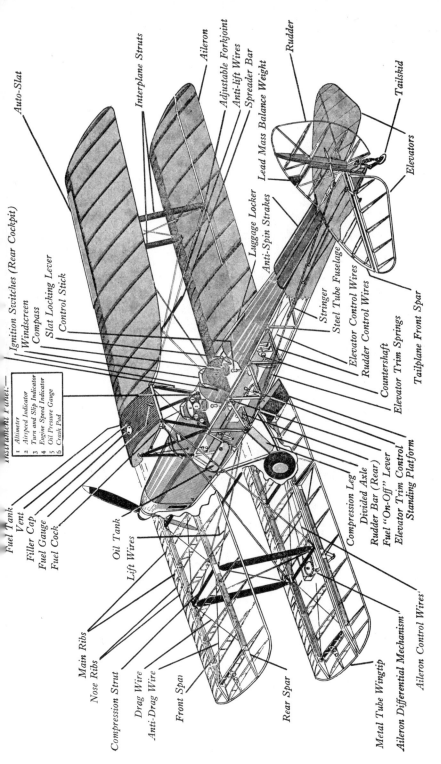

Auto-Slat

Ignition Switches (Rear Cockpit)
Windscreen
Compass
Slat Locking Lever
Control Stick

Interplane Struts

Aileron
Adjustable Forkjoint
Anti-lift Wires
Spreader Bar

Rudder

Tailskid

Elevators

Lead Mass Balance Weight

Luggage Locker
Anti-Spin Strakes

Stringer
Steel Tube Fuselage
Elevator Control Wires
Rudder Control Wires
Countershaft
Elevator Trim Springs
Tailplane Front Spar

Instrument Panel:—

1 Altimeter
2 Airspeed Indicator
3 Turn and Slip Indicator
4 Engine Speed Indicator
5 Oil Pressure Gauge
6 Crash Pad

Fuel Tank
Vent
Filler Cap
Fuel Gauge
Fuel Cock

Oil Tank
Lift Wires

Main Ribs
Nose Ribs
Compression Strut
Drag Wire
Anti-Drag Wire
Front Spar

Rear Spar

Metal Tube Wingtip
Aileron Differential Mechanism

Aileron Control Wires

Compression Leg
Divided Axle
Rudder Bar (Rear)
Fuel "On-Off" Lever
Elevator Trim Control
Standing Platform

The DH 82a Tiger Moth with seats removed for clarity

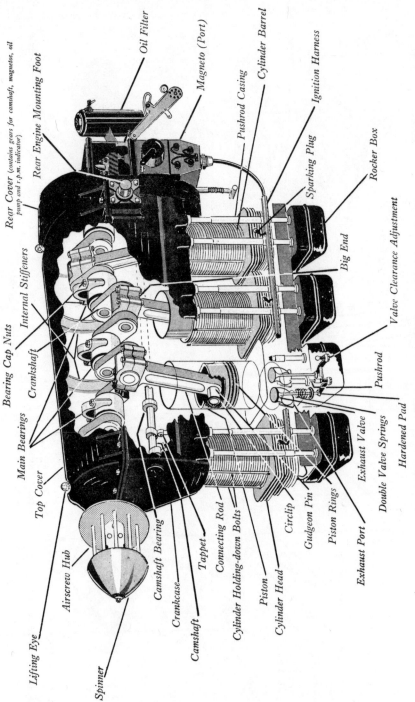

Lifting Eye

Airscrew Hub

Spinner

Camshaft Bearing

Crankcase

Camshaft

Tappet

Connecting Rod

Cylinder Holding-down Bolts

Piston

Cylinder Head

Circlip

Gudgeon Pin

Piston Rings

Exhaust Port

Double Valve Springs

Exhaust Valve

Hardened Pad

Pushrod

Valve Clearance Adjustment

Rocker Box

Ignition Harness

Big End

Sparking Plug

Cylinder Barrel

Pushrod Casing

Magneto (Port)

Oil Filter

Rear Cover (contains gears for camshaft, magneto, oil pump and r.p.m. indicator)

Rear Engine Mounting Foot

Internal Stiffeners

Crankshaft

Bearing Cap Nuts

Main Bearings

Top Cover

Gipsy Major 1 engine, cut away to reveal its main features

and some of the civilian manned Elementary and Reserve Flying Training Schools. Most of the machines from Kenley went to these civil units which were under Air Ministry contract, so that in effect production for the home market was confined to the needs of the Royal Air Force.

The R.A.F. order started at works number 3238, the sixty-fourth DH 82a to leave the factory, but the first sixty-three machines went to divers customers of interesting variety. Thirteen were delivered to various Elementary and Reserve Flying Training Schools. One of them, in fact the third DH 82a to see the light of day, was registered G-ACDC and is now in the hands of the 'Tiger Club' at Redhill aerodrome. This Tiger, the oldest in existence, has led a particularly dramatic life *since* the war and will receive more detailed attention in a later chapter.

Sir Alan Cobham was allowed to purchase G-ACEZ and G-ACFA to supplement his two DH 82 Tigers so heavily engaged on air display duties, and the Scottish Motor Traction Co. Ltd. bought G-ACDY with a view to starting an airline! One went to Holland (PH-AJG) and another to Australia. The remainder of these first sixty-three Tiger Moths were purchased by the air forces of Spain, Denmark, Persia, Portugal and Austria.

By now the Royal Air Force had committed itself to the Tiger Moth in so far as flying training was concerned, for, although 400 of the excellent Avro Tutor biplane trainers had been delivered to them during the period 1932–6, production ceased in May of that year and they were gradually replaced by the Tiger Moth II. Whilst it has not been possible to establish the official reason why the Tutor was dropped in favour of the Tiger Moth, there can be little doubt that the decision was taken in the light of both first and operating costs. A beautiful aeroplane to fly, the Avro Tutor was deservedly popular with Service pilots, but with economy a prime consideration its 240 h.p. Lynx engine could not compete with the 130 h.p. Gipsy Major. Nevertheless in 1934 the Tutor actually replaced the Tiger Moth at No. 3 Flying Training School, but this was a temporary reprieve and all Avro Tutors were withdrawn from service during the early years of the war.

The R.A.F. fitted their Tiger Moths with a rather cumbersome folding canvas hood which could be extended over the pupil in the rear cockpit confining his view to the limited instruments before him. Although it did nothing to enhance the Tiger's performance the hood certainly turned the aeroplane into an instrument trainer, providing its pupils with some periods of intense concentration with the turn needle of the Reid & Sigrist indicator as the only concession to gyro-operated flight panels. When it was eventually possible for de Havillands to supply the flying clubs with Tiger Moths, a situation arose where both military and civil pilots were trained on the same type of machine—a convenient arrangement for the country in times of emergency when vast numbers of pilots are required. Such a situation unhappily can no longer exist for, with the complex requirements of a modern supersonic air force to deal with, Service trainers have become so massive and expensive that no club could consider owning them.

With orders coming in from all over the world, in addition to the heavy demands of both R.A.F. and civil flying schools operating under Air Ministry contract, the DH 82a went into truly large-scale production at Stag Lane. By now the de Havilland Company had gone a long way towards becoming a big concern although it could by no means be described as an industrial giant. Nevertheless its growth was real enough, and it says much for the aeroplanes made at Stag Lane that a great deal of the de Havilland Company's progress occurred during the years of depression, which afflicted industry on both sides of the Atlantic. The strength of the company had been built up on Moths of various kinds and consolidated by the Tiger Moth itself, for without doubt it was the little biplanes that made the company. Unlike some of his competitors, de Havilland rarely pursued military contracts during the years preceding the war. Possibly this was because his main interest lay in civil aviation, but previous experience must have contributed to his absence from the pre-war military scene. Having suffered at the hands of officialdom on one or two occasions he was not prepared to see his designs ruined by an Air Ministry that changed its mind with the wind so that the project was assured of failure before it was flown. Aeroplanes, particularly good ones, do not materialize on their own but are entirely dependent upon men of outstanding talent in their own sphere. In acknowledging de Havilland's genius as an engineer it would be all too easy to overlook another factor of almost equal importance—his ability to surround himself with the right men. Frank Hearle was his earliest choice. They had shared digs together as young men at a time when Hearle was working in a Dalston bus depot, truing up crankshafts with, of all tools, a hand file! For this he was paid the then quite substantial wage of £2 10s. per week. When the young Geoffrey de Havilland decided to build his first aeroplane in 1907, Hearle joined him at the reduced salary of 35/-. From that time association between the two men strengthened and, but for brief periods, they were to remain together through two world wars and the uneasy peace that went between.

When work started on the first aeroplane, de Havilland and Hearle shared a flat in Kensington. De Havilland's sister Ione kept house for them and in later years she and Frank Hearle were married. Hearle eventually became Chairman and Managing Director of the company.

Another founder member of the de Havilland Aircraft Company was Arthur E. Hagg. With no formal engineering training, Hagg's genius for design eventually led him to be appointed as Chief Designer, a position he held for ten years until his retirement. Today no one lacking qualifications would be considered for such a position by an aircraft manufacturing firm, yet all the teaching in the world cannot give a man that special ability unless it is in-born.

It is often the case that as an organization grows larger so the link between staff and top management becomes more remote. Yet de Havilland succeeded in maintaining an almost family atmosphere long after the business had ceased to consist of a small number of people on first name terms.

While the flying clubs clamoured for Tiger Moths to replace their ageing equipment, instruction went on in Cirrus and Gipsy Moths along with the Avro Avian, Robinson Redwing and the other light aeroplanes of the day.

Anticipating future expansion de Havilland had purchased a number of open fields in the Hatfield area, and a new works and aerodrome was planned. The old Stag Lane aerodrome was finally sold for building land. Geoffrey de Havilland made the last take-off in July of 1934 and set course for Hatfield.

The Tiger Moth production line was gradually transferred to the new Hatfield factory, where its tempo was soon to be stimulated by events from Germany. Looking back on this lamentable period in our history there is an air of unreality surrounding the ostrich-like politicians of the day, none of whom seemed unduly perturbed about Germany's massive preparations for war. The lone voice of Winston Churchill consistently drew the attention of the House to our rapidly deteriorating position, warning the nation of the consequences of allowing a belligerent Germany to rise against an unprepared Britain. Such was the climate of British politics in the mid-'thirties that few Members of the House were prepared to treat seriously the facts and figures relating to German rearmament that were placed before them. Sufficient to say that when in later years Churchill's pre-war speeches were published in a book called *While England Slept*, they read like a history of the events leading up to the war although his pronouncements in the House of Commons had taken place some years earlier.

Eventually the hard realities of the situation struck home and, amongst other preparations, R.A.F. expansion was put in hand. This not only involved more personnel in various technical trades and more aircrew, but it became apparent that the existing civilian-run Elementary and Reserve Flying Schools were not enough to meet the urgent needs of a crash-rearmament programme. It was therefore decided to change the conception of these schools, affiliating them more closely to the R.A.F., and in 1937 the Royal Air Force Volunteer Reserve came into existence, the Tiger Moth playing an important part in the proceedings.

Pre-1937 flying training had been designed to provide the R.A.F. with first line pilots on a peacetime basis, but once the expansion got under way it was clear that a large reserve of aircrew would have to be trained to meet wartime casualties and provide a second line of defence.

The Volunteer Reserve was based upon a town centre which was under the command of a retired or reserve officer. He was assisted in his task by a local advisory committee which, amongst other functions, helped with recruiting. These town centres were attached to civilian-manned flying schools. Some were already training regular R.A.F. pilots, for it had been found more economical to carry out elementary training outside the Service and then transfer pupils to an R.A.F. unit for advanced instruction rather than operate elementary flying training within the Service. Other of these civil schools had been engaged on R.A.F. Reserve instruction and these too were brought into the scheme.

It was anticipated that members of the R.A.F.V.R. would do sixty hours flying per year, mostly at week-ends. After two years they would be converted to Service types of aircraft. Air Ministry contracts were put up for tender, and the aircraft industry, established flying schools and even retired R.A.F. officers with financial backing competed for them, sometimes before obtaining that prime and most important facility—an aerodrome.

Incredible as it may seem, it is on record that a contract was in fact awarded to a company without a suitable aerodrome—but the firm involved was Reid & Sigrist, a substantial concern with many years experience in the design and manufacturing of aircraft instruments. Starting with nothing but a series of fields and the necessary finance, the task of setting up a large flying school can only be realized when all the requirements are put on paper. The building of the school at Desford, Leicestershire, was recently recalled by Squadron Leader George Reid, D.F.C., now retired but at the time Chairman and Managing Director of Reid & Sigrist. The events took place several years before the formation of the R.A.F.V.R. at a time when civilian training of Service pilots was coming into vogue; nevertheless the problems involved follow closely those peculiar to the Reserve schools that took over in 1937. Indeed Desford came into the R.A.F.V.R. scheme on its inception, and if the following description gives an impression of over-lavish ground facilities for so few aeroplanes it should be remembered that the new aerodrome was designed for expansion in time of war—an expansion which when it came was hard to contain:

Reid & Sigrist Ltd. Training School at Desford, Leicestershire

A flying training school was required in Leicestershire and we obtained the contract for this against other competitors.

We bought land in a good position some ten miles from Leicester which was very suitable for a practical aerodrome, but it needed a tremendous amount of work which had to be done in a very short time. We started in August 1935 using machines to get the right levels and where necessary new grass was put down. Buildings were positioned so as not to interfere with the approaches. Fuel tanks were sunk under concrete and mobile refuellers bought to deal quickly with the aeroplanes. Ambulances and fire fighting vehicles were also acquired. We bought, I think, ten Tiger Moths on the advice of the Chief Instructor, George Lowdell.

Buildings went up for lectures, offices, messes and maintenance of aircraft. Tarmac roads were constructed and strong concrete positioned where the aircraft went in and out of hangars. Water was laid on from a distance.

A most advanced Tube and Bell sewage system was led away from the aerodrome by electric motors. This could deal

DH 82 Tiger Moths under construction at the Norwegian Air Force factory, Kjeller.

Line up of DH 82 Tiger Moths of the Royal Norwegian Air Force.

A Norwegian-built Tiger Moth on skis.

with two to three thousand people. Six- and twelve-room bungalows were built.

To keep the pupils interested and in a healthy condition we arranged for a good squash court, football and cricket pitch and two tennis courts.

The main electricity supply was fed through oil switches and arranged so that the whole installation could be shut off instantly.

The large buildings were steel framed and all the buildings had their own heating boilers.

Flying instructors were carefully chosen by George Lowdell and 'Taffy' Jones.

Obviously tremendous work had to be put in to get the place ready for 26th November with everything functioning satisfactorily by that date.

Lord Swinton, Air Marshal Tedder, Air Marshal Bowhill and others in authority were invited to an opening luncheon to see what had been accomplished in so short a time, and the Tiger Moths gave an exhibition of their readiness. On average the pupils were aged eighteen years, and under the Chief Instructor many became quite distinguished pilots, several obtaining high honours in the R.A.F.

Accurate records were kept of all pupils on their progress and examinations. These were often confirmed by their ability later in the R.A.F.

The Tiger Moths were fine aeroplanes for training purposes and were equipped with blind flying instruments and a hood which was pulled over the pupils when on instrument flying. The blind flying test consisted of an eighty mile triangular course.

The number of pupils at Desford grew to the point where we had to transfer the navigational course to Carlisle with their instructors and staff. This allowed more pupil pilots at Desford and many more Tiger Moths were required. The aerodrome was enlarged and more grass runways made. Four centres were built on the aerodrome, each under a separate instructional staff. Later we had one centre at Braunstone aerodrome where the Leicester Flying Club had been. This centre was on the south side whilst the Reid & Sigrist factory was situated on the north side of the airfield.

The addition of the centre at Braunstone took place

during the war and by this time we had about fifty Tiger Moths on pupil training. We also did night flying from the centres we had established.

The difficulty was obtaining staff; 90 per cent. came from near-by places and we had to run transport between their homes and the two aerodromes. We also established a system of technical training for both male and female staff.

It is interesting to note that in those days choice of aeroplane type was the prerogative of the contractor.

Sad to relate that when Squadron Leader Reid decided to retire and sell his interest in Reid & Sigrist, both Desford and Braunstone aerodromes ceased to exist, but there must be very many thousands of pilots and ex-pilots who took their first faltering steps in a Tiger Moth at Desford.

By August 1939 there were more than forty Reserve Flying Training Schools. With the exception of No. 4 which operated Blackburn B2 aircraft and No. 8 at Woodley equipped with Miles Magisters, all schools trained on Tiger Moths. Many of the units were closed on the outbreak of war, the remainder being renamed Elementary Flying Training Schools with Woodley and Cambridge producing flying instructors.

What was it like to be a pupil at one of these schools? Of course, during the 'thirties Tiger Moths were considered to be very much the last word in training aircraft, but the art of flying instruction, and it certainly is an art, was not so well developed as it is today. Like most other people flying instructors can, broadly speaking, be put into three basic categories: good, undistinguished and bad. Those answering to the last description can again be sub-divided into the instructor who never stops talking to his pupil from the moment of entry into the aircraft (so that the bewildered student pilot is swamped and learns nothing), and his opposite number, the flying instructor who prides himself on being a man of few words, maintaining a brooding silence until a moment of near crisis (and in consequence his pupils must learn by example or not at all).

Wing Commander P. R. M. Groom recalls the 'silent' instructor in these words:

> In September 1937, as a pupil-pilot, I did my R.A.F. *ab initio* training on dual-controlled Tiger Moths at Prestwick.
>
> My original instructor, when handing over control to me, invariably said, 'You've got her,' and I replied, 'I've got her.' During the course he was posted and I was given a different instructor, a sardonic man of few words.
>
> On our first trip together he demonstrated 'forced landing with engine', where one pretended to be far from home with only ten minutes petrol left. The drill was to fly low over a field, ensure it was free from obstacles, climb and make a glide approach.
>
> The instructor demonstrated. When we were nearly on the ground he opened the throttle and we began a gentle climbing turn. We continued the climbing turn, on and on until we were at 2,000 ft. when the instructor bawled at me, 'What the hell are you playing at?' I said, 'You've got her.' and he said, 'No, you've got her.'
>
> The instructor pointed out that, immediately after he had opened the throttle, he had waved his hands outside the cockpit. My head was in the office at the time, so I didn't see the signal (and probably wouldn't have cottoned on anyway).
>
> On looking back on that long, smooth gentle, perfect climbing turn from 0 to 2,000 ft., I realized that the Tiger Moth is such a stable aeroplane that she can fly herself—the pilot is superfluous!

Of course there are plenty of stable aeroplanes but there is something forgiving in the nature of the Tiger that can turn a misunderstanding of this kind into an amusing incident.

An interesting development of the Tiger Moth appeared shortly after the inception of the DH 82a in 1934 in the form of a radio-controlled version intended as an expendable and relatively inexpensive target for the benefit of both ship-borne and land-based anti-aircraft gunners. These pilotless target aircraft were operated mostly over water, the majority being fitted with floats. Partly in the interest of buoyancy but also in deference to cost, the familiar steel tube fuselage of the Tiger Moth was replaced by the wooden structure used on the DH 60 GIII and Moth Major. These wooden-fuselaged Moths represented the ultimate in the DH 60 Series of biplanes. Delightful and successful as they were, a relatively small number were built, production ceasing in 1935 when all Moth Major fuselages were diverted to the radio-controlled Tiger Moths, which were known as Queen Bees. Standard Tiger Moth wings, tail surfaces, engine mountings and undercarriage parts (land or water) went into the Queen Bee but in addition to the wooden fuselage there were these major modifications:

Strengthened fuselage to allow for catapulting.

Flying controls and instruments in the front cockpit only.

No mixture control.

No tail trimmer.

Rear cockpit covered by removable fairings.

Two axes automatic controls and radio receiver in rear cockpit.

No windscreen to rear cockpit.

Luggage compartment rearranged to take relay gear.

Original nineteen-gallon fuel tank replaced by one of twenty-four gallons capacity. No fuel gauge was fitted and the top of the tank was protected by ply covering against accidental damage during slinging operations.

Mounting for reel-type aerial on fuselage side near front cockpit.

Shelf behind front instrument panel carrying two accumulators for radio and auto controls.

'Eclipse' hand starting gear installed on the right-hand side of the engine and operating through a throw-out clutch.

Windmill-driven air compressor installed within the port wing bay. This was often mistaken for a generator although none was fitted.

Built-in handling lines, slinging and salvage gear.

The Air Ministry placed a contract for one prototype,

works number 5027, which emerged from the hangar for its first flight on 5th January 1935 wearing R.A.F. markings K 3584. On this occasion it was flown by a test pilot prior to the installation at Farnborough of the highly secret auto controls and radio equipment. The development flights were made with the Queen Bee under full radio control but with a safety pilot in the front cockpit. Although early demonstrations featured landing and taking off with the usual wheel undercarriage, in service this was replaced by floats for over-water operation, the danger of shooting the aeroplane down over the most open countryside being unacceptable.

Like many things in Service life, the Queen Bee on occasions provided some light entertainment for the less serious minded lookers on, two delightful instances being recalled by Air Commodore R. J. B. Burns, C.B.E., who spent the last few years before the war flight testing these aircraft. At the time the Mediterranean Fleet was using Queen Bees, and this particular launching occurred when he was on the flagship, H.M.S. *Queen Elizabeth.*

The weather was marginal for Bee operations, since there was a high wind blowing with rather too much cloud about which made seeing and controlling the little Bee very difficult. However, since practically the whole of the Fleet was at sea for this particular shoot, we took a chance and launched the little target aeroplane. The worst happened and to the consternation of the high priced help observing from the bridge, the Bee disappeared altogether. There was a safety device incorporated which should have caused the Bee automatically to go into a left hand glide and land itself if no W/T signals were received for a period of three minutes. After anxiously watching for some time without sign of the Bee, it was decided that she must have been carried out of sight downwind, and the *Queen E.*, accompanied by the majority of the then impressive Mediterranean Fleet, set off in hot pursuit at a considerable rate of knots. About half an hour later, after this impressive and extensive steaming in the wrong direction, we received a message that the Bee was gently sitting on the water intact off the Grand Harbour.

She was duly recovered, and lived to avoid the determined efforts of the Royal Navy to shoot her down on many subsequent occasions.

Catapults on ships of the Royal Navy were in those days by no means trivial affairs, being really designed to launch the very much heavier Supermarine Walrus amphibious biplanes. Sometimes they proved a little too rough for the relatively feather-light Queen Bee, not during the actual launching (for this could be regulated according to the weight of the aircraft) but whilst rotating the aircraft into wind.

On this occasion, in rotating the catapult with a Queen Bee on it into the fore and aft position, it was accidentally stopped with a violent jerk which we knew had probably done the rigging of the air frame a deal of no good. However, there was again an impressive Fleet at sea to join in the shoot, and we had no spare Bee aboard. So we decided to shoot it off, and the inevitable happened. The Queen Bee did a most spectacular slow roll off the end of the catapult, and disappeared into the blue waters of the Mediterranean, much to the uninhibited expressions of disgust voiced by the Royal Naval hierarchy who were done out of their shoot.

Some have argued that the Queen Bee was a Moth Major with Tiger Moth wings, but the manufacturers gave the type design number DH 82 B. Furthermore the then highly secret Queen Bee manual S.D. 147 described it as a modified de Havilland Tiger Moth. It was certainly more or less identical to the Tiger in outward appearance but how did the Queen Bee evade the gunners at the touch of a button? The handbook describes its basic principal as 'wireless control of an automatic pilot' and these few words summarize the complex subject both neatly and accurately. Put into non-technical terms what happened was this: The aircraft was fitted with auto controls based upon the MK IA Automatic Pilot in use at the time. Briefly, a single gyroscope controlled two compressed-air valves, one sensitive to changes of direction whilst the other came into operation whenever the aircraft assumed a nose up or nose down attitude in relation to the level flight position. These valves fed compressed air to small pistons, one controlling the rudder and the other linked to the elevators. There was no auto control for the ailerons and indeed this was unnecessary in view of the close relationship between the directional and lateral control of any aeroplane. You keep straight and the wings remain level. Put on a little right rudder and a bank to the right develops as soon as the nose yaws in response to rudder. This is elementary aerodynamics. Compressed air for the gyro and the servo controls was provided by a windmill-driven pump, situated on the port side of the fuselage within the slipstream area of the propeller, so that once the Queen Bee's engine was running at, say, cruising power, the windmill would rotate and provide the necessary 30 lbs. per square inch. The air went through a small chemical dryer to remove all moisture.

This simple auto pilot was pre-set to maintain the Queen Bee in a level attitude, but arrangements were made so that the gyro could be precessed or disturbed from its normally level plane when the air valves would open causing the Queen Bee to take up a new attitude.

The control box on the ground was provided with nine buttons, each for a separate command, e.g. left turn, climb, glide, etc. This in itself was an ingenious piece of equipment, and when a button had been used a light appeared adjacent to it confirming that the correct signal had been sent. These signals, in fact very similar to those produced by the dial of an automatic telephone, were made up of a dash followed by a series of dots. This was the code transmitted to the aeroplane by the control box:

— .	Navigation lights on
— ..	Navigation lights off
— ...	Right turn
—	Straight ahead
—	Left turn

— ••••••	Climb
— •••••••	Level flight
— ••••••••	Glide
— •••••••••	Dive

An automatic telephone dial was provided on the controller as a standby in the event of a failure in the pushbutton system. When the Queen Bee operated with the Fleet it was usual for these command signals to be sent to the aircraft over the ship's transmitter, but ground-based units had an MII 'mobile' transmitter. This was an enormous affair nearly six feet high and weighing 1,500 lbs. Transmission was in the frequency range 160–180 kc/s, for these were the days before V.H.F. radio.

Signals were received in the aircraft on a simple four-valve set (type R 1088) which fed them into a 'black box' full of relay switches which appear to have been standard G.P.O. equipment. Assuming the controller on the ground pressed the 'right turn' button the aircraft would receive a dash followed by three dots causing a relay switch to click around at each impulse. A final relay would come into play, operating a small valve on the gyro, upsetting its balance in such a way that it supplied air to the rudder servo control and made the Queen Bee turn to the right. When the command 'climb' was sent a separate air-operated throttle servo opened up the engine, and in the glide power likewise decreased.

Certain very clever safety devices were incorporated. For example in the event of engine failure or a breakdown on the transmitter or receiver the Queen Bee would automatically go into a gliding turn to the left so that it was kept within a confined area. But once it had descended below a pre-set height, known as 'altimeter height' the glide continued straight ahead providing better conditions for a safe landing. Furthermore, were the controller on the ground to select 'dive' and forget what he had done, the Queen Bee would level out on reaching its pre-set altimeter height and continue in cruising flight.

Final adjustments to the Queen Bee were made in the air by a test pilot who was provided with a large automatic telephone-type dial marked with the nine commands, climb, dive, etc. The dial, referred to as the Supervisory Control, was situated on the front instrument panel in the place usually occupied by the turn and slip indicator, each finger-hole lighting up whenever a command was made by the test pilot so that he was left in no doubt and could see the last instruction he had given to the auto controls. The dial merely fed impulses directly into the relay box and was a substitute for the radio signals normally received from the ground transmitter. This arrangement enabled the test pilot to give a command and then adjust the aircraft so that it gave the following performance:

Straight and level flight: Queen Bee would settle at 9,000 ft. cruising at 79-80 m.p.h. giving a duration of approximately $3\frac{1}{4}$ hours on 24 gallons.

Turns: adjusted to Rate I, i.e. 180 degrees change of heading in one minute.

Glide: speed 56 m.p.h. giving an angle of descent of 5-10 degrees.

Climb: 400 ft./min. at a speed of 65 m.p.h.

Dive: 130 to 150 m.p.h. at an angle of 25 degrees. Usually it took 4,000 ft. to settle at a steady airspeed during the dive and it was not uncommon to reach 170 m.p.h. in the early stages. 300-800 ft. was required during the recovery.

When the test pilot had completed these adjustments he would accompany the aircraft being controlled from the ground, the requirement being one hundred commands to be sent and answered correctly by the aircraft. A separate receiver on the ground fed a tape machine which recorded each signal on a half-inch paper ribbon so that an analysis could be made afterwards.

The extraordinary thing about the Queen Bee was that both take-off and landing were fully automatic and not under radio command once the initial instruction was given and the process started. During the take-off, either from its own wheels or a catapult, the gyro was spun by an outside supply of compressed air. This was disconnected once the Queen Bee's own windmill compressor became operative. 'Level flight' was selected on the controller followed by the radio command 'climb'. An indicator on the starboard side of the fuselage showed the position of the throttle. The launching of a Queen Bee involved a count down in the modern manner and when it took place on one of H.M. ships the ritual was accompanied by a complicated sequence of flag waving as each stage of the pre-take-off drill was accomplished.

In the early part of the take-off the controls were locked in the correct position, coming into play after a safety pin had been pulled by a fixed lanyard. A trailing aerial then wound out on an automatic winch and became fully extended during the climb. The aircraft was then ready to receive radio instructions.

The Navy operated the Queen Bee with two cine-camera-equipped chase planes which, needless to say, kept at a discreet distance during the actual firing. High-angle gunnery was practised first, followed by low-level simulated torpedo attacks flown at about 20 ft. The aircraft had a tendency to lose height during level turns and at low height it was usually put into a climb before a change in direction. Controllers were warne : not to select 'glide' when the Queen Bee was directly over the transmitter because it had a habit of going into a dive for some reason or other.

With space more or less unlimited at sea it was a relatively simple matter to guide the Queen Bee into wind and commence the landing from about 500 ft. Heavier demands were made on the controller when a landing had to be made on an aerodrome and a special sight was provided to ensure that the glide was initiated at the correct point in relation to the airfield. The Queen Bee would continue to descend in a glide until at a height of several feet the weight on the end of the trailing aerial struck the water (or aerodrome surface), bringing into operation the Landing Valve. This automatic device raised the elevators beyond their usual range of travel, putting the Queen Bee into the correct landing attitude, at the same time earthing the ignition so that the engine stopped.

By any standards the Queen Bee was a remarkable technical achievement, particularly when it is remembered that radio communications were in the early 'thirties nothing like so developed as they are today. It comes as something of a surprise however to realize that, marvellous as it was for its day, the Queen Bee by no means represen ed the beginning of the story of the pilotless aeroplane. This really began with that gifted engineer, Sir Hiram Maxim, who proposed automatic flight using gyroscopic principals in 1891—twelve years before the Wright brothers made their first powered flight. Another scheme was suggested in 1912 by T. W. K. Clarke, but the first serious trials occurred during the First World War. Attempts were made to fly an aeroplane without a pilot at Brooklands, Feltham in Middlesex and that historical airfield Upavon. None of these tests proved successful, but they were followed by an attempt to produce a Zeppelin destroyer based upon a small Folland-designed aeroplane which was powered by a 35 h.p. A.B.C. engine. It was to be launched off a special track constructed at Northolt, but the three examples tested failed to fly.

The first qualified success came in October 1921, when a Bristol Fighter carrying a test pilot was made to answer rudder signals from distances of up to eight miles. The transmitter was at Farnborough.

September 3rd 1924 saw the first really successful flight of a pilotless aeroplane under radio control and again the honour fell to the Bristol Fighter. It made a heavy landing in the sea at the end of a flight which included some fifty radio commands. The Americans managed a radio controlled flight twelve days later but the aircraft was wrecked on landing.

A pilotless flying bomb named Larynx appeared in 1925 with a designed range of 300 miles carrying a 250 lb. warhead. The speed of this miniature aircraft was more than

190 m.p.h. and it was arranged to fly entirely on automatic controls without radio command. A small transmitter was carried by Larynx, providing its operator on the ground with a means of estimating its position. Twelve were built and successful tests were made in this country and in the Middle East. In 1935 a jet version was suggested, but perhaps the most interesting thing about Larynx is that it preceded the German V I flying bomb by so many years and formed the basis of the weapon that was used against us in the final stages of the last war.

The first auto-control system as used in the Queen Bee was installed in a Fairey IIIF Seaplane late in 1931. It was if anything too successful in the eyes of the Senior Service, for in January 1933 the entire Home Fleet did its utmost to shoot it down finally running out of ammunition whereupon the seaplane was landed completely unharmed by gunfire. H.M.S. *Shropshire* of the Mediterranean Fleet brought it down in May of that year.

Much of the work on automatic control was conducted by Meredith, and the radio equipment was evolved by F. S. Barton and G. R. Joyce. The officer in charge of the projects leading up to and including the Queen Bee was G. W. H. Gardner, C.B., C.B.E., D.Sc., F.R.Ae.S. (now Sir George Gardner), who was at the time in the Physics and Instruments Department of the Royal Aircraft Establishment. The gifted F. F. Marshall designed the automatic controls and much of the experimental flying was entrusted to Flight Lieutenant C. McC. Vincent.

The first pilotless flight of a Queen Bee took place in the English Channel off H.M.S. *Orion*. The occasion got a little out of hand and in Sir George's own words:

> The aeroplane was successfully launched from the ship's catapult and various manœuvres were satisfactorily executed until, when the aircraft was flying at low height in a slow right turn and gradually losing height, it was found impossible to get any response to further signals. The aircraft continued to fly in a wide circle and at one critical point appeared to be about to crash into the bridge of the ship.

The Chief of the Air Staff and many other senior officials were on the bridge and tension built up rapidly. The Control Officer continued to press buttons, most of the Naval officers who were in familiar surroundings ran for cover, an R.A.E. official laughed hysterically, and the Chief of the Air Staff stood his ground and slowly turned up the collar of his greatcoat. The tension relaxed when the aeroplane just missed the ship and eventually crashed into the sea a short distance away. Tape records of the transmission showed that when the trouble began, the ship's transmitter had started to send a continuous signal and continued to do so until the end. This was subsequently found to be due to a key which had become stuck in the main transmitter circuit.

A total of 420 Queen Bees were built, 320 at the de Havilland Co. works and the remainder by Scottish Aviation who manufactured theirs in a Scottish Motor Tractor Co. disused garage. A Queen Bee base was situated at Manorbier and five other permanent units were stationed along the coasts of Britain, mainly for the purpose of providing gunner practice for the Army. The Navy used Queen Bees in the West Indies, as well as Malta, Hong Kong, Alexandria and Singapore. The Queen Bee version of the Tiger Moth was the first practical anti-aircraft target to be adopted by any country and it is generally accepted that it did much to improve the standard of gunnery both on land and at sea. It was not uncommon for a Queen Bee to become a veteran of twenty or more gunnery exercises before finally suffering the fate for which it was built.

Most of the Queen Bees remaining after the war were reduced to scrap and burned at Redhill aerodrome, although one fuselage is reported to be in a hangar on that airfield still.

While the DH 82a production line boomed at Hatfield a more leisurely operation was in progress at the de Havilland Technical School, where purely as an exercise in aeronautical engineering the students built three Series II Tiger Moths, G-ACPS, G-ADGO and G-AEVB, during the period 1934–6. The Svenska Aeroplane Company, by now part of the Saab organization, had already made three of the early Tiger Moths for the Swedish Government and with the emergence of the improved DH 82a version a batch of twenty machines was constructed under licence. The DH 82 had been known as the SK 11 in Sweden and now the DH 82a was given the designation SK 11a and Swedish Air Force registrations FV 509 to 520, FV 546 to 550, FV 553, FV 589 and 590.

The aircraft factory owned by the Royal Norwegian Air Force had by this time changed its name to Kjeller Fly-fabrikk. It had already produced seventeen of the early Tiger Moths, two of these, carrying service markings 157 and 159, being fitted with a .303 Colt machine-gun with an interrupter gear allowing it to fire through the propeller. Both aircraft were operated by the Royal Norwegian Air Force Flying Schools on gunnery instruction. A further twenty Tiger Moths were built to DH 82a specification and special skis had to be designed for use in the Norwegian snow. Some of these aircraft were equipped with hoods for instrument flying instruction.

Portugal now joined the other two foreign countries producing Tiger Moths under licence. Eleven of the Mark I machines had been imported for the Portuguese Air Force, but with the arrival of the DH 82a as many as ninety-one examples were manufactured by Oficinas Gerais de Material Aeronáutico, Alverca do Ribatejo.

In 1928 De Havilland Aircraft of Canada was formed in a modest plant at Mount Dennis. There were but fifty employees whose first task was the assembly of sixty-two Cirrus Moths, something of an achievement in a factory limited to 1,200 sq. ft. in area. This Canadian off-shoot of de Havillands progressed on to later Moths and then Dragons, simple twin-engined aircraft using standard Moth wings outboard of the motors. During the war years it employed over 7,000 people and built 3,257 aircraft (Mosquitoes, Ansons and Tiger Moths). The first Canadian designed aeroplane to be constructed by the factory was the Chipmunk, a highly successful Tiger Moth replacement.

A considerable number of Cirrus and Gipsy Moths had been in use in Canada and it is perhaps a little surprising to find that it was not until 1938 that the Royal Canadian Air Force received its first Canadian-built Tiger Moth. With the Canadian winter to face, the open cockpits of the Tiger were bound to receive attention, and a sliding canopy was added covering both cockpits.

After 227 DH 82a Tiger Moths had been built, a great many changes were made—some of an important nature with one or two altering the 'plane's appearance quite markedly. The more significant modifications were these:

Engine cowlings were redesigned to form two halves hinged along the top. These included the nose panel (fixed on the original Tiger), so that almost complete access to the engine was gained on opening the cowlings.

Exhaust system was redesigned to incorporate a cabin heater. A long extension pipe terminated behind the front cockpit.

Instrument panels were replanned to cater for different instruments and the curved top deck separating the two cockpits was shaped like a Gothic arch to improve forward view from the rear seat.

A pressure fire extinguisher was arranged to discharge into the engine bay in addition to the hand appliance situated in the rear cockpit.

An oil tank of greater capacity and fitted with a winter cover was incorporated. The yent on the fuel tank was altered to prevent icing.

Bendix brakes were fitted, operated by a hand lever on the left-hand side of each cockpit, with differential braking being effected through the rudder bar. To minimize the dangers of nosing over in the event of harsh application of brake, the main wheels were moved forward slightly by shortening the undercarriage radius rods.

A castering tail wheel replaced the familiar tail skid which, because of the brakes, was no longer needed.

A large windscreen was fitted to the front cockpit only and a sliding canopy arranged in two sections, one for each cockpit. Both cockpits had a blind flying hood.

Trim tabs were fitted to both elevators in place of the original spring-loaded device.

Document case was installed in the rear cockpit.

Bottom wings had a wider treadboard either side of the fuselage, an inset hand grip built into each wing tip and a plywood covered leading edge.

Interplane struts were of oval section steel tube in place of the original wide chord wooden struts.

Small skis could be fitted to the main and tail wheels.

These much modified Tiger Moths were given the type number DH 82c. They performed magnificently under the severe conditions to be expected of a Canadian winter, providing a major portion of the wartime elementary training capacity—the subject of a later chapter.

Most of the Canadian Tiger Moths were powered by the 145 h.p. Gipsy Major 1c which provided some 15 h.p. more than the standard DH 82a and in consequence endowed the aeroplane with a materially improved rate of climb. Although de Havilland Aircraft of Canada made a great number of Tiger Moths they were dependent upon the parent company in England for Gipsy engines, and at one period of the war, when supplies across the Atlantic were strictly limited in the face of constant U-boat activity, the American Menasco engine was substituted. One hundred and thirty-six Tiger Moths were built with these engines, but the 120 h.p. developed by the four-cylinder Menasco was bound to curtail their performance, and climbing to a suitable height for aerobatics or spins must have been a very prolonged business. One example, R.C.A.F. No. 4861, has been kept on display in a Royal Canadian Air Force museum.

The Canadian production line was no mere trickle. Two hundred and twenty-seven Tiger Moths were completed in the year up to August 1939, and when production ceased in 1942 the total had reached 1,747. The majority of these went to the Royal Candian Air Force which took delivery of twenty-six DH 82a's, 1,384 DH 82c Tiger Moths powered by the Gipsy 1c and 136 with Menasco engines.

DH 82b Queen Bee. The wooden fuselage is evident in this picture. The windmill-driven compressor supplying air to the auto controls is situated just behind the propeller.

Queen Bee control-box sending commands to the radio-controlled target aircraft flying overhead.

A Queen Bee floatplane on the launching catapult at the pilotless Aircraft Unit, St. Athan, *circa* 1941,

During 1938 the de Havilland Company at Hatfield ordered a substantial number of Tiger Moths fuselages from its Canadian off-shoot. The figure usually quoted is 200, and whilst there is little reliable information on the subject, works numbers 82584 to 82690 were reserved for the Tigers that were to utilize the Canadian-built fuselage assemblies. It is believed that only fifteen of these arrived from Canada and in fact one of the batch, British works number 82588 and Canadian fuselage number E 104, was only recently dismantled in this country, ending its life as G-AFSV. Three of these part-Canadian machines (works numbers 82596–8) went to Kenya, and although it was intended that they should fly as VP-KCT, KCU and KCV, on arrival they were impressed into the local air force and so far as is known never carried their civil markings. The remaining ninety-two numbers set aside (82599 to 82690) have defied all efforts to trace and are usually assumed not to have arrived in this country. It is known that part of the order for fuselages was diverted to meet the needs of the Canadian Government, but in any case by this time de Havilland Aircraft of Canada were committed to the DH 82c version of the Tiger Moth for it was more suited to local conditions than the British-built DH 82a. It is also believed that the American Government placed an order for several hundred Tiger Moths and that these too were diverted to the R.C.A.F.

Meanwhile hopes for peace in Europe continued to decline so that by 1938 the British Government felt impelled to bring into operation the Civil Air Guard, an organization intended to supplement the Reserve Flying Schools in that it introduced both men and women to flying from within the wide age group of sixteen to sixty. Like their R.A.F.V.R. opposite number they were required to go before a town selection committee and those who were successful signed an undertaking promising in the event of an emergency to give their services to the country as pilots in the capacity most suited to their ages and qualifications. The Civil Air Guard involved the flying clubs, which in consequence found themselves short of both fly-instructors and aeroplanes, the latter deficiency often being filled by new Tiger Moths. A subsidy was paid to the club for each member of the C.A.G. during his first six hours dual and then there was no further payment until the pupil obtained a licence. Members of the C.A.G. wore a simple uniform based upon blue denim overalls with Union Jack flashes on the shoulders, and a special brevet was awarded on obtaining an 'A' licence. C.A.G. pilots under training paid 5/- per hour for their flying and not unnaturally this was the cause of some resentment with the older established club members, for many had learned to fly at the pre-war rate of between 30/- and £2 per hour.

Nevertheless few would deny that the C.A.G. did in fact justify itself when the time came, providing considerable numbers of part-trained pilots, many of whom did invaluable work in the A.T.A. and the R.A.F.

The C.A.G. enjoyed a somewhat brief existence for towards the end of August 1939 the shadow already cast over Europe began to darken and but a few days later, secure in the misguided belief that Britain would never interfere in his plans for the enslavement of mankind, Hitler marched on Poland. By now 1,378 Tiger Moths and 210 Queen Bees had been built, numbers that were to become insignificant during the war that followed when the Tiger Moth was to make its biggest single contribution as trainer of the pilots of the Commonwealth—but that was by no means all it had to offer in time of war.

Within two years aircraft production in Britain had outstripped that in Germany, and the A.T.A. had delivered a great flood of aircraft to the squadrons and the now fully trained reserves went on to use them to good effect. But for the emergence of these reserve units in their various forms the seeds of disaster might well have been sown, for without them the enormous production from the aircraft factories would have languished impotent.

5. The Fighting Tigers

With Neville Chamberlain's historic declaration of war on
3rd September 1939, all club and sporting flying ceased
throughout the British Isles, and the Tiger Moths at the
Reserve Flying Schools were impressed into the R.A.F.
along with the multitude of club and privately owned light
aircraft of every type. For some time it was not uncommon
to see these aeroplanes in their new R.A.F. markings yet
still bearing civil registration letters. Whilst frantic preparations were made to put in hand pre-war plans for
large-scale flying training, other units were being formed
which were to involve the Tiger Moth on the edge of
battle and sometimes uncomfortably close to the very
centre.

The Communications Squadron, B.E.F., or to give its
later title, 81 Squadron, was formed at Andover some four
weeks before the outbreak of hostilities and placed under
the command of Squadron Leader George Ashton, A.F.C.,
who was incidentally a veteran of fifty-two at the time. Without delay 'A' Flight left Andover for France on 17th
September 1939. This involved a rather long water crossing for a pilot in a Tiger Moth without radio or even a
'Mae West', and refuelling stops were made at Shoreham
on the south coast with another at Poix before flying on
to Laval, where 'A' Flight remained until the end of the
month. The unit then moved to a tiny airfield near Amiens

called Mont Joie which had until just previously been privately owned.

Sergeant (later Flight Lieutenant) D. R. Bevis, one of the first pilots to join the squadron, returned to Andover with instructions to bring another Tiger over to France with the newly formed 'B' Flight. This second communications flight arrived at Amiens on 6th October, and the two flight commanders were Flight Lieutenant Smith and Flight Lieutenant Morgan. Tiger Moths were detached from Amiens to Arras, Abbeville, Poix and Metz on communication duties during the period popularly referred to as the 'phoney war'. Early in 1940 Squadron Leader Ashton left 81 Squadron to become O.C. R.A.F. Iceland and the communication Tigers came under Squadron Leader Hill.

The winter that led into 1940 was particularly severe and for a time the Tiger Moths were practically the only aircraft to fly. Under Sergeant Gauldie the ground crews pre-heated the engines with blow lamps, thinning the engine oil so that the Tiger Moths could be started.

When the Germans burst through the Low Countries the Tiger Moths were called upon to operate non-stop from daylight to sunset. As the roads became blocked with refugees military traffic was often brought to a standstill, and Tigers assumed a vital role, landing alongside roadways and providing one of the few reliable means of communication behind the battle area.

As the Dunkirk scene began to form most of the squadron drifted with the tide of confusion to Boulogne. There were not enough pilots to fly all the aircraft back to England so that two Tiger Moths and a C.40 autogyro had to be burned before leaving Arras. Many of the ground staff were able to leave Boulogne and returned home by ship.

When the Germans took Metz, G.H.Q. Army put through an urgent request for a Tiger Moth, providing their own pilot, an Army captain complete with wings on his tunic, who duly arrived to collect the 'plane. Sergeant Gauldie's offer to accompany the captain was declined, and in the event this was fortunate for him because on returning from the reconnaissance flight the captain reported being shot at by German tanks. It was then found that one bullet had penetrated through the front seat where Gauldie would have been sitting while another had squeezed between one of the centre section struts and the fuel line, fortunately without fracturing it.

About this time several of the pilots under the command of Flight Lieutenant Smith were detached to a field at St. Omer. By now the military situation in France had become desperate for the Allied forces, and in endeavouring to maintain some link between units Bevis and Mackay were sent to Norrent Fonte, although it had already been abandoned.

Without warning, German tanks drove on to the field. Fortunately both Tigers burst into life on the first swings of their propellers and a hasty take-off was made—down wind with the German armour lumbering towards them. The situation was little better when they returned to St. Omer, for by now the last six communication pilots from Flight Lieutenant Smith's flight were completely cut off. A take-off just before daybreak was planned and as the six Tigers approached Dover they suffered the indignity of being shot at by our own gunners, who by now were prepared to blast away at anything that didn't resemble a Spitfire or a Hurricane. Luck was with them on this occasion and they landed safely at Hawkinge, where the Hurricane pilots on stand-by were astonished to witness six scruffy and bearded pilots climbing wearily out of six very operational looking Tiger Moths.

A number of 81 Squadron pilots got back to England via Merville and one or two other points. Flying Officer Gautier, however, had a more exciting time. He ran out of petrol and was fished out of the Channel by a French destroyer, which spent the next few days bombarding the German-held coast. It is thought that he was eventually landed at Southampton.

The squadron finally collected at Hendon, and since Britain was by now out of Europe the need for B.E.F. communications was gone and the valiant little unit was disbanded.*

Following on Dunkirk at a time when to the outside world Britain seemed a beaten nation about to face the onslaught of a Nazi invasion, serious attempts were made to turn the Tiger Moth into a fighting aeroplane. The venture which received least publicity but certainly represented the most radical departure from convention involved some extraordinary experiments at the two aerodromes in Leicestershire operated at the time by Reid & Sigrist, but before describing them in detail the remarkable man responsible for the project must be mentioned again. His name is George Reid, an inventor and industrialist whose varied and colourful career would provide excellent material for a book in its own right.

George Reid joined the Royal Naval Air Service in 1914 and within twelve months was put in charge of a small unit defending London from the Zeppelin attacks. There were ten naval mechanics but only two other pilots, and Reid arranged that his two colleagues should be responsible for East and West London whilst he defended the centre. Pilots of the First World War, particularly during the early days, were indeed dedicated men. Reid's unit operated from a small aerodrome which developed a large pool in its centre after heavy rain, so that it became the practice to touch down on the adjoining field and hop over a small path on to a less watery part of the aerodrome. With Zeppelin attacks coming during hours of darkness much night flying was involved, often without landing lights or flare-paths. Engines being what they were in 1914, complete or partial power failure was accepted as commonplace, and during one such occasion Reid attempted to land in

* On referring to his log-book Bevis finds that he flew the following Tiger Moths during his eventful months in France:

K6846	N6803	N6949	N9154	N9159
N6749	N6846	N6964	N9155	N9206
N6799	N6847	N6965	N9156	N9433
N6801	N6853	N6987	N9157	N9442
N6802	N6946	N9125	N9158	N9444

a street near Tottenham, his engine bursting into life again before the moment of drama arrived. Anxiety was soon to return, however, for within a few minutes his instrument lights failed and he deemed it prudent to get back on the ground as quickly as possibly. His landing occurred on some ground near Chingford Reservoir, an area well known to him fortunately, for it was pitch dark at the time and as usual there was no flare-path. He made his way to some nearby Royal Naval Air Service huts, appearing in the doorway to the astonishment of the Officer of the Watch who was oblivious of Reid's unorthodox arrival. This same young officer later wrote the popular song 'Keep The Home Fires Burning' and attained fame and success in the theatre—his name was Ivor Novello.

Reid became senior pilot to the Vindex with the Harwich Light Squadron, and while flying seaplanes with that unit took part in the big raid on Zeebrugge. Some thirty land planes were detached to attack at 6,000 ft., and Reid and another pilot named Openshaw went in at 1,000 ft. in their seaplanes.

They arrived over Zeebrugge in the dark to witness what Reid describes as a 'Brocks Benefit Night', with the Germans firing everything that could shoot irrespective of calibre, the most alarming being the guns on their Monitor ships, whose 12 in. shells were set to burst at varying heights, scattering showers of red-hot metal into the paths of the aircraft. Reid's inventive mind had already shown itself and for the occasion he had made up four bomb sights to his own design which enabled the C.P.O. observers to guide their pilots to the target.

The searchlights caught Reid's seaplane as he approached the Mole and he had the unforgettable experience of actually seeing one of the relatively low-velocity 12 in. shells flash past his aircraft, glowing red hot as it went between wing and fuselage. Fortunately it burst well above him. After scoring several direct hits on the Mole they returned to their base practically unmarked. On the way back an attempt was made to drop one of their compressed-air cylinders (used for starting the engine) down the funnel of a German destroyer, but in view of their reception it was not thought advisable to await the results.

George Reid's war came to an end when he tried to rescue a British pilot who had forced landed on a beach during a raid on the island of Sylt. Some German soldiers witnessed the incident but seemed undecided about the identity of the aircraft, no doubt because some of their own machines were based nearby. The situation registered just as Reid was getting the pilot on to the float of his sea-plane, and they started firing as he moved off. Only a few minutes after leaving the water the engine failed, and although they managed to coax sufficient power out of it to continue taxiing towards their squadron, adverse winds caused them to run out of petrol and they were blown back to Sylt, where prison camp awaited them.

The opportunity arose for an escape attempt when Reid got wind of the Germans' intention to move a number of French prisoners to Osnabruck. Disguised as a French officer he got himself on the train and picking the most likely moment jumped from the carriage, badly hurting his left leg, an injury that was to trouble him for many years. The commandant stopped the prison train until Reid was found, thus delaying other rail traffic bringing urgent supplies for the front. All this took place when the battle of the Somme was at a critical stage for the Germans and when he returned home after the war Reid was able to confirm with Lord Weir that his attempted escape had temporarily disrupted German supplies to the front, much to the displeasure of the O.C. 10th Army Corps, General Von Hanish, who put the train commandant under arrest for blocking the line.

With the return to peace George Reid was put on the Air Inventions Committee. He had designed an apparatus for grading pilots medically and was invited to talk to the Royal Society of Medicine on the subject, an honour indeed for a layman.

Towards the end of his Service life Reid was posted to

the Air Ministry Training Department, where he wrote a manual of training for R.A.F. engineers. He retired from the R.A.F. as Squadron Leader Reid, D.F.C., in May 1926 and started a small factory in Hampstead, where he manufactured some of the earliest gyro instruments ever produced for aircraft.

One of Reid's first designs consisted of an air-speed indicator surrounded by gyro-controlled coloured lights which were arranged in such a way that the pilot obtained directional and lateral level information. Vickers took up the patent and examples were tried by at least one airline company based at Croydon.

Soon the business grew and a new factory was built on the Kingston by-pass to produce an instrument called the Rand. S. for Service aircraft. In 1936 Reid developed a five-barrel gun which fired a series of projectiles containing small wire-trailing parachutes, which were intended to deal with low flying aircraft, and a number of ships on the Atlantic run used the device during the Second World War.

But what of the experiments mentioned earlier in this chapter? These emanated from George Reid and were born of desperate times during 1940 when our fortunes (in the war against the Axis Powers) were at a low ebb. He visualized the Tiger Moth in the role of anti-paratroop attack plane, utilizing the experienced flying instructors stationed at flying schools up and down the country. With a German invasion imminent, an invasion which at the time of Dunkirk seemed inevitable, Reid's idea was that as soon as the German troop carrying Junker 52s appeared on our radar, instruction would stop at the flying schools and the Tiger Moths would be dispersed in large fields situated within an acceptable radius of their base; but they would be Tiger Moths with a difference, for they were to carry a weapon extraordinarily named the 'Paraslasher'. The equipment was the embodiment of simplicity and consisted of what amounted to a farmer's hand scythe on the end of an 8 ft. long tube. When not in use the assembly lay along the underside of the fuselage and in no way interfered with flying training. A release lever in the rear cockpit allowed the knife to drop below the aircraft on the end of its pole and it was held in this extended position by a length of $2\frac{1}{2}$ in. bungee cord. So armed, the flying instructors would then fly amongst the invading paratroops slashing the canopies of their parachutes with devastating results. Those who escaped this terrible fate would be harried on the ground as they endeavoured to set up their equipment. Certainly the name Paraslasher was a fitting one.

Reid's imagination had been triggered by a pre-war incident when a criminal on the run was chased and finally cornered in a field by Tiger Moths which continually dived at him until the police arrived. It was of course a fantastic idea and like most revolutionary schemes attracted its fair share of ridicule. Nevertheless George Reid was convinced that his idea had possibilities and was determined to take it a stage further. Reid & Sigrist operated Tiger Moths at Desford and Braunstone aerodromes and it was not long before one of their machines was fitted with an experimental Paraslasher.

The Commanding Officer of 7 E.F.T.S. Desford during this period was Squadron Leader (now Wing Commander) George Lowdell, A.F.M. He had opened up Desford for Reid & Sigrist before the war and his considerable experience of crazy flying at air displays made him a natural choice for the flight tests, the first of which took place on 12th June 1940.

The Tiger Moth concerned, G-ADPG, was still in its civil markings and amongst other tests George Lowdell attacked life-sized pictures of Hitler and Mussolini painted on canvas screens and stood on the ground. He proceeded to cut these into shreds without difficulty. Further experiments were carried out on man-sized sacks of straw, and of some two dozen positioned on Braunstone aerodrome, half were destroyed during the first 'attack'.

By now George Lowdell had become expert with his incredible Paraslasher. He could fly low over the ground cutting a neat furrow into the grass without effecting the performance of the aeroplane. Strange to relate, there were no jolts or shocks felt by the pilot. During practice he would make the Tiger Moth appear suddenly from behind a hangar. The possible effect on the morale of enemy troops of a wicked looking knife approaching at 100 m.p.h. needs little imagination.

Encouraged by these results Reid & Sigrist invited the Air Ministry to inspect the Paraslasher and a demonstration was arranged on 7th July 1940.

The main advantages put to them by George Reid were that the Paraslasher did not interfere with training. It could attack paratroops on the way down and on the ground, it was simple to make and fit, used no ammunition at a time when we were desperately short of it and would only cost about £10 for each aircraft. He also made the point that flying instructors' morale would be improved and they would be better employed operating the Paraslasher than hiding in shelters.

The Air Ministry was certainly impressed by the demonstration, but a request by Reid & Sigrist to be allowed to try the weapon at Henlow against a parachute carrying the equivalent weight of a man was turned down. The very experienced Lowdell had put up a convincing show with the Paraslasher but the Air Ministry felt it would be an ineffective weapon in the hands of a less accomplished flying instructor.

So ended an extraordinary episode in the life of the Tiger Moth. How effective would the Paraslasher have proved in the event of an airborne invasion? It is difficult to reach a conclusion since so many conflicting factors are involved. As a parachute destroyer there is little doubt it would have done its job well. How it would have fared against troops on the ground is another matter, for a Tiger Moth flying in open country is something of a sitting duck. On the other hand its sheer manoeuvrability would have made it a menace had it been given the opportunity to attack from behind buildings or trees. Certainly it would have been an object of terror to troops caught on the ground before they were able to organize their fighting equipment.

In these days of highly complex weapon systems the Paraslasher will to many seem Heath Robinson in conception, but it should be remembered that this was the period when our Army had lost the bulk of its equipment at Dunkirk and our factories were desperately trying to meet the needs of the fighting Services—a backlog resulting from political folly in the pre-war years. Such was the situation that we were reduced to making petrol bombs in old lemonade bottles while bits of steel were being welded into pike heads for fitting to broom handles. Viewed against this background the Paraslasher ceases to be grotesque in conception and becomes something inspired at a time when without doubt our backs were to the wall.

(After the war George Lowdell became chief production test pilot for Vickers at Weybridge doing valuable work on Viscounts while his old chief, Squadron Leader Reid now retired and in his seventies, continues to invent—a gyro control for ships being one of his current projects.)

Around the same period as these experiments another project was put in hand with a view to giving the Tiger Moth teeth. Initiated by the de Havilland company this scheme was more conventional than George Reid's but was nevertheless influenced by the same factors that had led to the Paraslasher. Small racks of the type originally designed for the DH 84 Dragons delivered to Iraq in 1932 were fitted to take eight 20 or 25 lb. bombs released by Bowden Cable and a four-position lever. The idea was that flying instructors would fly their Tiger bombers solo and would proceed to the beaches and bomb the invading troops. The scheme was given the code name 'Banquet Light' and the thought of Tiger Moths without cover of any kind bombing well-armed troops on the beaches hardly bears thinking about. Nevertheless de Havilland's fitting shop worked around the clock to make some 1,500 sets during the invasion scare, although not all of these were fitted. Early experiments were made by Geoffrey de Havilland's brother Hereward and at a number of the flying schools; inter-flight bombing competitions were organized using 8½ lb. practice bombs. The cross bracing wires in the centre section were used as a sight during dive bombing. They also flew dawn patrols looking for enemy troops who may have been dropped from aircraft overnight.*

During July 1940 tests were started with the bomb racks at Boscombe Down, and these went on for several months culminating in the following report:

Test Report 586g of 30th Oct. 1940

Take-off and Landing. Unchanged.
Stalling. Normal.
Level Flight. Normal except when C. and G. was full aft Trim was insufficient at full throttle.
Dives. With throttle less than ⅓ open speeds reached were 160–170 m.p.h. at a diving angle of 50–55°. Drag of bombs limited speed.
No trouble in recovery.
Bomb dropping. No fouling of undercarriages (a) in level flight, (b) in prolonged dive at 160–170 m.p.h. at an angle of 50–55°, (c) in a dive following a half roll.
Spinning. These were tried with pilot in front and rear cockpit. No passenger carried and bombs were removed leaving the racks and supporting crutches. Eight turns were made to left and right losing 2,000 ft. Recovery was normal.

The test report was reassuring enough and with the Tiger Moth's reputation for predictable handling characteristics one would have thought that the bomber version would be fit for flying instruction, provided of course no bombs were fitted. Certainly this had always been the intention, but during August 1941 a number of rather alarming reports came through to the effect that some Tigers were showing a marked reluctance to recover from a spin. Intensive spinning trials were put in hand at Boscombe Down during September 1941 using three machines which had collected somewhat vicious reputations for themselves. These were R4760, R5129 and N6221. The various reports

*See additional note at end of chapter, page 109.

of the time convey the impression that the misbehaviour of these Tigers was something of a mystery, the problem being still further complicated by the fact that only R5129 had bomb racks. It is on record that on one occasion this particular machine took thirteen turns to recover from a spin and the test pilot who sat through the performance must surely be admired for continuing the experiments. As no conclusions could be reached at Boscombe Down it was decided to continue the trials on a rather larger scale at Farnborough. The now notorious R5129 was accompanied by N5468 and R5180 along with two more Tigers from a recent production batch, T6035 and T6615.

The original Tiger Moths had impeccable spin recovery characteristics and Farnborough made a detailed comparison between the early machines that had been cleared for civil and military use at Martlesham Heath during 1931–5 and the troublesome examples in their possession. This revealed that gradually over the years certain minor changes had taken place. The R.A.F. had asked for mass balance weights on the ailerons, the aileron box and the spars had been reinforced and three separate camouflage schemes (Mods. 62, 76 and 93) had added layers of paint to the aircraft. All this extra weight, much of it out on the wings, had the flywheel-like effect of perpetuating rotation during a spin, the aerodynamicists referring to the condition as 'increased rotary moments of inertia'. The situation had not been improved by the installation of bomb racks as these appear to have disturbed the airflow over the rear fuselage and fin. The tests also revealed that the spin tended to flatten unless the ailerons were in the neutral position.

These findings were confirmed by tests on BB727, an ex-civilian Tiger Moth that had somehow or other avoided putting on weight. R5129, the worst offender, had its aileron mass balance weights removed and anti-spin strakes added —small flat surfaces either side of the rear fuselage fitted adjacent to the tail-plane. The removal of the aileron mass balance weights reduced the flywheel effect and the addition of strakes slowed down the rate of spin so that even R5129 would recover without fuss. Check tests at Boscombe Down during December confirmed that the Tiger had been tamed, and instructions were issued to all units calling for Mod. 112 (fitting of anti-spin strakes) and Mod. 103 (deletion of aileron mass balance weights) and the addition of a notice in the cockpit limiting the maximum speed to 170 m.p.h., a limit imposed by aileron flutter and not the strength of the aeroplane as a whole.

The civil Tigers originally had three hinges to each aileron, but when the R.A.F. requested mass balance weights an extra hinge was added. Although aileron mass balance weights were removed from all Tiger Moths by 1942, they continued to be manufactured with four hinges to each aileron, and it is perhaps a constant reminder of the time when the Tiger ran wild that to this day it is always the fourth or extra hinge that wears before the others.

There were two racks fitted to Tiger Moths, each carrying four bombs. The racks were arranged in two ways: one installed under each wing, or alternatively both could be fitted under the rear cockpit when, in bomber form, the 'plane had to be flown solo from the front cockpit. In practice this arrangement had the disadvantage that once the bombs were released the Tiger became very nose heavy, since the rear cockpit was unoccupied, and it was difficult if not impossible to get the tail down on landing. Indeed it is for this very reason that a Tiger Moth must under normal conditions only be flown solo from the rear cockpit. This type of installation had been fitted to some of the original DH 82 Tiger Moths sold to Persia during the 1931–2 period. It was in this form that the Tiger bomber went through its tests at Boscombe Down and, although many were so fitted, the alternative method (using the same type of bomb racks under the bottom wings) was tried and later found favour since the machine could be flown solo from the rear cockpit even when carrying its eight 25 lb. bombs. The bomb racks were attached to the bottom wing spars by bolts and saddle plates. The method of release was common to both under-wing and under-fuselage configuration. A small lever in the cockpit released the bombs either in one drop or four stages.

On another occasion a Tiger Moth was modified to accommodate one quite large bomb weighing 240 lb. and Hereward de Havilland carried out several tests from Hatfield, including one to determine the ceiling performance of the Tiger with its heavy load, but although he managed to stagger up to 7,000 ft. nothing came of these trials.

Yet another scheme was put forward, again no doubt prompted by thoughts of an impending German invasion. A tray specially designed to carry Mills bombs was to be added under the instrument panel in the rear cockpit. When the need arose the pilot was expected to take a Mills bomb from the tray with one hand, remove the safety pin with his teeth and then drop the bomb down a small chute or tube let into the floor within his reach. The scheme got to the trial installation stage before someone asked the inevitable question, 'What happens if he drops the bomb on the cockpit floor after he has pulled out the pin?' The scheme was abandoned!

The possibility of a German invasion becoming increasingly remote as the state of our own armed forces improved, the bomb racks which had precipitated the deletion of aileron mass balance weights were themselves removed and, like the Paraslasher, never saw use in anger.

With the thought of all these attempts to project the Tiger Moth into the tide of battle, it is strange to reflect that when the little biplane went operational in World War II it did so completely unarmed. The submarine had formed the keystone of the Kaiser's naval offensive during the 1914–18 conflict, when it had been found advantageous to employ DH 6 biplane trainers as U-boat spotters. Any doubts that Hitler intended to put his trust in the U-boat once more were soon to be dispelled, for within a few hours of Chamberlain's declaration of war came the sinking of the *Athenia* on 3rd September 1939.

Canadian Tiger. The picture reveals some of the main departures from the original DH 82a: the metal interplane struts, the tail wheel, elevator trim tabs and, of course, the sliding canopy.

The Paraslasher. George Lowdell practising on a life-size canvas of Mussolini.

The blade
retracted . . .

. . . and its contr
in the rear cockpi
the T-handle w
lifted and th
pushed downwar
to lower the blad

The DH 6 had been the workhorse at our flying training schools during the Kaiser War and history was to repeat itself when a quarter of a century later the Tiger Moth, following the example of its distant ancestor, flew the grey seas acting as spotter and discouraging the U-boat captains into the bargain. Here the similarity ends, for whereas in 1917 the DH 6 lost its place to the Avro 504 when it became the leading R.F.C. trainer, the Tiger Moth was to outlive all challengers during its war service and even hold the stage for several years after the return of peace.

It is a well-known fact that prior to attacking its target the submarine must raise its periscope above water, this optical instrument forming the sight for the torpedoes. In this attitude the submarine begins to give away its position for the tell-tale whisp of turbulence created by the periscope is there to be seen without the help of asdic or other submarine detectors. The tactics were simple in so far as coastal waters were concerned—keep the U-boats down below periscope height and they would be unable to attack our shipping as it entered and departed from the major ports handling vitally needed supplies.

Such was the state of our unreadiness for war that during December 1939 it was found necessary to form six Coastal Patrol Flights for the purpose, using unarmed light aeroplanes, it being argued that although they would be unable to attack in the event of a contact the noise of the engine would be sufficient to keep the U-boat submerged, and the light 'planes could perform a valuable function as spotters. In any case no other aircraft could be spared during the opening months of the war. Coastal Patrol Flights were located at suitable aerodromes in relation to shipping:

No. 1. Dyce (Aberdeen)
    2. Abbotsinch (Glasgow)
    3. Hooton Park (Birkenhead)
    4. Aldergrove (Belfast)
    5. Carew Cheriton (Tenby, Pembrokeshire)
    6. St. Eval (Newquay, Cornwall)

All Coastal Patrol Flights used Tiger Moths, with the exception of No. 6 which was equipped with Hornet Moths, a much sought after private aeroplane of pre-war days. It seems odd that the authorities should have allowed Coastal Patrol pilots to suffer the open cockpits of the Tiger Moth in Scotland whilst their colleagues in the milder climate of Cornwall enjoyed the enclosed cabin of the Hornet Moth, but no doubt there was a reason.

Each C.P.F. had six pilots and nine aircraft to allow for servicing which, in the face of the most severe winter conditions, was of a very high order, there being no reported case of engine failure or part failure up to June 1940 when the Tiger Moths were replaced by more advanced aircraft.

The Coastal Patrol Flights provided unorthodox entry into the Royal Air Force for at least one pilot. R. A. Carter had like so many young men before and since the war, scraped and saved so that he might learn to fly. He went solo in June 1935 after buying less than ten hours flying instruction at Marshalls Flying School, Cambridge, a modest total which due to financial considerations took him twelve months to amass. When war came in 1939 he had reached the relatively advanced age of twenty-nine and it took much persuasion and perseverance on his part before the R.A.F. finally and somewhat reluctantly accepted him as a pilot. He was posted to No. 2 C.P.F. Abbotsinch where he arrived, a Sergeant Pilot without stripes or wings, attired in plus fours, and pork-pie hat and with little or no knowledge of the Royal Air Force. He recalls that another newly arrived pilot by the name of Perkins very kindly sewed the sergeant's chevrons on to his as yet unworn tunic. Pilot Officer Tillet, the equally new Commanding Officer, greeted him with the words, 'Whatever have they sent to me now—pilots without wings?' Tillet led him to the flight line for the usual check ride that formed part of a pilot's introduction to a new unit and Carter had his first glimpse of the nine brand new Tiger Moths as they stood on the tarmac, looking very business-like in their camouflage and operational numbers.

On landing he was issued with one Tiger Moth and two mechanics with instructions to fly whenever he liked so that he could become accustomed to the local area—quite a change from snatching a quarter of an hour here and there whenever finances permitted.

Within a few days the pilots were summoned to the C.O.'s office and made conversant with the aims of the unit and how they were to be accomplished. It was soon clear to Carter that his free flying paradise had another side that was not so attractive. Pilots received their operational instructions on a document called 'Form Mauve' which detailed such information as time of take-off, position of the patrol area (in code), and times of arrival and departure, height to fly, etc. Pilots reported sightings on a 'Form Orange', giving their information in this order:

1. Name of vessel sighted
2. Nationality
3. Tonnage
4. Position
5. Course
6. Speed
7. Time observed
8. Description

As has been already mentioned, the winter of 1939–40 was particularly severe. The sea spray froze on to the Tiger Moths as they carried out their patrols so that it was necessary to smear the vulnerable areas of the wings and tail surfaces with a special paste developed to prevent severe icing. On the front seat of each Tiger was a small wicker basket containing two homing pigeons made comfortable on a layer of wood shavings. In the event of a forced landing at sea the pilot was supposed to write his position on a slip of paper, attach it to a pigeon and hope for the best, since there was no radio. A part-inflated motor inner tube filled the luggage locker and was attached to a marine distress signal by a 30 ft. length of string. A signal pistol and cartridges were fastened to the right-hand door of the rear cockpit, and with nothing more than heavy flying clothing and an all-important Mae West, the pilots of the Coastal Patrol Flights flew sortie after sortie under conditions of poor visibility and almost indescribable cold. The rear cockpit of a Tiger Moth is always more draughty than the front and in the cold air of a Scottish winter each eddy thrust like a blade of ice, so that not unnaturally strenuous attempts were made to reduce the freezing blast. The removal of the front windscreens effected a partial improvement, although much of what had buffeted the pilot's head now found its way into the front cockpit and blew into the rear—carrying with it feathers and wood shavings from the pigeons' basket together with bird droppings which caused almost constant sore throats. It would have been an easy matter to cover the front cockpit with a detachable canvas or ply sheet, but for some reason the authorities witheld permission.

In his book *So Few* David Masters records an incident when one exhausted pilot fell asleep in his Tiger to awake only as his wheels touched the water, and another pilot landed back at base trailing yards of seaweed from his tail-skid. In each case the pilot was not aware of any act of self preservation, but reaction on the controls must have been instinctive and more or less instantaneous, for both pilots brought their Tigers home undamaged.

Undoubtedly the Coastal Patrol Flights provided valuable movement information on shipping, and the sound of their engines must have made many a U-boat commander keep his submarine below the surface, for how was he to know whether the aircraft overhead was merely a defence-less Tiger Moth or an aeroplane carrying a depth-charge? It was this part of the operation that earned it the unofficial title 'Scarecrow Patrol'.

It is a commonly held belief that from a height it is possible to see into the depths of the sea. The pilots of the Scarecrow Patrol, however, found that although this may be true in certain areas the not very clear water around these shores obscured submarines, even when their position was known with certainty. With no radio the Scarecrow Patrols were flown in pairs, the idea being that when a suspicious object was sighted one Tiger Moth would continue to circle the spot while the other returned to base and reported the matter so that the information could be sent by radio to naval and merchant ships in the area. Alternatively, when a sighting was made within signalling distance of a naval vessel the pilot would fire a green cartridge and continue to circle the spot, in this way marking the area for the attacking ships.

There is so often an embarrassing gulf between theory and practice and this was certainly the case on the occasion of Carter's second operational sortie, an occasion (he related afterwards) made the more embarrassing by the presence of his Commanding Officer who happened to be flying in the accompanying Tiger. Before take-off Pilot Officer Tillet impressed upon Carter that he was to stay with any object he considered to be suspicious. It was no day for a light aeroplane without radio. The snow and sleet were driven by the wind and there were patches of sea fog. Just off the Mull of Kintyre Carter sighted a vessel approaching the Clyde and to his consternation some thousand yards behind followed an object, something—a periscope! At this very moment Pilot Officer Tillet broke formation and disappeared into the mist leaving a by now very excited Sergeant Carter to make what he could of the situation. He circled the object for over one and a half hours convinced that Tillet would be sending naval forces to finish the U-boat. By now all the coldness and discomfort of the Tiger's open cockpit had been forgotten; his mind was completely occupied by the object in the water below. Occasionally he had visions of gaining an immediate D.F.M. when the sub had been dealt with, although often as he flew over the boat a sailor in a white roll-neck sweater waved his arms at him in a way that under more normal circumstances would have registered 'go away' or something less polite. It was with approaching exasperation that the skipper finally ordered his crew to pull the 'sub' alongside the ship, and it was then that Carter could see that his German U-boat was in fact a paravane of the type towed behind ships to cut mine cables.

He returned to Abbotsinch, having been in the air for two hours and forty minutes and as a result very short of fuel. Naval H.Q. was not amused by the incident and Carter was subjected to some criticism by his Commanding Officer. News of Carter's non-existent U-boat reached the other Coastal Patrol Flights and the following morning he was presented with a toy submarine, formally mounted, with the inscription, 'Sunk by R. A. Carter on 11th December 1939'.

The normal route followed by No. 2 C.P.F. was Abbotsinch – Ardrossan – Isle of Arran – Mull of Kintyre – Rothlin Isle (Northern Ireland) – Ailsa Craig, and then back to base down the railway line on the mainland. When the snow lay deep on Abbotsinch a plough was borrowed from Paisley town council and it was not uncommon for the snow on either side of the runways to be above the level of the Tiger Moths wings. Carter's big moment with No. 2 C.P.F. came when he was chosen to escort the *Queen Elizabeth* on her maiden voyage across the Atlantic. As the greatest liner in the world left the Clyde she was accompanied as far as Ailsa Craig by three Tiger Moths piloted by Flying Officer Virgin, Pilot Officer Birt and Sergeant Carter.

Both Sergeants Carter and Perkins flew a number of sorties without their pilots wings until they were presented them in February 1940.

The original pilots of No. 2 C.P.F. were Pilot Officer Tillet (killed in action shortly after the flight was disbanded), Pilot Officer Birt, Sergeant Perkins and Sergeant Carter. They were later joined by Sergeant Langston, Flying Officer Virgin and a South African, Flying Officer Potgeiter. Carter flew eighty sorties with 2 C.P.F. and when the unit disbanded in June 1940 was responsible for ferrying the Tiger Moths to various maintenance units. Happily Carter is still flying in South Africa what he describes as his favourite aeroplane, Tiger Moth ZS-BGL.

To Flying Officer Hoyle, the Commanding Officer of No.
1 C.P.F., must go the distinction of being involved in what
is believed to be the only sinking of a U-boat that resulted
from the intrusion of a Tiger Moth. Hoyle sighted a submarine immediately below him, fired a 'green' when naval
forces closed in to the attack with depth charges leaving
behind them a vast area of oil and bubbles that continued
to rise to the surface for several days. The brass ring from
the base of the green signal cartridge fired by Hoyle is still
kept as a valued souvenir in the officers' mess at Dyce.

But the Tiger Moth was having its moments of drama in
more exotic parts of the world, where it experienced extreme temperatures at the other end of the scale to those
encountered during the Scottish winter. Later in the war,
during the closing part of 1944 when we were involved
with the Japanese in Burma, between six and ten Tiger
Moths were turned into ambulance 'planes, the extensive
modification being undertaken at Comilla, East Bengal.
The luggage locker lid was enlarged and made to hinge on
the left-hand side of the fuselage, and a separate lid about
four feet long was cut out of the curved ply that formed the
top deck behind the luggage locker, the floor of which now
extended some six feet towards the rear of the aircraft. The
casualty was placed with his head adjacent to the back of
the rear cockpit, his feet pointing towards the tail of the
Tiger Moth. The long door was closed over his legs, and
final entombment was completed by shutting the now enlarged locker hatch. Little was done to provide windows
other than a small rectangular perspex panel which allowed
light to enter near the injured man's feet. The tail skids
were modified to increase braking effect on the short strips
often visited by the ambulance Tigers.

Patients were, on many occasions, flown to a strip near
the big hospital at Gonchwein. Sometimes the ambulance
Tigers would feed a Dakota which awaited casualties on
one of the larger airfields. But often the Tigers were called
upon to fly in and out of small and badly prepared strips

offering no choice of wind direction, usually with a bad slope thrown in to enliven what was already a hazardous operation.

These valiant little ambulance 'planes were flown by 224 Group Communications Squadron, the unit being based at an aerodrome near Chittagong which rejoiced in the delightful name of Cox's Bazaar. Later the ambulance Tigers moved to Akyab in Burma. One of the 'ambulance drivers', now Flight Lieutenant William Moxon, remembers that they were 'rather tricky' to fly when loaded. The elevator trim was unable to cope with the extra weight in the rear, and some pilots incorporated their own unofficial devices to overcome this extreme tail heaviness, the most popular being a length of rope attached to the stick in such a way that the pilot could obtain additional leverage. Tiger Moths were later replaced by the American Stinson light ambulance aeroplanes.

At about the same period one Flight Lieutenant T. G. Hicks found himself in the role of Wing Armament Officer, an appointment which amongst other responsibilities involved making routine visits to six airfields in the Imphal Valley, Assam. One of these, an airstrip at Palel near the Burmese border, meant a not too comfortable and almost unimaginably dusty thirty mile drive from his base, so it was with some gratitude that he accepted the offer of a lift in a Tiger Moth piloted by the Wing Commander Flying.

As they were about to finish their business at Palel an air-raid warning was sounded clearing everyone from sight as if by magic. The Wing Commander decided that if they were in for trouble they might as well have it in the comfort of their own home, and without wasting any time the Tiger was started and both men strapped themselves in.

They taxied to the end of the narrow strip, so narrow in fact that the Tiger Moth, without brakes and relying entirely upon the scraping action of its swivelling tail skid, found itself with insufficient room to turn into the take-off direction. Normally a member of the ground crew would have held one wing tip while the pilot gave the Tiger a burst of throttle, but the air-raid siren had, temporarily at any rate, secured the disappearance of all ground crew. 'Get on the wing,' shouted the Wing Commander, a reasonable enough request under the circumstances and one that would present no difficulty to an aircraft hand or another pilot. Hicks, choosing to accept the Wing Commander's order literally, got on the wing which gave way beneath him in a little welter of splintering wood and tearing fabric. Fortunately not having heard the noise the incident went unnoticed by the Wing Commander. Hicks took hold of himself, realized his mistake and, removing his backside from the damaged area, pulled the Tiger round. Very wisely the Wing Commander had elected to make the return journey at nought feet in deference to Japanese Zeros that might have been in the area. Flight Lieutenant Hicks was completely unaccustomed to low flying and his alarm was not diminished by the appearance of an ominous tear in the wing fabric which suddenly appeared in the place where he had so recently sat. For the rest of the journey his attention was rivetted to this depressing development, all concern for low flying and Japanese fighters being driven from his mind. Fortunately the tear spread so far and no more but Hicks has never forgotten his feeling of gratitude for the robustness of the Tiger Moth when they landed safely at base.

*Flying instructors at the Elementary Flying Training Schools were often bored with their occupation and anxious to go on operation, so that the introduction of practice bombing represented a heaven-sent opportunity to let off steam. Up and down the country Tigers were to be seen hedge hopping towards imaginary targets. After releasing the bombs they would depart the way they had arrived—as low as possible. They flew up rivers below bank level, between woods, around hills and anywhere considered impossible for an aeroplane to venture. Occasionally a Tiger would return to the home airfield trailing fifty or more yards of telephone wires from its tailskid and at one time the G.P.O. were hard pressed to maintain communications over the Cambridge area until steps were taken to curb the more boisterous among the instructors.

6. Tigers in Training

For some time the de Havilland Company had been working on a design study for a fast, high flying, twin-engined light bomber, so fast in its day that no armament was to be carried. Such a concept was rather ahead of Air Ministry thinking at the time and there was much active opposition from certain of the Air Marshals. The project was turned down and de Havillands were offered a not very attractive sub-contract as a rather patronizing consolation prize. But out of stupidity came wisdom, for, nettled by the unimaginative attitude of those concerned with the nation's military aircraft, Geoffrey de Havilland made one of his characteristic far-reaching decisions. He would build the bomber as a private venture and in great secrecy to ensure that no interference would be forthcoming from official quarters. A prototype was built at Salisbury Hall, an old country house near Hatfield aerodrome. Shortly before the first flight it survived a particularly determined air raid which nearly put back the clock by many months. The aeroplane was the now legendary Mosquito, an all wooden masterpiece that was the envy of every air force on both sides of the war and the delight of both bomber and fighter pilots who flew it in each version.

Following on the maiden flight, official hostility gave way to official enthusiasm and the entire resources of the de Havilland aeroplane factory was ordered over to Mosquito

*Sir Geoffrey de Havilland died in 1965

110

production. This meant the end of the Tiger Moth production line at Hatfield, but an alternative factory had to be found without delay, for the Tiger Moth was vitally necessary and more and still more were needed for the war effort.

The gigantic facilities of Morris Motors Ltd. were under committed at the time and it was decided to transfer the Tiger Moth production line to their works at Cowley near Oxford. It was only to be expected that the home of one of Britain's leaders in the sphere of mass production would bring a fresh approach to the task of aircraft manufacture. Not for them the 'one off' attitude that was a feature of most pre-war aircraft workshops, although this comment does not in any way detract from the magnitude of de Havillands' own effort. By the time production ceased at Hatfield a total of 1,975 Tiger Moths and 320 Queen Bees had left the workshops

When Morris Motors received their first contract for Tiger Moths early in 1940, they immediately set about translating the rather detailed structure of the little biplane into a series of repeatable operations so that it could be manufactured on the 'flow line' principle so successfully adopted when mass production of cars had been their daily bread. The flow line technique had not been applied to aeroplanes before and there were many raised eyebrows and sceptical comments from the old hands in the aircraft industry. Nevertheless by April 1940 the first Tiger Moth emerged from the motor works at Cowley, passed all tests without difficulty and led the way for the biggest line of Tigers ever to come out of one factory. By 15th August 1945, when the last Tiger Moth left the Morris works, over 3,500 complete aeroplanes had been made.

Not that the transition from motor-cars to Tiger Moths was made without difficulty. Morris Motors had lost most of their 5,000 assembly staff on the outbreak of war and a school had to be opened in the factory to train welders and other technicians capable of working to aircraft standards.

Remembering how the Tiger Moth was evolved from another aeroplane without drawings it will come as no surprise to learn that the blueprints made after the Tiger Moth had come into existence were not always clear to the engineers at Morris Motors groping in unfamiliar country with their first aeroplane. Try as they might, the men at Cowley found themselves unable to fit the first set of cowlings around the engine of their near-completed Tiger Moth. Drawings were checked and found to accord with the finished article. The impasse was finally resolved when an inspector arrived from Hatfield with a pair of tin snips and cut off two small pieces of sheet metal. The cowlings then closed. But the Tiger had grown up at Stag Lane and Hatfield during an era when blueprints were not always so explicit as they might have been, and what was clear enough to the Hatfield men occasionally baffled those working feverishly to establish a new production line where cars had poured forth before.

The flow line system is based upon mass production of each and every part, so arranged that the correct item arrives at the correct point on the main assembly line at the correct time. It is the aim of the production engineers to keep moving large numbers of the product in hand in all its stages of construction. Even a light aeroplane such as the Tiger Moth is a complex and detailed structure when compared with a family car, and there were many problems to be solved before large scale production could commence. To instance one important development, the jig welding of tubular steel fuselages was pioneered at Cowley and proved completely successful under the arduous service conditions met by the Tiger Moth all over the world.

The project at Morris Motors was in the hands of the following key personnel:

Joint Managing Directors	H. Seaward
	H. A. Ryder
General Manager	S. V. Smith
Works Manager	H. T. G. Smith
Production Manager	W. E. A. Cullum
Planning Engineer	F. Stott

Chief Inspector	A. F. Houlberg
Liaison Officer, with emphasis on Spares (went to Morris Motors Ltd. from de Havilland)	G. E. Plummer
Test Pilot (seconded to Morris Motors Ltd. by de Havilland)	T. Tucker

As production of Tiger Moths gradually diminished at Hatfield, so the volume increased at Cowley. An airfield was constructed adjacent to the works and as each machine came off the flow line it was pushed across a small road to the airfield, test flown and delivered without delay. Seventeen Tiger Moths were completed at the end of the first week of production, but as the pace quickened thirty-five and even forty came out of the works each week—many times the production rate as it was before the flow line method was introduced. There were never any failures and at the time the flow line at Cowley was in advance of American manufacturing practice. Vast quantities of spares and complete assemblies were made in addition to the Tigers delivered in flying condition, and eventually it was considered unwise to keep this enormous stock under one roof. Great efforts were made to disperse the parts around the countryside into what was called 'purgatory storage', and barns, sheds, garages, church halls and in fact anything with a roof to keep out the weather was requisitioned for the purpose. The last Hatfield-built Tiger Moth had de Havilland constructors number 83124 and carried the service registration R5265.

There is some confusion about the actual number of Tiger Moths completed at Cowley. In his authoritative book *An Outline of de Havilland History*, C. Martin Sharp credits Morris Motors with 3,210 aeroplanes, whilst A. J. Jackson's *De Havilland Aircraft Since 1915* gives a figure of 3,216. However a complete record of Tiger Moths built for the R.A.F. by Morris Motors exists and 3,433 registrations are listed. Furthermore the works at Cowley produced

113

an additional seventy-five Tiger Moths against overseas orders, twenty-four going to New Zealand (NZ775 to 798) ten to the Persian Air Force, five to South Africa and twenty-six were delivered to India in civil markings (VT-AMI to VT-ANI). It has not been possible to trace the remaining ten machines from this overseas batch, but in any case the registrations available give strong evidence that Morris Motors produced 3,508 Tiger Moths, mainly to meet the insatiable appetite of the flying schools.

Arrangements had been made to transfer elementary and basic flying training to those areas within the Commonwealth least likely to come under direct enemy action. It was essential to keep the restricted air space over the British Isles clear of training aircraft and of course too many aerodromes could not be diverted from operational needs. Furthermore the close proximity of these isles to the Luftwaffe meant that a serious flying training programme was bound to become a target of some priority in the eyes of the German High Command: it would be all too easy for them to stop the flow of new pilots to the squadrons when the R.A.F. would surely become paralysed. Then again there was the traditional British weather—hardly ideal for a non-stop training programme.

From these thoughts emerged the now famous Empire Training Scheme with its scores of elementary and service flying schools operating away from enemy reach.

Obviously the cost of transporting thousands of aircrew across the seas was high, both in terms of real money and, what was perhaps of more importance at the time, valuable shipping capacity. Then there was the attendant risk of sending thousands of the nation's above-average young men through U-boat-infested waters—young men who had already assumed a degree of national importance, for prior to shipment they had completed six months or so at one of the Initial Training Wings where a very thorough pre-flight training had been given them.

Pilot training during the war was based upon a policy of progressive elimination of all but the best candidates. Not unnaturally nearly everyone wanted to be a pilot, and whereas during the early stages of the war the home flying schools were busy coping with the remnants of the C.A.G. and part-trained direct R.A.F. entrants, once the Empire Training Scheme got under way it was vitally necessary to have some arrangement which would prevent square pegs from getting into round holes; it is one thing to consider oneself a future bomber or fighter pilot but quite another matter when the training starts. Unlike peacetime club flying, these pupil pilots were to be put through a rapid and highly concentrated course, getting their wings after two hundred hours flying, when they would be expected to pilot some of the most complex equipment put into the hands of man at that time. No civil airline would consider placing a nineteen-year-old in command of a four-engined aircraft weighing the wrong side of thirty tons, sending him over Europe in hail, rain or snow with but a few hundred hours in his log book. Yet this is precisely what did happen time and time again, and the fact that generally the boys were able to cope is a true measure of the success of the Empire Training Scheme.

To separate the square pegs from the round holes all candidates were later accepted for aircrew under the classification P. N. B. or Pilot/Navigator/Bomb Aimer. So labelled, the cadets went to I.T.W. for comprehensive ground courses and on successful completion progressed to Grading School. Here they received twelve hours flying instruction and a proportion of the most promising came forward for pilot training at one of the overseas flying schools. Those considered below the general level of aptitude for pilot training continued their service in one of the other aircrew categories.

The Grading Schools were in reality pre-war civil-operated Elementary Flying Training Schools, with one or two exceptions already equipped with Tiger Moths, so that the important task of categorizing all the war-trained aircrew for the R.A.F. fell to the lot of the little biplane. It is because of its Grading School activities during this phase of the war that to fly a Tiger Moth became part of the experience of almost every R.A.F. pilot.

Life at the Grading Schools was hectic for the instructors with cadets arriving constantly for what amounted to a probational period of flying training. There were times when the Tigers were operated in marginal weather conditions in an effort to keep up to schedule. On these occasions, however, it was impossible to send cadets solo even when they were ready to go. During one rather lengthy period when the little airfield at Theale near Reading was plagued with continuous Thames Valley haze, across the walls of the cadets' lavatory were scrawled the words, 'Lost Horizon, a Theale Production', an announcement no doubt inspired by the famous film of that name.

Since flying instructors at these schools were confined to flying around the airfield and the local area, a small number of flying hours were allowed them so they might keep in practice with cross-country and instrument flying. It was usual to save this practice flying time for some specific occasion, such as a week-end leave when the Tiger Moth provided convenient free transport. One bright and sunny day at Theale a Tiger landed with a bicycle tied to the side of the fuselage with its wheels resting on the lower wing. The pilot in the front cockpit got out, untied two pieces of string, removed his cycle and rode off as his colleague taxied away for home.

At the end of their twelve hours on Tiger Moths the now graded cadets were posted to Heaton Park, Manchester, there to await shipment abroad. A great proportion of the training was concentrated in Canada where both R.C.A.F. and R.A.F. units turned out countless thousands of aircrew. Other flying training took place in South Africa and Rhodesia. The Australians, New Zealanders and Indians trained at home. A limited number of cadets learned to fly in the U.S.A., and because of America's early neutrality, civilian clothes had to be worn. With America's entry into the war in 1941 the Arnold Scheme, as it was called, gave way to an organization known as the Washington Delega-

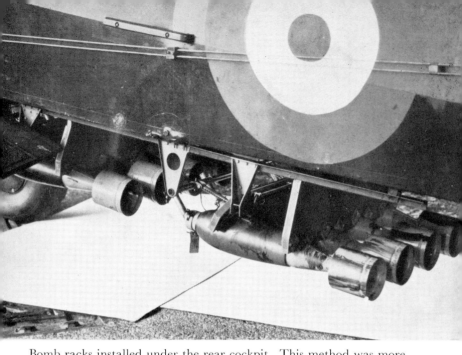

Bomb racks installed under the rear cockpit. This method was more common than the under-wing arrangement.

Operational Tiger pilots. *Left to right:* Sergeant Carter and Sergeant Langston of the 'Scarecrow Patrol' with Flight Sergeant King.

The Tiger Moth coupé, a very beautiful cabin conversion designed and executed in New Zealand.

tion which controlled a number of civilian-run R.A.F. administered British Flying Training Schools. The lucky ones trained at these glamorous stations had the benefits of civil catering, civil Link instructors (many of them attractive girls!) and American civilian flying instructors who wore a special B.F.T.S. uniform. The Commanding Officer was an R.A.F. Wing Commander who was assisted in the administration of the school by a Squadron Leader Chief Ground Instructor, a Flight Lieutenant Chief Flying Instructor, an Adjutant and a Navigation Officer. The pupil pilots were largely responsible for their own discipline, cadet officers or N.C.Os.' being appointed for the purpose with the rank of Cadet Wing Commander downwards. British Flying Training Schools were situated at Terrell, Texas; Clouston, Florida; Ponca City, Oklahoma; Miami, Oklahoma and Phoenix, Arizona. The cadets completed seventy hours elementary instruction, mostly on P.T. 17 Stearman biplanes, before progressing on to AT6A Harvards (often known as North American Texans) for basic and advanced flying.

All this has little to do with the Tiger Moth other than to establish the interesting fact that when the newly qualified pilots came home from America and were sent to Elementary Flying Training Schools again for acclimatization or pre-A.F.U. (Advanced Flying Unit) many found to their dismay that the help of a flying instructor was needed before they could again go solo on the Tiger—and how the little brute magnified every fault!

The home-based Tiger Moths, most of which spent their working days grading cadets under the P.N.B. Scheme, by no means led a tranquil life. They were subjected to almost continuous harsh treatment at the hands of pupil pilots. Incredible stories about Tiger Moths at the flying schools are almost inexhaustible. For example, there was the incident one crystal clear morning in the late summer of 1941 when Sergeant Chandler and his pupil climbed in a Tiger to some 4,000 ft. in preparation for some aerobatic instruction. Chandler was a relatively new flying instructor on rest from operational flying. A fellow instructor, R. R. Lewis, glanced up casually as Chandler commenced his dive for a 'roll off the top'. The Tiger was perhaps half way round the loop when one starboard mainplane fell off, then the other. Almost immediately both port wings parted company with the now spinning fuselage. The wings, released of their burden, fluttered like sycamore leaves over the town of Peterborough while the fuselage, now divested of all means of support, plunged to the ground like a dart. To the relief of Lewis and others watching on the ground first the pupil and then Chandler baled out, the pupil landing unhurt on the edge of the aerodrome and his flying instructor descending alongside Wagon Repairs Ltd. with nothing more than slight grazes to show for his ordeal. Meanwhile the wingless, pilotless fuselage plummeted down, finally ending its unorthodox return to earth with the propeller boss resting on the living-room floor of a Peterborough house and its tail unit sticking out of the roof. The glass on the instruments in both cockpits remained intact, fortunately the petrol tank did not burst and no one suffered injury. It was afterwards discovered that the wrong type of nut had been fitted to the wing bolts at the maintenance unit concerned. Most of the Tiger Moths at Peterborough were grounded for inspection as a result of this incident and flying training was disrupted for two days.

The Tiger Moth figured prominently at two schools charged with the very responsible task of producing elementary flying instructors. Trainee instructors were drawn from many sources: ex-operational pilots, pre-war club instructors and even newly qualified pilots who, by virtue of certain characteristics, displayed special aptitude for teaching. At one stage of the war most of the flying instructors' courses were handled at Cambridge and Woodley. The course was an exacting one, designed to improve the trainee instructor's flying, increase his knowledge of ground subjects and, above all, teach him the necessary 'patter'. Each exercise such as Effects of Controls, Climbing, Stalling, etc., had to be explained on the ground and demonstrated in the air with every sequence accompanied by the standard commentary as laid down by the Central Flying School. It took much practice to be able to synchronize what was happening with what was said, particularly during a landing when the instructor finished the actual touchdown with the words '. . . until the aircraft sinks to the ground on all—three—points'. On the word 'points' it was the aim of every good instructor to make contact with the ground, and hours were spent 'pattering' in the air, sometimes with the instructor but more often in the company of a fellow student. This was fairly hard work, communication between cockpits being restricted to accoustic-type Gosport speaking tubes. Each pilot was connected to the system by an arrangement not unlike a doctor's stethoscope which led into the earpieces of the leather flying helmet. Both cockpits had a flexible pipe which emerged from behind the instrument panel and terminated in a rubber mouthpiece. As these became aged they could be relied upon to blacken the face of the user so that at the end of a busy day's flying the instructors often looked as though they had been down a coal mine. Particularly during take-off and landing it was essential that the speaking tube should remain in the position set by the instructor, since both hands were on the controls and he was unable to support the mouthpiece. With constant use much of the rigidity would disappear from the speaking tubes and they would droop like jaded flowers and have to be tied up with string. It was always necessary to speak slowly, deliberately and above all loudly, and on occasions when moisture collected in the system it was almost impossible to hear. In retrospect it seems unbelievable that practically all the pilots of the R.A.F. and their Commonwealth colleagues received their elementary training on Tiger Moths with complete success.

If the Gosport tubes could exasperate, on occasions they were good for a laugh, a particular instance being the time when the middle-aged and slightly deaf Chief Ground Instructor at Shellingford was given a lift to the West

Country in a Tiger Moth. As they flew over the spectacular Avon Gorge and its graceful Clifton suspension bridge, the pilot felt moved to break silence and shouted, 'Look at all the boats coming out of the Avonmouth.' This seemed to upset the Chief Ground Instructor and in the mirror (installed for the benefit of the flying instructor so that he might watch his pupil) the pilot could see his passenger peering anxiously first left then right.

'What did you say?' asked the C.G.I. 'I said look at all the boats coming out of the Avonmouth,' repeated the pilot. 'My God!' came the reply, 'I thought you said look at all the bolts coming out of the ailerons.' Fortunately for all concerned, later in the war quite efficient electric inter-comm. replaced the rather Victorian plumbing system that had grudgingly allowed conversation between instructor and pupil.

So that student flying instructors could concentrate on the job of learning the various exercises, arrangements were made to give them a brief spell at pre-F.I.S. (Flying Instructors' School) for in most cases they had but recently come off Spitfires and Lancasters or such-like and the transition back to a Tiger Moth often came as something of a shock. The E.F.T.S. at Theale handled much of this work which was later shared by No. 3 E.F.T.S. Shellingford. It is perhaps surprising that such a procedure had to be adopted, but whereas the Tiger is the most forgiving aeroplane imaginable, it can deflate a pilot's ego in the shortest possible time—as many were to find at first hand.

It became the practice to take these ex-operational pilots for a short ride whilst they became accustomed to the open cockpit of the Tiger and the very different handling technique associated with light aeroplanes. One, Flying Officer Miller, joined the pre-F.I.S. course at Shellingford in 1945. He was, by wartime R.A.F. standards, an experienced pilot with 1,500 hours in his log book and two operational tours on Halifax four-engined heavy bombers. After twenty minutes or so his instructor landed and invited him to do a circuit of the aerodrome. The take-off was a long drawn out affair using most of the airfield, the throttle opening slowly and gradually as though the Tiger was about to bite. A lengthy climb at shallow angle was followed by a circuit of the airfield that seemed to take in most of Berkshire. How different it all must seem to sit in a Tiger Moth with the minimum of controls; what a contrast after the Halifax with its four throttles, four mixture controls, four pitch controls, massive instrument panel and complex fuel system! With these thoughts in mind the instructor felt moved to get Miller's reactions to the joys of Tiger flying. 'What do you think of it?' he asked, and the strained voice of the ex-bomber replied, 'I haven't had time to think!'

As a tactical exercise low flying is of great value, and indeed its practice can be the difference between success and disaster when a pilot is caught in lowering cloud without radio. R.A.F. pilots rarely needed much encouragement to practise this exhilarating form of aviation, and, in an effort to confine hedge-hopping to those parts of the countryside least likely to be upset by the sudden appearance over the garden wall of a steeply banked Tiger Moth, low flying areas were designated for the purpose. No. 3 E.F.T.S. Shellingford had an excellent one situated on the edge of the Berkshire Downs and running alongside the main London to Bristol railway line. Opportunities to let off steam were many and some of the flying instructors developed a technique that must have been a source of entertainment for many a passenger on the Great Western Railway, as it was then called. The idea was simple: one waited until a fast train came into the low flying area and then dropped down in line with the guard's van. The throttle would be opened slightly and as the Tiger, by now more or less at window level slowly overtook the train, a line of excited passengers would appear, their heads turning in unison towards the front of the train as they watched the aeroplane creep forward—it was rather like watching a troup of well rehearsed chorus girls. And then as the pilot drew abreast of the engine he would throttle back a little, allowing the speeding passenger train to draw ahead, and this time the line of faces would turn the other way as the Tiger Moth appeared to move backwards in relation to the train.

A task of prime importance was allotted the Tiger Moth when it was decided to train large numbers of glider pilots for the forthcoming invasion of Europe. The glider pilots were to be men in khaki, and both officers and men were posted to R.A.F. flying schools from various Army units. Obviously it would be more convenient to teach these men to handle an aircraft flying under its own power, the alternative being the time-wasting procedure of glider towing and cable retrieving after each landing. The soldiers were given seventy hours flying on Tiger Moths followed by a period of training on Hotspur gliders; then they were converted to the massive troop-carrying Horsa (which could lift a jeep) or the even bigger Hamilcar.

When the first Army entry marched into Shellingford under the command of its own officers the flying staff was impressed by two things: their smartness in comparison with the usual R.A.F. cadets, and their enormous clanging boots. They were wonderful lads, smart, alert and always ready to please. Many had come straight off tanks and much time had to be devoted to the task of making clear that, robust little aeroplane as it may be, the Tiger was no tank. The boots were certainly a handicap, effectively preventing any suggestion of 'feel' on the part of these Army pupils, and one or two of the spectacular first solos that resulted are unlikely to be forgotten by those who were there at the time. Fortunately the Tiger Moth will stand any amount of being dropped from a height provided it lands on both wheels. This, the Army was not always able to arrange!

Later these same Army glider pilots distinguished themselves at Arnhem and during the Rhine crossing, and information filtered back to Shellingford where proud flying instructors could be seen discussing the exploits of their pupils. The senior Army officer under training with this particular entry was Captain Morrison, an old school friend and classmate of one of the authors. To everyone's dismay, news came that he had been killed during the Rhine crossing. Shortly after the war a very much alive Morrison, still in uniform, and a somewhat dazed Flight Lieutenant pilot met by chance in the busy streets of Liverpool when the Captain was able to assure his old school friend that, in the words of the famous explorer, his death had been grossly exaggerated.

With pupils going round and round the airfield in an endeavour to master circuits and landings, many of the Elementary Flying Training Schools had satellite fields at their disposal where pupils under instruction could be diverted, relieving the aerodrome proper of at least some traffic. Nevertheless at around 10 a.m. each day when the N.A.A.F.I. van was known to be visiting each flight with tea and cakes it was nothing to see thirty or more Tiger Moths jockeying for position to land in time for the morning cup.

No. 3 E.F.T.S. was fortunate in having a particularly delightful relief landing ground near the village of Pewsey in charming countryside so typical of Berkshire. It was within a few minutes flying of the aerodrome and at certain times of the year passers-by on the road from Charney Bassett to Faringdon would witness a strange early-morning ritual: several figures clad in full flying kit would be seen wandering aimlessly about the landing field in a head-down attitude followed in each case by a Tiger Moth. In fact the man on foot was a flying instructor looking for mushrooms while his pupil followed in the aeroplane ready to receive the proceeds of the morning's harvest. Neither officers' nor sergeants' mess at Shellingford ever bought mushrooms.

Most of the adjoining fields at Pewsey were under cultivation and the land girls making this valuable contribution to the war effort sometimes found themselves the target for a little boisterous attention—which culminated in Sergeant X taking off from Pewsey with a pupil under instruction and making a pass at a likely-looking land girl. As the young lady went about her task the wheel of Sergeant X's Tiger literally caught her bending and she later complained to the local police of being thrown full length to the ground. Wing Commander Garnons-Williams, at the time Shellingford's Commanding Officer, recalls that he had a lot of explaining to do in an effort to prevent the incident developing:

> Although one of the girls claimed she was hit, she refused to have her bottom examined by the M.O. or anyone else, and she eventually accepted an apology from the individual concerned. After this incident, we issued an order that simulated engine failure after taking-off was to be carried out only from Shellingford—this being the 'getaway' excuse offered by Sergeant X.

The Fleet Air Arm entrusted its cadet pilots to the Tiger Moths of the R.A.F., many receiving their elementary flying training at Clyffe Pypard, a large wartime flying school south of Wootton Bassett.

Tiger Moths were used on the Junior R.N. and R.M. Officers' Air Course at Royal Naval Air Station, Gosport (H.M.S. *Siskin*), whilst in far away Trinidad the local flying club gave up its Tigers to R.N. Air Station, Piarco (H.M.S. *Goshawk*), so that Observers could be trained for the Fleet Air Arm. These particular aeroplanes were also used for target towing and from all accounts it seems they were well cared for by the Senior Service who returned them to the Trinidad Aero Club towards the end of 1945.

Many were the wartime flying instructors who bitterly resented their inability to take an active part in the fighting, either as bomber or fighter pilots, and the fact that their own contribution to the total war effort was a vital one did little, in many cases, to quell a feeling of dissatisfaction. It is a weakness suffered by all types of humanity to imagine that what is on the other man's plate is better than one's own. When they were not too busy and too tired to care, it was only natural that those who visualized themselves as operational pilots should become bored with the routine of flying instruction. The by-products of boredom are many. At its best it can lead even responsible people into trouble, and when allied with a restlessness to get on to operational flying the results can be, and sometimes were, near tragic. But the demarcation between tragedy and comedy is often slight, and out of a potentially serious incident often came comedy as a flying instructor sought relief from monotony during the war.

There was 'Dusty' Miller, deputy flight commander of B Flight, 3 E.F.T.S. Shellingford. His repeated applications to be taken off instructing and sent on 'ops' were turned down—which was understandable enough because he was, in those days, on the wrong side of forty. One day in a moment of frustration and despair he took it into his head to fly his Tiger Moth between the flight office and another small building on the edge of the aerodrome. Unfortunately the gap between the buildings didn't quite fit the Tiger's wings and he ended his brief journey slithering along an adjoining field in a wingless fuselage—fortunately without serious injury.

One of the most amusing incidents occurred at Fairoaks in Surrey, although it, too, might well have ended in disaster. One day in 1941 the telephone rang for the Commanding Officer, Wing Commander C. E. F. Arthur, A.F.C. It was the officer in charge of a nearby balloon-barrage site at Brooklands. One of his balloons had just descended in flames on the golf course and he suspected a Tiger Moth may have something to do with it. 'Was there,' he asked, 'a Tiger Moth unaccounted for at Fairoaks?' Arthur gave his caller a somewhat unceremonious 'no' and hastily replaced the receiver. But a few minutes later his attention was drawn to a Tiger Moth parked within sight of his office window. There seemed to be something rather special about this Tiger for it was surrounded by a number of animated spectators—instructors, pupils and one or two civilian aircraft engineers (maintenance was in the hands of civilians at the E.F.T.S. establishments). He went to investigate and to his utter amazement found that a third or more of the fabric had been burned off the starboard lower wing and tailplane, also the right-hand side of the fuselage and fin were badly scorched.

Arthur sent for the pilot who duly arrived. He had no eyebrows other than a thin, singed line. His explanation was that he had gone to the forced-landing field at Merrow. It was a thundery day and the cloud came down rather suddenly, forcing him to return home on instruments. He must have got off course because on the way home he 'hit a balloon or something!' Eyeing him rather suspiciously Arthur told him that if Group H.Q. would accept the story it was good enough for him, but it was only after the war that Bernard Barton, the flying instructor concerned, was able to relate the true version of what happened.

Apparently B. Flight at Fairoaks had its share of bored instructors, some of whom organized a little competition to pass the time of day. The idea was to wait until a layer of cloud appeared just below balloon height, obscuring them from the ground but leaving the great bulbous objects in full view of those flying above. With these conditions giving them privacy from the ground the aim was to run the wheels of the Tiger over the top of the balloon. Barton had done this successfully before—'a nice run in up wind, throttled back to about 60 m.p.h. A lovely squelch as the wheels ran along its back and turning round—saw it fairly heaving about from the impact.' On the day in question he was accompanied by a Rhodesian pupil called Chisholme. The balloons were half in and half out of cloud like basking whales in the sun. But things went wrong, the Tiger sank into the balloon which burst around him and was ignited either by static electricity or the Tiger's exhaust. The whole aircraft seemed to be enveloped in flames and in the confusion that followed Barton pushed up his goggles to get a better view of the situation, an action which, temporarily at any rate, cost him his eyebrows. By now the trailing edge of the starboard wing was emitting dozens of little flames perhaps an inch or so high, rather like Bunsenburner jets. Barton dived the Tiger gently in an effort to put out the flames. At first full of enthusiasm for the idea, both instructor and pupil now returned to Fairoaks very badly shaken and holding on left aileron for all they were worth in an effort to keep the aeroplane level. The Tiger Moth involved was K4291, one of the original machines delivered to 18 Elementary and Reserve School, Fairoaks, in 1937. It lived to fly many more hours with a witch's head painted on its rudder.

Early in 1945 attempts were made to devise special equipment which would enable night flying training to continue during daylight hours. Night flying could at times present something of a bottleneck when a heavy training programme was in progress, for experience had shown that four or, at the most, five light aircraft without radio were all that could be handled around the flare path at any one time. The Two Stage Amber system was evolved, therefore, and experiments proceeded at various flying schools engaged in advanced and elementary training. The principle was a simple one based upon the properties of polaroid transparent sheeting. The pupil wore special polaroid goggles which enabled him to see his instruments in the normal way. The usual blind flying hood was modified to carry polaroid panels so that, when the pupil looked out of the aircraft through two thicknesses of polaroid, vision was darkened to the point where night conditions prevailed, whilst his instructor acted as safety pilot in daylight. Later, detachable amber screens were fitted to the windscreens and canopies of more modern aircraft and the pupils wore amber or blue goggles giving the same effect as polaroid— hence the name Two Stage Amber.

The officer in charge of these experiments at Shellingford, Flight Lieutenant 'Jock' Lamb, was a popular young Scots flying instructor who was later killed in a night flying accident. His pupil recovered from the crash but was unable to remember anything besides being lifted out of the wrecked Tiger Moth. Although the cause of the accident has remained a mystery, it was thought likely at the time that the Tiger Moth had flown into the slipstream of a low-flying heavy aircraft and had been unable to recover before striking the ground. This is a possible explanation since during the war aeroplanes flew without navigation lights to avoid attracting the attention of German night fighters, and there must have been many 'near misses' with neither pilot being aware of the fact.

Of all the assignments handled by Flying Training Command one of the most interesting brought it into contact with a neutral country. The war was at its height with the tide of events just beginning to move in favour of the Allies in certain theatres and the fortunes of the Axis powers were in the balance.

Von Papen, the German Ambassador in Turkey, was bent on a campaign to bring the Turks into the war on the side of his country. Strenuous efforts were being made to complete an agreement whereby a number of Turkish Air Force personnel would be sent to Germany for training with the Luftwaffe. Such a move was looked upon as a vital stepping-stone towards involving the Turks in war. The Turkish Air Force had German equipment and it seemed that with practically everything in their favour the Nazis would succeed in at least the first stage of their plan.

It is believed that Winston Churchill was able to persuade the Turkish Government that such a move would be to their disadvantage, and at the eleventh hour the Turkish flying training programme was diverted from Germany to Britain. The full significance of this diplomatic victory may never be revealed, but at the time it must have been interpreted by the outside world as a vote of confidence in the Allies in general and the Royal Air Force in particular.

The Turkish trainee officers were carefully selected by their Government. They were being sent to wartime Britain as representatives of their country and a great deal was expected of them. On arrival in the U.K. they were sent to No. 5 I.T.W. Torquay, where they will long be remembered for their splendid uniforms and quiet, almost shy manners. Those who passed the final ground subject examinations were transported from the beauties of Torquay to the less attractive and highly industrial Wolverhampton area, the home of No. 28 E.F.T.S. at that time under the command of Wing Commander H. A. Roxburgh, A.F.C., A.R.Ae.S. Of his Turkish pupils he has this to say:

> As officers they were very rigorously treated by our standards; failure to learn to fly was barely tolerated, failure on ground subjects was a definite black-mark and the treatment meted out for any disciplinary shortcomings was very severe indeed. In the latter case the individual was sent straight back to Turkey and reduced to the ranks forthwith.
>
> To illustrate the type of treatment meted out to them, I recall once complaining to their Turkish officers-in-charge that they were late in reporting for their Link training programme. He promptly stood at the door of the Link Trainer room at the next session and fined each officer £1 for each minute that he was late. Although they were very well paid by our standards (I believe a 2nd Lieutenant got £60 a month) this did ensure punctuality at lectures, etc.

The Turks were completely lacking in natural ability, which is perhaps not surprising for theirs was an agrarian nation with little knowledge of modern machinery. In consequence they took longer to go solo than the average European, needing some eighteen or nineteen hours dual before they could fly alone. Flying instructors found them completedly unpredictable in the air. At times Wolverhampton's Tiger Moths were scattered all over the countryside in the odd aerodromes and fields that had appeared to offer refuge to the Turks when they became lost. Nevertheless, although some hair-raising passes were made at the aerodrome from time to time, there were no serious accidents.

If Roxburgh had certain difficulties to contend with, his unusual pupils did on occasions repay the moments of anxiety, albeit unconsciously:

> 'On the light side I do remember giving a Turk an instrument flying test and, after wallowing around the sky to the point where my patience was more frayed than it should be, I asked him what bloody course he thought he was on; he replied, "Number Thirty-four War course, sir." '

It was the practice at Wolverhampton to run rather up-stage officers' mess balls at quarterly intervals. The Turkish officers were excellent dancers and their charming manners and generous pay made them popular at the local dance halls. As Wing Commander Roxburgh stood by to receive his guests at one of the mess balls he was dismayed to see that a number of the young Turkish officers had brought along as partners girls who can best be described as 'shop soiled'. It was an embarrassing situation for, whilst the other guests may well have been offended, there was no doubt in Roxburgh's mind that the young men concerned, far away from home in strange surroundings, were quite innocent in their approach to the matter.

I endeavoured to explain afterwards to the Turkish officer-in-charge the standards expected but, with his limited English, he had some difficulty in grasping what was meant by the term 'lady'. At last the penny dropped and he said, 'I see, sir,—no public women.' I agreed that perhaps this was the best way to leave it.

Through sheer determination and hard work most of the Turks learned to fly the Tiger Moth and progressed on to other aircraft, bringing to a close what must have been one of the most unusual training programmes ever to be entrusted to the Tiger Moth in Britain.

Throughout the turmoil of wartime flying instruction, Tiger Moth serviceability remained at a remarkably high level with both engine and airframe absorbing seemingly unlimited punishment. One minor component, however, did become troublesome. During mid-1944 a batch of replacement tail skid springs were given the wrong heat treatment, and the flying schools were forever having to change them for they broke at the slightest provocation, even while taxiing. This in itself was of little consequence except that on occasions the bottom of the rudder became distorted causing the fabric cover to wrinkle. Even this was nothing more than unsightly, making not the slightest difference in the air.

While the Elementary Flying Training Schools went about their business grading R.A.F. aircrew candidates by the thousand, flying training proceeded at the overseas schools away from the interruptions of war and weather. Very considerable numbers went to Canada, those destined to continue on pilot training being posted to an E.F.T.S. manned by Service personnel as opposed to the civil contract basis favoured in Britain. Of the twenty-five Elementary Flying Training Schools in Canada, nineteen were operated by the Royal Canadian Air Force, the other six being administered by the R.A.F.

Many of the Canadian schools were equipped with the elderly Fleet Finch trainer, but these were gradually replaced by Tiger Moths as production got under way at de Havilland's Canadian factory.

The magnitude of the vast Canadian training programme is perhaps hard to appreciate, for it cannot be thought of in the same terms as the flying club movement even in its busiest form. Every one of those twenty-five flying schools was a large organization in its own right, flying day and night seven days a week. Small wonder that when a wartime pilot is asked where he received his training the answer is so often, 'Canada'. Many Canadian trained pilots won distinctions as the war progressed, and one school, No. 19 E.F.T.S., kept a record of the honours gained by their ex-pupils:

1 D.S.O.
30 D.F.C.s.
1 A.F.C.
1 C.G.M.
8 D.F.M.s.
1 A.F.M.

To this impressive list must be added the decorations won by the school's flying instructors after they had finished instructing and gone on operational service.

When No. 33 E.F.T.S., Caron, Saskatchewan, commenced

training on 9th January 1942 the airfield was under snow. Instructors and pupils alike experienced considerable difficulty in taxiing, particularly when, as so often happened, a Tiger Moth became stuck in the snow. On a number of occasions desperate attempts to get the aeroplane moving with bursts of throttle ended with the Tiger standing on its nose and a shattered propeller in the bargain. Strict instructions were then issued by the Chief Flying Instructor to the effect that when a Tiger Moth became stuck the engine was to be switched off and the occupants were to await the arrival of help when the aeroplane would be towed in. The instruction ended with a clear warning of what would happen to anyone disobeying the order. The next person to find himself stuck was none other than the C.F.I. himself. He was obviously a believer in the slogan 'don't do as I do—do as I say' for in defiance of his own rule the throttle was opened wide putting the Tiger on its nose with its tail in the air. When next morning he arrived at the flight line some cadet with a flare for artistic appreciation had painted a picture on the nose of his aircraft—a baby ostrich with its head in the sand. It so happens that the name of the C.F.I. was Gosling.

Squadron Leader C. A. Garretts was a cadet on the first course at Caron during January 1942. Shortly after the opening of the school an instructor and his pupil became so ill in the air they were forced to abandon their Tiger Moth which crashed in open country. On examination both occupants were found to be suffering from carbon monoxide poisoning caused by fumes from the exhaust system seeping into the enclosed cockpits of the Canadian Tiger. For a time the canopies were removed until the exhaust system had been modified.

During 1943 a number of the schools in Canada converted from Tiger Moths to Fairchild Cornells, a monoplane trainer fitted with a 160 h.p. Menasco engine; No. 5 E.F.T.S. made the change rather earlier, receiving the first of its new aeroplanes during November 1942.

In addition to their principal role of pilot training, Tiger

The Hoppity, a clipped wing Tiger built in Southern Rhodesia to provide safe taxiing practice for the local A.T.C. cadets (1942).

An unorthodox landing at Mount Hampden, S. Rhodesia, involving Tiger Moths 680 and T7673 on 14 May 1942. Four occupants, only one injured.

Opening ceremony of 'The Tiger Moth', an inn on the Maidstone-Rochester road.

Moths were used at four Wireless Schools in Canada: St. Hubert, Province of Quebec; Calgary, Alberta; Winnipeg, Manitoba; Guelph, Ontario. With its enclosed cockpits the Canadian Tiger Moth provided an inexpensive means of flying a trainee wireless operator while he practised the various radio procedures before going on to larger and more lavishly equipped aircraft. It was at one of these schools that a young wireless operator under training won the first George Cross to be awarded a member of the R.C.A.F., unfortunately under the most tragic circumstances.

On 10th November 1941 a Tiger Moth of No. 2 Wireless School returned to its base at Calgary after a routine training flight. The pilot, Flying Officer James Robinson, an experienced R.C.A.F. instructor, was making a normal approach prior to landing when the aircraft dived into a field short of the aerodrome and immediately burst into flames. Leading Aircraftman Karl M. Gravell, the trainee wireless operator, got clear of the blazing Tiger Moth his clothing alight. Medical evidence later revealed that he had lost one eye on impact, yet despite this grievous injury and serious burns he deliberately returned to the flaming wreckage and set about trying to rescue the trapped pilot. It is believed that had he considered his own safety and put out the flames burning away his clothing L.A.C. Gravell would have lived. As it was he gave his life trying to save a dead pilot for, unknown to him, Robinson had been killed during the crash. On 11th June 1942 this fine young Canadian was awarded a posthumous George Cross.

While production of Tiger Moths continued in Canada and England, de Havilland Aircraft Pty. Ltd. of Australia was likewise engaged many thousands of miles away. The outbreak of war found the Royal Australian Air Force badly in need of a suitable training aircraft, and plans were immediately put in hand for the large-scale production of the DH 82a version of the Tiger Moth. As an interim measure early in 1940 a number of part-completed DH 94 Moth Minors was shipped from Hatfield to the de Havilland factory at Mascot. The Moth Minor was the last light aeroplane to be designed by the parent company, and hopes that this graceful little monoplane might blaze the trail, carrying on where the biplane Moths left off, were lost forever because of the war. A total of fifty-nine Moth Minors was delivered to the R.A.A.F. and a few have survived the war to fly as private aeroplanes.*

Meanwhile preparations went ahead at de Havilland's Brankstown factory in New South Wales, and towards the end of 1940 the first of the Australian Tiger Moths began to emerge. During December of that year three were exported to the Madras Flying Club and two went to the Government of Burma. The following year sixty Tiger Moths were exported to the then Dutch East Indies and a further twenty-five were sent to India. The Royal New Zealand Air Force received twenty and gave them serial numbers NZ 1400 to 1419, but the largest export order was placed by the R.A.F. for delivery to South Africa and Southern Rhodesia. There is a degree of uncertainty about

---

* Additional to pre-war deliveries, which were numbered A17-1 to A17-20, one hundred Tiger Moths were sent by Britain to Australia, arriving between 22nd February and 9th September 1940, and it seems likely that they retained their R.A.F serial numbers which were:

N6882	N6900-1	N6903	N6905-6
N9129-30	N9135-6	N9139-40	N9173
N9257-61	N9263-4	N9266	N9269-70
N9376	N9403	R4835-44	R4879-93
R5181-6	R5256-65	T5360-1	T5384
T5409-13	T5458-63	T5482-7	T5525-31
T5555-61			

Spencer's Gulf Aero Club gave up VH-AAI and VH-UXC on 4 January 1940 whilst a few days later the Broken Hill Aero Club relinquished VH-AAX. These three club Tigers became A17-21, 22 and 23. The other Australian flying clubs handed over their precious Tigers six months later, eighteen joining the R.A.A.F. during the period 8th July to 19th August 1940. These were:

VH-AAJ	ADH	UDT	UYL
AAP	ADI	UVZ	UYQ
AAR	ADK	UYJ	UYR
ABM	ADO	UYK	UZT
ACP			UZV

They were given serial number A17-674 to 691.

134

the numbers involved but the Australian company quotes a figure of 395. With the exception of one Tiger delivered to the Broken Hill Aero Club in April 1941, all other aircraft from the Australian production line went to the R.A.A.F.

In all 1,085 Tiger Moths were built in Australia, and although some seventy local modifications were incorporated, by and large these were of a minor nature and the aeroplanes were more or less identical to the British-built DH 82a. One interesting departure from the original was the use of plastic covered lift and anti-lift wires. All Royal Australian Air Force Tiger Moths were given serial numbers with the prefix A17, the highest number being A17-759. Most of these machines were allotted to the E.F.T.S. establishments which reached their peak in 1942, there being twelve in operation by that time.

Not content with producing well over 1,000 Tiger Moths, the Australians provided their own engines, some 1,300 Gipsy Majors being manufactured by General Motors Holdings Ltd.—a remarkable achievement bearing in mind the limited technical resources at their disposal in 1940.*

Not to be outdone by their Australian neighbours, de Havilland Aircraft of New Zealand Ltd. (now Hawker Siddeley International N.Z. Ltd.) started their own production line during the early days of the war, and it was not

---

* On 7th March 1942 Tiger Moths PK-VVQ to VVV arrived from the Dutch East Indies, the six machines joining the R.A.A.F. as A17-621 to 626. The Royal Australian Air Force received a total of 861 Tiger Moths from all sources and these were delivered at the following rate:

1939	20
,, 40	323
,, 41	230
,, 42	172
,, 43	79
,, 44	27
,, 45	10
Total	861

long before it was providing Tiger Moths for the four
Elementary Flying Training Schools operated by the Royal
New Zealand Air Force. The number of Tigers produced
in New Zealand has been variously quoted between 132 and
345. Attempts to clarify the situation have revealed that
supporters of one figure are convinced of the inaccuracy of
the other. These differences of opinion were put to R. W.
Jamieson, Sales Manager of the New Zealand Company,
who replied:

> The number of Tiger Moths built in New Zealand during
> the war was definitely 345.
> In the initial stages there were obviously some components
> sent from England, but it is not possible to draw a dividing
> line between English and New Zealand production on such
> a basis. In any case the assemblies imported were very minor
> ones and could be considered as being not more than the raw
> materials.

Tiger Moths were used at the R.N.Z.A.F. Central Flying
School based at Tauranga in addition to the four Elementary schools which operated from five aerodromes, so that the
345 production figure seems more likely than the lower one
sometimes quoted.

With a Japanese invasion seemingly imminent the Royal
New Zealand Air Force followed the British example and in
1942 fitted seventy-two of its Tiger Moths with light series
bomb racks for use against enemy troops landing on the
beaches. Fortunately they were never required.

Two E.F.T.S.s were established in India mainly engaged
in training Indian pilots, and at one time plans were made
to produce the Tiger Moth in Bombay. Serial numbers
BS900 to 936, BS949 to 997, BT111 to 136, BT153 to 183,
BT197 to 241 and BT261 to 272 were allotted and,
although official records mention these as 'manufactured in
Bombay', no one has ever seen a Tiger with a BS or BT
serial number. It seems very unlikely that production was
ever commenced, possibly because both Britain and Australia were able to supply sufficient aircraft for the two Indian

schools. Additional to the Tiger Moths shipped in Indian markings were those destined for Nos. 2 and 10 E.F.T.S. in Britain. These vanished somewhat mysteriously early in the war, only to arrive in India where they became VT-ANU to VT-AOP.*

During the early days of the war when the Air Ministry was busy impressing civil aircraft into R.A.F. service, twenty-eight Tiger Moths remained civilian and were exported by W. S. Shackleton Ltd. to India, some going to New Zealand and South Africa.

On a similiar scale to the New Zealand programme was the compact but nevertheless extremely valuable training scheme undertaken by the Rhodesian Air Training Group. Tiger Moths were shipped from Australia to equip the four Rhodesian Elementary Flying Training Schools (Nos. 25, 26, 27 and 28) and No. 33 Flying Instructors School.

The outbreak of war inspired a number of acts of patriotism: Mr. and Mrs. G. R. Milne of Salisbury presented three Tiger Moths to the Southern Rhodesian Air Force, and these were named 'Mary Ann', 'Sheila' and 'Jennifer' after their three daughters. 'Mary Ann' was given air force serial number T7513 but the other numbers are not known. Three more Tiger Moths, T7532 'Firefly', T7533 'Bindura' and T7666 'Roich' were each presented by residents of Salisbury. All six aircraft carried a silver plate proclaiming their origin. Yet another Tiger Moth named 'Rumbarvu' was loaned to the S.R.A.F. on the understanding that it would return to its owner at the end of the war, but unfortunately it was written off by a pupil during 1944. It is believed that this Tiger Moth was replaced by EM204, but it is not known if the original owner received his aeroplane at the end of the war.

Like most flying schools the world over those in Rhodesia

---

* There is also evidence that the following are representative of Morris-built Tiger Moths that were crated on leaving Cowley and shipped to India:

DE133	DE150	DE216	DE233
DE234	DE236	DE237	DE251
DE406	DE407	DE413	DE448 and others.

had their claims to make and stories to tell. The Tiger Moths of 28 E.F.T.S. were enhanced by a red and white chequered band painted round the fuselage, the reason being quite simply that the maintenance officer had once served with the famous 56 Squadron.

During 1942 the same unit received from Portuguese East Africa a very battered Tiger Moth which had been involved in a crash. Originally registered CR-AAG, the aeroplane arrived at Mount Hampden in a depressing heap of small and rather distorted pieces. New fuselage side frames were drawn from the stores of 28 E.F.T.S. and the rear fuselage from another crashed Tiger, Australian-built DX-544, was salvaged and incorporated in the extensive rebuild. To everyone's amazement the result was a Tiger Moth some 15 m.p.h. faster than standard—and no one ever knew why!

Later that year time-expired Tiger Moth components were used to construct a training aid designed for the express purpose of teaching boys of the local Air Training Corps to taxi. The top wing was removed and the bottom wing, which had its span reduced, was braced to the fuselage with interplane struts. The propeller was cut in diameter and the engine limited to a maximum of 1,200 r.p.m. The 'Hoppity', as it was called, behaved like any other clipped bird and was incapable of flight, so that the aspiring cadets could be turned loose without fear of an unscheduled take-off. At the same time it enabled these future trainee pilots to master the art of taxiing and so prepare them for more serious instruction in the future.

By and large, wartime flying training proceeded on a vast scale throughout the Commonwealth with a commendably low accident rate. This was particularly so at the elementary schools, although when the immensity of the task is considered it is perhaps to be expected that serious accidents were at times bound to occur. On 14th May 1942 Tiger Moths T7673 and 680 were being flown by pupil pilots accompanied by their instructors. They approached to land at Mount Hampden airfield, oblivious of one another's presence. During the landing one pupil let down on top of the other yet in the crash that followed only the pupil pilot in T7673 was injured. Tiger Moth 680 was rebuilt and flew again. Exactly twelve months later there was a repetition involving T7938 and T7512, the pupil in the second of these two aircraft being killed.

Rhodesia was not very kind to the Tiger Moth. The sandy soil was hard on the engines, accelerating wear, so that overhauls came rather more frequently than usual. Sand or not, there were no reported cases of complete engine failure other than those attributed to mishandling. During the nine-month-long Rhodesian summer the Tigers baked all day in the sun, and when the appropriate season arrived had to face the most intense rain storms. In 1943 Tiger Moths were replaced by Cornell monoplanes and those having flown more than 2,000 hours were reduced to scrap.

The less used Tigers were transferred to the Union (now Republic) of South Africa, but while the formalities were being completed shortage of hangar space made it necessary to park the surplus aircraft in the open for a number of weeks. They were to be flown to Induna for dispatch to South Africa, but when the time came the wings were badly warped and the aircraft had to be re-rigged. C. Nepean Bishop made thirty-four test flights on the sixteen surplus Tigers from 28 E.F.T.S. before they were deemed fit for tuition again. After the first stage of the flight to South Africa the Tigers remained in the open for several weeks at Induna and must have reached South Africa in a state of extreme distress.

Along with the other Commonwealth nations, South Africa made its contribution to the vast Empire Training Scheme by providing amongst other facilities seven Tiger-equipped Elementary Flying Training Schools. It goes without saying that in common with the Rhodesian Tigers those in South Africa were subjected to intense heat, but it is not always realized that the Transvaal can produce a freezing winter. Although most were kept in the open the

Tigers maintained their usual high standard of reliability despite such extremes of climate.

Up to September 1939 forty-two Hatfield-built Tiger Moths were delivered to the South African Air Force and various civil owners, all machines going into air force service on the outbreak of hostilities. They were given military serials below number 1000. During the war Hatfield delivered a further six machines and Cowley another five, but the main source of equipment for the South African schools came from de Havilland's Australian factory and these were numbered from 2400 upwards. Some South African Tigers had tail wheels but *no* brakes and were therefore impossible to stop in an emergency. As such they provided many a moment of drama on the ground.

During a routine progress check, the C.F.I. and a pupil from 7 E.F.T.S. Kroonstaad had a frightening experience in Tiger Moth 2232. The flight was perfectly normal until in an attempted 'roll-off-the-top' the wings began to fold upwards, slackening the landing wires to the point where, devoid of tension, they took up the appearance of a neat letter 'S' on either side of the fuselage. An emergency landing on the Karoo plateau followed at an altitude of 4,500 ft. whereupon it was found that the flying wire attachment bolts were pulling through the wooden main spars of the wing. Such a failure had never been experienced before and it can only be assumed that Tiger Moth 2232 may have been wrongly assembled on arrival.

And so the Tiger Moth became the indispensable tool of what may prove to be the most ambitious flying training programme in the history of aviation, for it is very unlikely we shall ever see anything quite like the Empire Training Scheme again. Besides the many advanced schools of one kind or another, at its peak the wartime elementary training complex numbered some eighty-two flying schools situated in Britain, Canada, Australia, South Africa, Southern Rhodesia, New Zealand and India. Based as it was upon a concept of progressive elimination of all but the best material, the Tiger Moth may bring a reminder of disappointment to those who failed to get their pilot's wings, for the average rejection rate was no less than 22 per cent. Times were desperate and time was short during the war, so that training schedules were constantly under pressure. Nevertheless Tiger Moth write-offs averaged only 2.5 per cent per 10,000 hours flying, as opposed to double that rate at the Service Flying Training Schools operating more advanced types of aircraft. The work capacity of more than eighty large flying schools operating a concentrated training programme, day and night, seven days a week, is truly enormous; the four New Zealand elementary schools alone trained 7,154 pilots during the war.

When it is realised that up to 1970 there were only some 14,000 holders of the Private Pilots Licence in the U.K. (the product of pre and post-war training at the flying clubs) the production of over 7,000 qualified pilots by New Zealand was no small achievement. True, the peacetime pilot must usually learn at his own expense, thus limiting the numbers able to realise an ambition to fly but equally true is a 12-1 population factor in favour of Britain. Such is the impetus of war that mountains are moved by nations large and small and given the right tools the impossible becomes reality. The Tiger Moth certainly earned its keep in New Zealand.

With the arrival of the atom bomb hostilities ended even more suddenly than they had begun, and the vast and throbbing enterprise in which the Tiger had played so vital a part became a liability overnight. When production finally ceased in 1945 over 9,200 Tiger Moths and Queen Bees had been completed. Perhaps Arthur Hagg the designer was thinking of the first Tiger and how it was built in a modest shed on Stag Lane aerodrome when, some thirty-two years later, he remarked, 'We little visualized the numbers that were eventually produced.'

7. The Post-War Tiger

The shooting and bombing had stopped, the wild parties and celebrations were over and the grim task of clearing up the debris had to be faced. All over Europe, the Middle and Far East, hitherto busy aerodromes became crowded with aeroplanes—immobile, inert objects which seemed to reflect the strange mood of depression that afflicted their pilots and aircrews. For with the sudden collapse of Japan flying more or less ceased. There were, of course, ferry trips and communication flights, but air traffic was reduced to a tiny stream in contrast to the flood that had existed before.

At the flying schools a limited amount of instruction carried on, but the writing was on the wall for many of the units and it was not long before some of the airfields built during the war reverted to farmland. One of the biggest schools, No. 14 E.F.T.S., had the distinction of flying from a runway equipped aerodrome as opposed to the usual and more suitable grass field. Tiger Moths are not particularly happy on runways, for unless there is little or no wind the tail skid is unable to maintain directional control on the ground. On the outbreak of war ten Tiger Moths were transferred from Barton to Elmdon and another ten came over from nearby Castle Bromwich to form the nucleus of No. 14 E.F.T.S. under the management of Airwork Ltd. Eventually no less than seventy-two Tiger Moths were operated until 1946, whereupon the School closed and Elmdon became Birmingham Airport once more.

The thousands of Tigers built during the war had, by any standards, made their contribution to victory, but what of the older ones, those impressed into the R.A.F. when civil flying stopped so abruptly that September Sunday in 1939?

The prototype DH 82, G-ABRC, went into R.A.F. uniform as BB 723. It was used at No. 1 E.F.T.S., the de Havilland operated school, where it was given the local number 43. On 26th May 1943 it was sent to No. 5 Maintenance Unit prior to joining the Navy with 758 Squadron, Hinstock. Later that year it was transferred to 781 Squadron, Lee-on-Solent and in November 1944 moved with them to Heathrow—now London Airport. Next came a posting to Heston (May 1945) followed by another move on 22nd March 1946 to R.N.A.S. Stretton. So the 'first ever' survived the war. Unfortunately it was to find the return to peace harder than life in the Forces. After completing its Service life at Gosport it was sold on 31st January 1951 to Rollasons and was last seen in 1953 at Croydon airport in a dismantled condition. Regrettably efforts to trace this historic aeroplane have proved fruitless and its fate may never be known.

Another DH 82, Sir Alan Cobham's G-ABUL of 'Air Circus' fame, joined the R.A.F. as BB 792 and went to No. 6 E.F.T.S., the school operated by Brooklands Aviation Ltd. On 23rd June 1944 it struck and killed a cyclist during a low flying exercise. G-ABUL eventually crashed and was written off at Wollaston, Northants.

The oldest Tiger Moth on the British register is the third DH 82a to leave the factory, G-ACDC. It is unique in having led a particularly hazardous life *since* the war! ACDC was already six years old when it entered the R.A.F. as BB 726. It remained at No. 1 E.F.T.S. until 1st November 1941 when it was transferred to 28 E.F.T.S. (remember the Turks?). It continued flying until July 1947 and then followed six years in storage at R.A.F. Cosford. On 6th

November 1953 it was bought from the Ministry by A. J. Whittemore Ltd. who restored it to the civil register in its original serial letters. By this time it had flown 4,978 hours 30 minutes. An uneventful life and, indeed, so far no accidents had been recorded, but in 1957 it was bought by the Tiger Club and the now twenty-three-year-old aeroplane entered a new era.

It was loaned to the Surrey Flying Club at Croydon and within a few months someone managed to invert it on the aerodrome. New wings and a new rudder were fitted but soon afterwards while it was being taxied by Mr. Jack Piercy a member of the Surrey Flying Club ran into it and another new rudder was required. In 1959 a member of the Tiger Club using a somewhat unorthodox starting procedure managed to stand G-ACDC on its nose on Sandown aerodrome. A new propeller was fitted. Several months went by without incident until 28th February 1960. C. Nepean Bishop, the Tiger Club's veteran Chief Flying Instructor, was flight checking a member when a rather fundamental part of the under-carriage collapsed during take-off. Bishop got the Tiger off the ground but the emergency landing that followed resulted in further damage, and one wing, the propeller and of course the offending undercarriage had to be replaced. Mr. Dennis Hartas used G-ACDC on 24th June 1962 for a crazy flying display at Wolverhampton which unfortunately ended with the old warrior on its nose. Another new wing and a propeller were fitted. Very nearly finally in every meaning of the word the aeroplane was seriously damaged at the Rochester air display on 9th September 1963. The weather had been particularly unkind over that week-end with poor visibility, high winds and low cloud threatening to ruin the event. In an effort to do something to entertain the patiently waiting public Mr. Neville Browning took off to give his well-known demonstration of crazy flying. Caught by severe gusts while at a low airspeed near the ground the Tiger touched the airfield and completed several somersaults within a few yards of the crowd. To everyone's surprise Neville Browning emerged from the wreckage almost unhurt. Such was the damage that had it been any other aeroplane the thought of rebuilding would have been out of the question. But G-ACDC has been listed as historic by the Royal Aeronautical Society and is in any case the pride and joy of the Tiger Club. Under the supervision of Mr. Deverall of Rollasons it has been rebuilt yet again.*

If ACDC had led a tranquil life in the Services, its near relation G-ACDG could justly claim the opposite. As BB 728 it too went to No. 1 E.F.T.S. where it remained until May 1941, when a heavy landing at Hatfield sent it to British Taylorcraft (later Auster Aircraft and then Beagle Auster) for repairs. From there it went to No. 4 E.F.T.S. but on 2nd July 1941 the almost unheard of happened— the engine failed and the Tiger overturned during the forced landing that followed at Newbold near Brough aerodrome. Back it went to British Taylorcraft for repairs. It was then delivered to 414 Squadron but during its stay with that unit someone made a heavy landing at Croydon on 28th June 1942, breaking the undercarriage and sending ACDG back to British Taylorcraft for the third time. In 1944 it was invalided out of the Service and sent to Vosper Ltd. who had it re-registered G-ACDG and flew it under a Ministry of Aircraft Production permit. On 1st January 1946 Marshalls Flying School at Cambridge bought G-ACDG and it became the first aeroplane in Britain to provide a civil flying lesson after the war. It was sold to a Dutch owner in 1947 and has since been fitted with the extended fin required by the authorities in Holland. Now registered PH-UAY it is still going strong in spite of a hard life.

Not all of these vintage Tigers have had such a happy ending. For example G-ADGS took part in flying training with the R.A.F., flew with the Navy at Worthy Down and Ronaldsway in the Isle of Man and indulged in glider towing at Culham near Didcot. Sad to relate in 1956 it was burned on Guy Fawkes Night at the Five Ways night-club, Purley.

*See additional note at end of chapter, page 162.

G-AFGT spent the war with the R.A.F. and was bought by Rollasons in 1949. It was restored to the register as G-AMEA until someone managed to make out the original registration faintly discernible under layers of paint and it reverted to its pre-war G-AFGT again. In 1951 it was sold to the Thailand Navy.

Individual case histories such as these are probably endless, but they illustrate vividly the hard wearing qualities of the type, for many of these pre-war Tigers were already eight years old when they were impressed into service. That a number should have amassed a considerable total of flying hours during the vigorous conditions of war, and then continued in harness some twenty years after the return of peace and still give indication of a long future, is all the more remarkable.

The Tiger's return to peace was by no means an all British phenomenon. Australia, to quote but one example, had its long line of veteran Tiger Moths, and there were many willing buyers for the old biplane. A17-12 and its ex-R.A.F. cousin R.4884 were bought by the Shark Patrol Service Co. Ltd., of Sydney, on 9th April 1946, while in August of that year the Methodist Inland Mission of Echo Island, Darwin, acquired A17-16. The Kuala Lumpur Flying Club purchased A17-24 and A17-404, and A17-84 is listed as having been issued to the R.N. on 3rd December 1945. This Australian-built Tiger continues flying in Britain as A1784.

In common with their British-built relations not all the Australian Tiger Moths survived the war, and A17-293, 296 and 297 were on 20th March 1942 lost in action in the Far East. Others were, of course, written off in training accidents.

All over the world people were ready to buy the now ageing biplane, and not unnaturally Britain figured high on the list of would be purchasers.

Why has the Tiger enjoyed this success? There is no simple answer, only a number of possible reasons. After the

146

austerity and tension inseparable from six years of war, the nation turned its attention to the serious matter of enjoyment. No doubt fired by the achievements of the Royal and other air forces, those with the money to spend found themselves able to take up flying possibly for the first time in their lives. As private flying slowly gained momentum there was a more or less immediate demand from the flying clubs and prospective private owners for suitable light aeroplanes. De Havillands, the most successful light 'plane manufacturers in the world during the years leading up to the war, had turned their attention from this market to other more ambitious projects, for within weeks of the defeat of Japan the prototype Dove had flown, and they were already heavily involved in Vampire jet fighter production. Then there was the Comet, the first jet-powered airliner in the world. Small wonder the de Havilland Company found it impossible to give thought to the little aeroplanes. Had this not been the case an entirely new breed of light aircraft may well have emerged from Hatfield to capture world markets.

As it was, economic difficulties and official opposition were to have a damaging effect on private and club flying during the immediate post-war years, and it was not long before Miles of Reading, the largest British manufacturer of light 'planes, fell prey to these unfavourable conditions and stopped production. This left the wartime British Taylorcraft Company with a virtual monopoly on the home market in so far as new light aeroplanes were concerned. By now trading under the name of Auster, the works at Rearsby, Leicester, continued to produce an improved version of the old American Taylorcraft design, a robust, fabric-covered high-winged monoplane which had done good work as an army spotter during the war. The more refined post-war Auster Autocrat was sold in appreciable numbers to flying clubs and private owners both in Britain and countries overseas, but it is significant that when the R.A.F.V.R. schools re-formed in 1947 it was to the old Tiger Moth that the Air Ministry turned for equipment—for it was fully aerobatic and the Auster was not.

The renaissance of the Reserve Schools did much to perpetuate the Tiger by giving it a new and important job to do. By and large, the post-war R.A.F.V.R. offered ex-wartime pilots the opportunity to keep in flying practice in an almost flying club atmosphere. Unlike the Auxiliary Air Force which expected its members to devote most weekends to the cause, V.R. pilots were committed to a modest training programme which could be undertaken in odd days here and there or continuously if this was more convenient. At a later stage the Reserve Flying Schools trained both navigators and wireless operators, at first in the veteran Anson I with its hand-wound retractable undercarriage. These were soon replaced by the much refined Anson 21 version. Reserve training for pilots continued on the Tiger Moth until 1950 when its successor, the Canadian designed de Havilland Chipmunk, began to appear. No. 1 R.F.S., the de Havilland run school at Panshangar, was amongst the first to re-equip, taking delivery of its Chipmunks in April of that year. Woodley and Cambridge received their Chipmunks during April but continued to use Tiger Moths as well. No. 16 R.F.S., Derby, changed its Tigers for the much larger and heavier Percival Prentice, but No. 2 R.F.S., Barton, having changed over to Chipmunks in January 1951 reverted back to Tiger Moths eleven months later.

As the post-war R.A.F.V.R. pinned its faith in the Tiger Moth so did many of the reawakening civil flying clubs. Considerable numbers of ex-Service machines were put up for tender by the Air Ministry, and these rugged little biplanes provided the clubs with an ideal opportunity to re-equip with cheap and reliable trainers. G-AINU of the Luton Flying Club was just such a Tiger. H. D. Burke learned to fly on it and, on 10th May 1947 using the same machine, took part in the first Royal Aero Club sponsored post-war air race at Portsmouth. Several weeks of intense preparation preceded the race; the fabric was polished, the angle of incidence was reduced and tight turns were

Formation Flying. *Top*: 15 R.F.S. Redhill (1950). *Bottom*: C. Nepean Bishop leading Tiger Club members in the 'Bishop'.

Post-war flying instruction in New Zealand. R.N.Z.A.F. Tiger Moths at No. 1. E.F.T.S. Taieri (November 1951).

Over the hedge. Pupil under training at post-war New Zealand E.F.T.S.

practised. Finally the engine oil was drained and replaced entirely by Redex, so that it is not difficult to believe Mr. Burke when he claims that 'the maximum revs obtained were well in excess of the "permissible" '. Later that year Burke ran out of petrol and forced landed on a narrow strip of grass which happened to be a practice horse race track on a Pottersbury farm. He managed to obtain five gallons of tractor fuel, took off and landed safely at Luton. Unfortunately several months later G-AINU flew into telegraph wires near Lympne and was written off.

Possibly the oldest flying instructor in the world, C. Pashley, C.F.I. of the Southern Aero Club, continued to fly Tigers at the age of seventy-four (1965).

Most of the aircraft servicing companies, big and small, found themselves overhauling Tiger Moths with a view to having them put on the civil register. Rollasons of Croydon handled eighty and will continue to turn out these old ex-Service machines like gleaming new pins so long as parts are available; fortunately to this day de Havillands are able to supply all drawings.

Rollasons is one of several companies that has rebuilt Tiger Moths for export. Four went to Sweden as recently as 1963, all equipped for glider towing. Others have gone to Holland where a modified and rather ugly elongated fin is demanded by the Dutch authorities, although the general opinion is that this does no more to reduce rate of spin than the strakes fitted during the early part of the war.

Tiger Moths supplied to Italy have been the cause of some amusement at Croydon because the authorities in that country allow private owners and clubs to choose (within reason) their own registration letters. Thus ex-Morris-built DE 486 entered civil aviation as G-APRY. Rollasons rebuilt it for L'Aero Club, Bologna, who collected it in May 1959, complete with Italian registration I-BANG. A Hatfield-built example delivered to the R.A.F. as N 5474 went on the civil register after the war as G-ANKA. It left Croydon during February 1960 registered

I-LUNI which we are advised means 'I'm moonstruck' in colloquial Italian, or less politely 'I'm nuts'!* *

Belgium too joined the ranks of post-war Tiger Moth customers, eleven being purchased by the government Administration de L'Aeronautique which in turn put them at the disposal of the Ecole d'Aviation Civile, a flying school run jointly by the Administration and the Belgian airline, Sabena. The Tigers are used for primary pilot training.† Some of these Tiger Moths have the luxury of an electric starter, an addition which, if fitted, would have prevented the mishap that befell OO-SOF. Fortunately the incident caused little damage and in retrospect has its amusing side.

It happened on 23rd September 1952 when a young pilot on a cross-country flight landed to refuel at Gosselies airfield, near Charleroi. The take-off was preceded by a lot of taxiing, and just before reaching the runway he had the misfortune accidentally to stop his engine. The pilot was on his own and rather than face a mile-long walk for help the decision was made, quite wrongly of course, to start the engine without chocks in front of the wheels and with no one in the cockpit. The engine fired on the first crank but the pilot had forgotten that, only minutes before, the throttle had been opened in an effort to catch the engine before it stopped and it had been left in that position. Now the engine roared into life and wound up to full power, the

---

* Other Tiger Moths rebuilt by Rollasons for Italian customers left Croydon with these registrations:

Factory	Service Serial No.	British Civil Registration	Italian Registration
Cowley	T6256	G-APLR	I-JENA
Cowley	DE516	G-APOC	I-PUMA
Hatfield	N6739	——	I-NONO
Cowley	T7276	G-APTV	I-MOMI

† OO-SOF, OO-SOM and OO-SOY are in use at the national gliding centre at Saint-Hubert. They bear these registrations:

OO-SOA	OO-SOI
OO-SOB	OO-SOJ
OO-SOE	OO-SOW
OO-SOG	OO-SOX

**See additional note at end of chapter, page 162.

Tiger lurched forward giving the pilot little time to jump away from the advancing propeller. It gathered speed in a more or less straight line with the pilot running in desperate pursuit. The wheels left the ground in a perfect take-off when, fortunately for SOF, they made contact with the top wire of the airfield fence, turning the Tiger gracefully through a 180 degree outside loop. The aeroplane came to rest upside down just outside the airfield boundary with both upper wings damaged, a dented fuel tank, a broken propeller and a rather tired-looking rudder. It was not very long before OO-SOF was repaired and flying again.

During 1963 there were thirty-six Tiger Moths registered in Belgium, all of the DH 82a variety.

According to the *Luton News* of Thursday 19th December 1957, possibly the last aeroplane to land at the old and historic Hendon aerodrome was Tiger Moth G-AISR, and from all accounts it was hardly a voluntary arrival. The aeroplane, which incidentally sported a canary yellow colour-scheme, belonged to the Luton Flying Club. Twelve forty-five p.m. on 15th December 1957 saw it at 3,000 ft. over the Welsh Harp. Paddy Ryan, the pilot, suddenly became aware of a drop in engine speed followed by violent vibration. Instinctively he opened the throttle when the voice of his passenger, Hugh Copelin, came across the intercom. with a clear if brief observation—'We're on fire!'

Ryan was unable to see evidence of this until a gentle turn revealed an alarmingly dense trail of smoke behind the aircraft. He cut the ignition switches and turned off the petrol, at the same time requesting Copelin to operate the fire extinguisher in the rear cockpit. This is arranged to discharge through a long extension tube into the engine bay. It may also be removed from its bracket for use within the cockpit and it sometimes happens that, unless the extinguisher is positioned close to the extension tube, embarrassing leaks occur and attempts to discharge into the engine bay can have surprising results. Such was now the case and Copelin found himself drenched in extinguisher fluid—much to his own and Ryan's amusement. In explanation of such ill-timed mirth Ryan says: 'This may be accounted for by putting an Irishman and a Scotsman in an English aeroplane.' The luck of the Irish now revealed itself in the shape of Hendon aerodrome where they landed safely to be wined and dined by the R.A.F. First examinations on the ground revealed no sign of burning and the cause of all the smoke in the air remained a mystery until the engine had been dismantled. Half of one piston had disappeared without trace allowing engine oil to be pumped through to the hot exhaust pipe, so causing a private smoke-screen.

When teaching a student to fly it is the usual practice to demonstrate all elementary exercises first and then introduce instrument and night flying after the pupil has gone solo and achieved a fair degree of competence. Late in 1947 Wing Commander Lindsay, Chief Flying Instructor to the flying group operated on behalf of the employees of Short Brothers Ltd., suggested that certain benefits might result from conducting *ab initio* training at night. Both he and another experienced flying instructor, Mr. C. Dash, agreed to try the experiment using as guinea pig Mr. A. C. W. Rattle, A.F.R.Ae.S., an aeronautical engineer with no pilot experience.

Night flying training began on 2nd January 1948, using a Tiger Moth of the Rochester Flying Club. All the exercises usually demonstrated in daylight were completed in nine lessons after dark and at ten hours and forty minutes dual the pupil was sent on his first solo during the night of 11th February. Night flying both dual and solo continued until 10th April when Mr. Rattle made his first attempts to fly in daylight, some twenty minutes dual being needed before the instructor sent him off alone. The experiment was later repeated with other types of aircraft, but *ab initio* night training does not appear to offer any real advantages and these experiments, interesting as they may be, have failed to bring about any change in general flying training procedure.

During March 1950 the Tiger Moth became involved in

the world of crime. In December 1949 the police were
called upon to investigate the disappearance of a number
of Christmas trees from two plantations in Northumberland at Haydon Bridge and Fourstones. Those concerned
were tried before Judge T. Richardson at Northumberland
Quarter Sessions when, according to the local newspaper,
aerial photographs of the scene of the crime were used in
evidence in a criminal court for the first time. The photo-
grapher, Detective Sergeant William Bee, used an old ex-
U.S. Air Force camera purchased by him for £4, and the
pilot was Mr. E. Fail, a member of Newcastle Aero Club.
The aeroplane was G-AHWG—a Tiger Moth of course!

As if the world had not had its fill of war and destruction,
troubles of a more localized nature persisted in different
corners of the world. Former enemies became friends and
wartime allies took sides against one another in what was
to become known as the 'cold war'. There were times when
animosities ceased to be cold and a decidedly hot shooting
war materialized overnight. Such was the case in Malaya
when Communist-inspired terrorists began to disrupt the
country. Actions of this kind have become fashionable since
the 1939–45 War and experience has shown that given
suitable country in which to operate a relatively small band
of well-trained guerillas can hold the attention of considerable numbers of uniformed troops. Many of the plantations
in Malaya are isolated and so had to be defended by the
local management and staff. As a result it became increasingly difficult to get money to the sites for payment of wages.
By now constant attacks by bandits had made the roads
unsafe for travelling without an armed escort, and such
facilities were stretched to the limit.

One Danish-owned plantation in particular posed severe
problems for it was situated at Ulu Bernam in north-west
Selangor and the journey involved a dangerous river crossing in addition to the usual bandit-infested roads. Arrangements were made to take advantage of the extraordinary
mobility which is one of the prime virtues of the light aero-

plane, and a Tiger Moth of the Kuala Lumpur Flying Club was hired to make the first pay drop, which occurred during August 1948.

It was a great success for, if the little Tiger didn't exactly get the pay to the plantations under the noses of the terrorists, it most certainly did so over their heads, and there was nothing they could do about it. Most of the sorties were flown by Mr. Glassborough, Chief Flying Instructor of the Kuala Lumpur Flying Club. He was frequently accompanied by a Malay clerk named Yasin who became an expert 'dropper'. Other members of the club taking part were J. Wagstaff, W. Stubbs, J. Field, G. H. Hurst and Dr. Peter Tasker. One or two women became skilled droppers.

Shortly before the first drop Mr. K. G. Hamnet, O.B.E., President of the Kuala Lumpur Flying Club, advised the secretary of the United Planting Association of his club's intentions. The project was readily accepted by estate and mine managers who entered into the spirit of the operation with great enthusiasm. Such was the demand for light 'planes that the Singapore, Perak and Penang flying clubs combined with the Kuala Lumpur members to provide a unique pay dropping service that was to continue throughout the twelve years of terrorist activity; the Perak Flying Club continued to operate the service until September 1963, for the method had proved convenient even in peaceful times. During the emergency leaflets were dropped urging the terrorists to surrender, and the Tiger Moth belonging to the Perak Club can claim one 'convert' with a fair degree of certainty.

Some $750 million was dropped during the emergency and whereas the clubs were paid for the use of their aircraft, pilots and droppers were volunteers. Tiger Moths VR-RAA, VR-RAB and VR-RAC, together with Austers and Cessnas took part, and in some ways the cabin aircraft with their side-by-side seating proved more suitable— because the pilot was thus able to keep an eye on his dropper and so avoid what happened to one Tiger pilot whose assistant persisted in throwing the money into the Pahang jungle in spite of his cries of 'No, no—not here!' (Fortunately the money was insured, although the rates were understandably high.)

One or two of the estates cleared their own landing strips which certainly made the task of delivery more easy. Pay dropping was fairly straightforward in the coastal areas but the inland mountain ranges provided something of a hazard, particularly to the Tiger Moths with their limited range. Once when the weather had deteriorated a Tiger was forced to land on the airstrip at Bentong during a period when the area was active with terrorists, an exciting experience for Mr. and Mrs. Clements Burnett-Rae, the husband and wife team who formed the 'aircrew' on this occasion.

Two other members of the Kuala Lumpur Flying Club faced an even greater ordeal when they experienced engine failure and had to force land in the jungle while flying pay packets to three estates in the Bahau area of Negri Sembilan. Dr. Tasker, the pilot, had no choice other than a landing in impossible country and both he and his dropper, Mr. Tyrell, were injured during the attempt. They managed to limp half a mile or so with the pay sacks, but when Tyrell could go on no longer they hid the money in the undergrowth. Dr. Tasker managed to get to Bahau and returned with the police—to the profound relief of Tyrell who was standing guard.

Meanwhile back in England the long and successful R.A.F./Tiger Moth partnership was coming to an end. A new trainer had arrived, one that was equipped with radio, full instrument panels and hydraulic disc brakes, so that from 1950 onwards the Tiger Moth gradually gave way to the Prentice throughout the R.A.F., and the Chipmunk in the University Air Squadrons and most of the Reserve Schools. Although the last Tiger Moth was withdrawn from R.A.F. service in 1955, six continue to serve the Royal Navy, towing gliders at Roborough for cadets of Dartmouth College. Three of these machines, ex-G-ADGV, G-ADPC and G-AFWI, originate from pre-war days. The Navy also keeps a Tiger at Yeovilton and Lossie-mouth. Civil gliding enthusiasts were quick to see in the Tiger a cheap and reliable tug aircraft and one or more of the breed could almost invariably be seen leading a sail-plane at such places as the Lasham Gliding Centre.

Release from the R.A.F. now final, considerable numbers of Tiger Moths were once again put up for tender by the Air Ministry. At one time some 200 were parked in long rows at Croydon airport, and during the severe gales of the 1953/54 winter picket rings were torn away from the wings of a number of these Tigers leaving them free to blow away and cause untold confusion. One wrapped itself round a transformer house on the aerodrome and four more were found next morning on top of one another near the control tower. NL880 left the airfield altogether and deposited itself on Purley Way, causing something of a traffic hazard, for it was dark at the time. Fifty or so of the 198 Tiger Moths parked at Croydon suffered damage in varying degrees.

Many of the surplus Tiger Moths were bought by Vis-count Yves le Gallais of Paris for use at the French aero clubs and up to January 1963 there were 109 of the type on the French civil register. Initially the task of collecting and handling the Tigers in this country was undertaken by A. J. Whittemore Ltd. but not all of the surplus machines made the grade and went to France; for example some were dismantled and reduced for spares.* Then again DE610 and T6531 were just 'scrapped' whilst both NL989 and R5176 were 'lost believed stolen'. Prince (now King) Baudoin of Belgium bought G-ANLC (originally R.A.F. serial T6945).

* These were:

DE474	R5139	DE356	N6845
DE376	N6586	DE263	NL764
NM132	N5489	BB800	R5103
R5208	N6592	DE637	T7445
DE524	T5880	DE938	NL913
			DE268

The Tiger Moth had its name perpetuated at an unusual ceremony which took place on 14th April 1959 at Rochester aerodrome. After a display of aerobatics by Squadron Leader Holt, Tiger Moth G-ANLR (ex-R.A.F. N6856) was wheeled onto the Maidstone–Rochester road and positioned outside a new Courage and Barclay inn. Colonel R. L. Preston, C.B.E., at the time Secretary General of the Royal Aero Club, unveiled the inn-sign whilst standing in the rear cockpit, and the newly opened pub was henceforth called 'The Tiger Moth'.* Apparently the picture of the aeroplane painted on one side of the sign was the subject of so much criticism from Tiger Moth pilots that the brewers felt obliged to have it changed.

Until it was prohibited by the authorities, aerial advertising formed a useful source of extra revenue for the flying clubs and it was not uncommon to see a light aeroplane towing a banner proclaiming the opening date of someone's July Sale or the name of a particular detergent guaranteed to wash whiter than white. Group Captain Gordon Carey, R.A.F. (Ret.), could on occasions be seen flying Tiger Moth G-APIP from Biggin Hill with a long trailing message on the end of a length of cable connected to a special release hook near the Tiger Moth's tail skid. The banner had a marked retarding effect on the Tiger's progress, and although a Queen Bee tank holding an extra five gallons was fitted to this particular aeroplane, endurance was marginal and the return journey home against a headwind with the fuel gauge reading near zero could provide anxious moments after blazing the trail along the south coast of England.

The immediate post-war years saw the growth of a new industry in which the Tiger Moth played a vital part. The aeroplane as a tool of agriculture had long been accepted in America, and now more and more farmers were becoming attuned to the idea of aerial top dressing as a rapid and economical means of treating large acreages of crops with chemical fertiliser. Additionally, similar techniques could be employed to treat affected areas with insecticide. The

* Another Tiger Moth pub was opened in October 1964 at Meir, Stoke-on-Trent.

possibilities were particularly attractive abroad where farm areas were often much larger than in England and not always well served by roads. Long before aeroplanes were specially designed for the purpose the Tiger Moth presented itself as an excellent crop duster. It had good lifting power, was of rugged construction and could operate from small fields near the spraying area. Furthermore the type was at the time both numerous and cheap. When used as a top dresser, phosphates were carried in a commodious hopper installed in the front cockpit and arranged to discharge through a controllable vent under the fuselage. Other Tiger Moths were equipped with a tank feeding insecticide to a spray system. Pressure was generated by a wind-driven pump which either forced the liquid through a system of under wing perforated piping or, in a later form, utilized rotary sprays.

And so the Tigers went to work on the farm alongside the tractor and plough. They sprayed and dusted in many parts of the British Isles, the African continent, Australia, New Zealand and other countries. New Zealand in particular took advantage of the fact that Tiger Moths were available in vast numbers and lost no time harnessing them to the land. A typical example was ZK-AJO, an ex-Royal New Zealand Air Force Tiger which over a period of a few years flew 6,500 hours and dropped over 6,000 tons of fertiliser.

But top dressing like any other business must of necessity keep up productivity if it is to prosper, and a desire to make the operation pay sometimes resulted in chances being taken in the interest of speed. At the end of each run it became the practice to pull up into a stall turn in an effort to clear trees or some other obstacle on the boundary of the field, at the same time reversing direction quickly for another pass over the dropping area. Small wonder that the crop-dusting industry has become the graveyard of the Tiger Moth, and in New Zealand alone the numbers employed on aerial work of this kind dwindled from 200 machines in 1955 to fifteen in 1963. Although accidents must have accounted for most of the losses, the appearance of new agricultural aircraft specially designed for the purpose has inevitably had its effect. Indeed, the appearance of modern aircraft has had a similar effect on the flying club movement which in New Zealand employed forty-one Tigers in 1955 and only fifteen in 1963. Nevertheless even those operators who have re-equipped with more modern agricultural machines keep a Tiger in the corner of the hangar perhaps for a special job—or maybe as a reminder of how a group of young pilots founded the industry with war surplus Tiger Moths each carrying a few hundredweight of chemicals. Today the industry drops one-half million tons per annum.

In addition to the club and top dressing Tigers, quite a number are privately owned in New Zealand and the civil register published on 31st March 1963 listed ninety-six DH 82a's and three of the now very rare DH 82 examples.

In Australia the story is very much the same and is best described by Squadron Leader P. G. Marman, A.F.C., R.A.F. (ret.), an agricultural pilot operating in that part of the world:

> A growing industry, lacking initial capital, owes its existence to the availability of this low cost aircraft. I have heard many men experienced in the business say that without the Tiger Moth, aerial agriculture in Australia could never have found its financial feet. The Tiger is now [February 1964] being pushed out of operation in favour of aircraft specifically designed for the work. The Tiger lacked a mechanism for quick jettisoning of its load of spray liquid or fertilizer. It also lacked the margin of surplus power for operation off improvised strips, usually positioned on the interior plateau at 1,000 ft. frequently in high ambient temperatures. Nevertheless she is the mother of an industry in this continent, one more task fulfilled by the greatest work-horse of them all.

The air-racing bug invaded South Africa as it did most countries with a sporting aviation fraternity, and between 1st and 3rd September 1962 a new event called The State

President's Trophy had its first meeting. The course was an ambitious one, contestants having to fly the 1,042 miles from Vereeniging to Grahamstown with an overnight stay at Aliwal North on the Saturday.

The trophy presented by State President C. R. Swart is a magnificent one mounted on a 2 ft. diameter cross-section of that beautiful South African timber unflatteringly named stinkwood. It is covered with a map of South Africa executed in beaten silver with each coastal town marked by a blue sapphire, while those inland are picked out in rubies. Kimberley is represented by a 10-point diamond and a gold nugget marks Johannesburg's place on the map, which is itself surmounted by a rampant springbok with gold horns and hooves and ruby eyes. The map is encircled with a line traced by a gold aeroplane. With the trophy is a first prize of R1,400 (approx. £680), second prize R800, third prize R400, and a fourth prize of R200.

The first meeting was well supported by a wide variety of aircraft types which included several Cessna 210's, a Beech Bonanza, Piper Tripacer and one or two older designs like the Fairchild Argus. But older by far were the Tiger Moths taking part. There was ZS-CJM flown by Commandant Jan Blaauw of the Defence Flying Club while another Tiger from the same club, ZS-CNR, was in the hands of P. J. Bruyns. Tiger Moth ZS-CJM, handicapped at 104 m.p.h., was never overtaken, beating the other thirty aircraft in the field, and Blaauw received his prize and the magnificent trophy from the State President. The race was controlled throughout by 'hams' of the South African Radio League.

Up to 1964 there were forty-three Tiger Moths on the South African register and the old biplane is from all accounts as popular as ever.

Given an unpredictable pupil the safest aeroplane in the world cannot always prevent an accident, even at a well run flying school. There was the case of the visiting official from the Civil Aviation Department of British Guiana anxious to complete his training for a private pilot's licence in England before returning home. The Ministry of Aviation recommended him to Fairoaks aerodrome, scene of much flying instruction under the guidance of Wing Commander C. E. F. Arthur, A.F.C., for more than sixteen years Commanding Officer of 18 E.F.T.S. (or as it became after the war, 18 R.F.S.) When the Reserve School closed in 1953 he was able to devote more of his time to the Fairoaks Aero Club and in the face of official Ministerial interest Cyril Arthur decided to take on the man from British Guiana himself rather than entrust him to his assistant instructors. Apparently the pupil had more than usual difficulty in keeping the Tiger straight during take-off, but eventually the persistence of both instructor and pupil won through and the moment of triumph, first solo, duly arrived. There followed a few uneventful hours of flying until 18th August 1958 when the man from British Guiana, practising solo landings at about 6 p.m., bounced rather heavily and opened up the engine to 'go round again'. The take-off direction that evening was northerly with the control building and signals area several hundred yards to the left. It so happened that Arthur was watching his pupil from a nearby building and he remembers the events following the bounce in these words:

> . . . he left the ground, flat turning moderately to the left, coming toward the signals area and control tower. He struck the top of the mast in the signals area with his starboard wings, this inverted him and he flew in the inverted position straight into the ground floor doorway of the control building. The aircraft slid to the ground and burst into flames. I dashed round the corner of the adjacent office block expecting I don't now what—a dead man I think, trapped in the blazing wreckage. As I came round the corner at full speed I collided with somebody. I started to say 'what the hell', then dumbfounded I recognized the pilot, all complete except for one shoe. I then made the inane remark, 'What are you doing here.' The crash wagon was within a few yards, got the fire out and all was well.

Trainer of the pilots of the Commonwealth in times of peace and war, crop duster, glider tug, aerial advertiser, bomber, coastal patrol plane, aerial ambulance—there seemed to be hardly any job unfit for the Tiger even in standard form. But when the modification experts became interested the old biplane was able to show that it still had a few new tricks up its sleeve.

*On January 9th 1966 G-ACDC was involved in another accident. During a practice forced landing without power a misunderstanding arose regarding the position of the fuel cock, so that on opening the throttle for the climb away from the selected field silence greeted the two occupants. Practice forced landings usually terminate 500 feet above ground level. The check pilot was therefore in the unfortunate position of being too high for a landing yet too low for a circuit and another attempt. Fortunately neither pilot was hurt but repairs included new bottom right and top left mainplanes. The paintwork was barely dry before the old Tiger was crashed during another crazy flying demonstration at Wiley on 5th June, 1966. Restoration included a new front fuselage and engine bearers, and three new wings. Not content with two serious accidents in one year the old veteran next came to grief on May 12th, 1968. While attempting to take off from Goodwood the pilot allowed a bad swing to develop with the usual result—extensive damage to CDC but none to the pilot. So back again it went to Rollasons of Croydon, for yet another re-build under the supervision of Adrian Deverall!

**In 1969 a most beautiful example was delivered to Colerado, U.S.A. with the registration N126B. Built by Morris Motors as DE 712, ex G-APJL, it emerged from the Croydon works in a high gloss off-white finish with R.A.F. roundals and tail flashes, burnished cowlings and other aluminium parts and instrument panels in polished teak. The new owner, Mr. O. E. Bartoe, Junior, supplies components for the Apollo space project and his visit to Rollasons coincided with the astronauts first circle of the moon. Deverell felt moved to ask the American—"is it true that the first things they saw on the other side were two Tiger Moths on the surface"?

8. The Tiger Changes its Stripes

It has become fashionable to convert. No sooner does a new motor-car appear on the road before one of the specialist companies announces a highly tuned version or an alternative body so removed from the original design that the result might almost be a totally different vehicle. Such conversions are by no means confined to cars; people convert houses, remodel expensive fur coats and even reshape themselves. In so far as the urge to convert affects aeroplanes, certain American companies have for some years done substantial business revamping existing designs— usually in the light, twin-engined business aircraft category. Usually an aeroplane of improved performance and comfort results, and whereas the modifications may include various aerodynamic refinements, bigger engines and even completely new tail units, none of these American conversions presents such a transformation as that given the Tiger Moth at Thruxton aerodrome near Andover.

With private flying at a low ebb in Britain it is hardly surprising that few light aircraft carrying four people were being built during the mid 1950s. Furthermore it was at that time difficult, if not impossible, to import examples of the excellent American light family 'planes. It was against this background that Squadron Leader J. E. Doran-Webb (Managing Director of the Wiltshire School of Flying Ltd.) conceived the idea of a cheap four-to-five-seater using as many Tiger Moth parts as possible. Needing the help of a qualified designer for such a project and on the advice of Colonel Preston of the Royal Aero Club, he aproached Mr. Ronald Prizeman, D.C.Ae., A.M.I.Mech.E., A.F.R.Ae.S., a graduate of the Royal Aeronautical College.

Doran-Webb's original idea was a five-seat, high-wing monoplane using the lower wings of the Tiger, its undercarriage, propeller, control systems and tail unit, but a detailed examination proved the structural and aerodynamic impossibility of the project. Doran-Webb had endeavoured to interest various professional organizations in his idea, but general apathy towards the light aeroplane was deeply ingrained at the time. Although his first assessment of the scheme had not been encouraging Prizeman was persuaded to take on the task of redesigning the Tiger to carry four people in an enclosed cabin. He was living in Buckinghamshire at the time, and since the Wiltshire School of Flying (actually in Hampshire) was to be the scene of operation, the project developed by post with letters and drawings passing between the two counties every few days. That the Tiger was capable of lifting four people was soon established by preliminary calculations; in any case this aspect was never in doubt, for many years earlier in 1932 the DH83 Fox Moth had been built around Tiger Moth wings, engine, tail unit and undercarriage and it had done even better, carrying four passengers in a cabin in addition to the pilot seated in a separate cockpit which was open in the earlier versions. The passengers' cabin was reminiscent of a four-wheeled cab with the passengers sitting in facing pairs. Inserted in the pilot's instrument panel was a Victorian-looking oval window through which he could wave reassurance to his passengers.

Prizeman was Chief Technician with another company but he agreed to handle the design work for Doran-Webb on a spare-time basis. There were, of course, bound to be technical problems and as time went on they ran into hundreds. If the weight lifting capabilities were assured, the ability to keep the four occupants within the centre-

Dutch Tiger Moth with the extended fin demanded by the authorities in Holland.

The 'Canon' one of the Tiger Club's 'Super Tigers' powered by a 145-h.p. Gipsy Major 1c modified to run inverted. The fuel tank has been removed to the front cockpit from its original position.

Rhodesian scene. Over 6,500 pilots were trained in Southern Rhodesia during the war on British and Australian built Tiger Moths. An Australian-built model is in foreground.

Tiger Moths, assembled at Brindisi, being serviced before their flight across the Adriatic to Yugoslavia.

of-gravity limits of the Tiger Moth was quite another matter. Indeed this very problem was to be Prizeman's main concern. He began by arranging for a Tiger Moth to be completely dismantled so that every part could be weighed separately. Using an 'Aeromodeller' plan he took measurements for the standard Tiger Moth, and this information, together with the list of weights prepared from the dissembled machine, enabled him to prepare an outline drawing of a four-seater biplane using as much of the existing aeroplane as possible. The weight calculations, taking every possible load combination into consideration, were completed by 29th September 1956, only a few weeks after Doran-Webb's original approach.

Meanwhile at Thruxton aerodrome a mock-up was prepared using Tiger Moth components and the doors and windscreen from an old Percival Proctor. Although most of the components were held together by wire, it was substantial enough for four people to climb aboard. This first structural test was a success!

It was anticipated that there might be a difference in flying characteristics between the four-seater Tiger Moth and the original version. The fuselage was now 37 in. wide, an increase of 13 in. made necessary by the need to provide two pairs of side-by-side seats, and this modification alone was bound to alter the stall. Then again, since the original wings were to be used, the wider fuselage would increase the span of the aeroplane and very likely its rolling and spinning characteristics would alter. By now Prizeman was beginning to feel that his modification was turning into a new aeroplane, but to avoid having to meet the stringent new design requirements called for by the authorities he was determined to treat the four-seater Tiger Moth as a modification. He continued making strength calculations with measurements from various bits and pieces of a Tiger Moth kept in his garden.

That aeroplane designing in 1931 was, in comparison to present-day practice, free and easy is understandable, and the *ad hoc* basis of the Tiger Moth's design as described in

Chapter 2 was soon to be confirmed by Prizeman in his quest for more detailed structural knowledge of the breed:

By means which I do not propose to reveal, we acquired a copy of the Tiger Moth strength calculations. They amounted to little more than a few pages of rough pencilled calculations. Their crudity was something of a shock to me, because it meant that I would have to calculate the strength of the Tiger Moth from first principles, according to modern practice.

At a later stage Doran-Webb acquainted de Havillands with details of the project and they were most co-operative, providing numerous drawings. Many were based upon the old DH 60 Metal Moth, with dozens of alterations to make them applicable to the Tiger Moth. To this day the Tiger Moth incorporates various lugs which, although of no relevance to the aeroplane, were important when the components were part of a DH 60 with folding wings.

Prizeman's new four-seater emerged as a Tiger Moth fuselage increased in width from 24 in. to 37 in. by a pair of welded steel tube space frames. The back of the cabin tapered sharply to blend into the rear fuselage giving a tadpole effect to the aeroplane. The following additional alterations were made:

Distance between mainplanes and tail increased by rear space frame to provide better control.

Engine moved forward by front space frame to preserve balance with four occupants.

Extensions either side of petrol tank to make the centre section conform to the new fuselage width.

Undercarriage widened by using two of the normal V-shaped axle pivots welded together. The undercarriage was made up entirely from standard Tiger Moth components.

A Fairey Reed metal propeller replaced the original wooden airscrew.

Addition of a large windscreen and enclosed cabin fitted with two hinged doors.

Four seats fitted in cabin arranged in staggered pairs to increase elbow room.

Spring-loaded rudder control adjustable in flight.
Lengthened exhaust pipe extending behind the cabin.
Wing attachments covered by fairings.

Having finalized the layout, a meeting was held with the Air Registration Board on 10th October 1956 when the scheme was submitted with a view to obtaining approval to go ahead. All aircraft design work must be subjected to an independent check if it is to conform with the regulations, and Mr. E. H. Smith was appointed for the purpose.

Under the active leadership of Squadron Leader Doran-Webb work proceeded on the aircraft at full speed, with Prizeman flying or driving down to Thruxton most weekends. During this hectic period Doran-Webb was involved in a serious skiing accident in Switzerland and spent several weeks there as a result. Nevertheless progress was good and on 2nd March 1957, exactly nine months after the project had started, the prototype G-AOEX made its first flight in the hands of Lieutenant Commander G. P. Shea-Simonds, at one time a Fairey Aviation test pilot. At the end of an uneventful trip Shea-Simonds commented, 'It reminds me of another aeroplane. Can't think what—oh yes, a Tiger Moth.'

The second prototype G-AOEY flew within a few weeks and later tests were handled by Commander 'Doc' Stewart, a Boscombe Down test pilot.

With success more or less assured, the project became the target for officialdom and Prizeman recalls this frustrating period in these words:

When the A.R.B. [Air Registration Board] staff gave us approval to go ahead, I do not think they thought seriously that we would ever succeed in the enterprise. After the prototype flew they had second thoughts and flung the book at us. For example, we had to produce a Pilot's Manual and Maintenance Instructions in lavish details, in spite of the fact that hundreds of Tigers were on the Civil Register without such benefits. Worse still, we had to produce a Type Record of a thoroughness which contrasted ironically with the original de Havilland calculations for the prototype, written (almost) on the back of an envelope.

By now the A.R.B. was treating the aeroplane as a new design and some 170 detail drawings were called for. Although the Special Category Certificate of Airworthiness had been issued without much difficulty, Prizeman was beginning to despair of ever getting the full C. of A. Although nearly 9,000 Tiger Moths had been produced, to say nothing of Queen Bees, the type did not meet with post-war A.R.B. approval, unbelievable as this may seem and one cannot but wonder how the organization was able to convince itself that a Tiger Moth was unsafe because it failed to meet standards drawn up for modern aircraft. Prizeman continued:

> We pressure tested the canopy and the door jettison mechanism, besides static loading certain parts of the structure. The most farcical suggestion was that we would have to take the machine to Farnborough to have the windscreen tested for its bird resistance!

Amongst those to sample the prototype during its development period was Air Commodore Alan Wheeler, a test pilot of great renown with a long and distinguished career at government establishments. There was never any pretence that the four-seater Tiger would be fast or even moderately rapid, but Doran-Webb and his colleagues were a little crestfallen when the great man landed and expressed the view that taking everything into consideration the aeroplane was 'a bit slow'. It then transpired that Wheeler had been under the impression the air-speed indicator was reading miles per hour. In fact it was calibrated in knots.

Doran-Webb had always seen his Tiger conversion as a potential agricultural machine, and an alternative version embodying a separate detachable top decking and open cockpit was offered. It was envisaged that agricultural pilots would prefer this arrangement to the enclosed cabin, but in practice this was not so and in any case it proved easier to install the tank or hopper next to the pilot leaving him totally enclosed.

Mr. J. C. C. Taylor, newly returned from a tour of Australia and New Zealand, suggested that the much converted Tiger be named 'Jackaroo', Australian slang for 'Jack of all trades' or 'new chum'. Spraying versions have a sixty-gallon steel tank and a Stuart Turner centrifugal pump feeding insecticide to a pair of 15 ft. under wing Allman spray bars, each fitted with fifteen nozzles. By changing the size of the Allman nozzles, spray intensity may be altered allowing the sixty gallons of insecticide to cover between $7\frac{1}{2}$ and 120 acres. At a spraying speed of 70 m.p.h. with the Jackaroo ten feet or so above the ground the spray width is approximately 50 ft. In this version two seats are removed.

It was the original intention to offer the four-seat version of the Jackaroo for £1,000, but production machines were sold for £1,270, or £1,595 the agricultural version. Alternatively an existing Tiger could be converted for £700. Gipsy Major I engines were standard but for another £200 the 145 h.p. Gipsy Major X could be installed. Brakes were offered at £50, electric starter £60 and night flying equipment only increased the price by £30.

That conditions should have encouraged any company to seriously contemplate converting a 1931 vintage biplane into a family four-seater may be a depressing reminder of the depths to which Britain's once flourishing light aeroplane movement had sunk by 1957, but it was a meritorious achievement nevertheless.

Twenty-six Jackaroos were built at Thruxton and their last known location is as follows:

G-AOEX—original prototype, sold to and still in use at the Wiltshire School of Flying.

G-AOEY—prototype, sold to a Mr. Tamanti of Italy and subsequently flown from Italy to Ghana, believed now to be still in Ghana.

G-ANZT—sold to Messrs. Rollason Aircraft.

G-APRB—sold to Messrs. Rollason Aircraft.

G-APAI—sold to Captain Rosborough.

G-APHZ—sold to Airspray Colchester.

G-AOIO—sold to Air Navigation Ltd.

G-AOIW—sold to J. Dumas, Holland.

G-AOIV—sold to E. Gravenhorst and shipped to Buenos Aires where it was re-erected by Messrs. De Havilland Aircraft and is still operating.

G-APJV—sold to Glamorgan Aviation.

G-AOIT—sold to E. Swanson and still operating in Scotland.

G-APAL—sold to Captain Watson.

G-APAO—sold to J. Read.

G-APAM—sold to Miss Sheila Scott.

G-APAX—dismantled and sold to Madras Flying Club, India, where it was re-erected and is still in operation.

G-ALIV
G-AMTX
G-APRC
G-AMPC
G-APSV
G-APSU
—also completed and were due to be exported to India (Madras Flying Club) but unfortunately import permits into India were not available. These aircraft therefore were taken back into stock and transferred to the Wiltshire School of Flying where they are now held mainly for spares.

G-AOIR
G-ANFY
G-AOIX
G-APAJ
G-APAP
—sold to Wiltshire School of Flying—still in use as training aircraft.

Rollasons of Croydon built a Jackaroo registered G-APOV (ex. R 5130) which departed from the original Thruxton design by incorporating a fuselage of constant taper from cabin to tail unit, thus avoiding the 'tadpole' effect which is a characteristic of the type. Seriously damaged on 1st July 1961 when it became involved in a bog in Wales, it was brought back to Croydon by road, but on inspection considered to be beyond repair. If G-APOV will never fly again it has certainly not reached the end of its useful life for the local spastic children decided they wanted their own aeroplane and it is being reassembled to become an object of endless fun for these unfortunate youngsters.

The Jackaroo can be regarded as an ingenious attempt to produce a cheap four-seater aeroplane from the components of an existing design. That the finished article should look so like a Tiger Moth is a measure of Ronald Prizeman's success in achieving his aim—to use as much as possible of the original machine which had inspired the project. Although certain new assemblies had to be added to produce a cabin of sufficient width, the Jackaroo would seem to have inherited many of the characteristics of its lusty forebear, including the most priceless one of all—reliability. Between 1958 and 1963 the ten Jackaroos in service at the Wiltshire School of Flying have amassed nearly 40,000 hours between them without a single modification.

On a less ambitious scale than the Jackaroo was the conversion by Rollasons of G-AOXS which was refitted as an inexpensive single-passenger air taxi. The passenger occupied a fully upholstered front cockpit covered by a small canopy and the pilot sat in the open rear cockpit. Unfortunately this unusual Tiger had a short career for it was written off in an accident.*

With the aeroplane becoming more and more involved in all walks of life it is natural that it should become a necessary ingredient in the making of films. It is hardly possible to see any picture with contemporary background that does not involve an airport scene, for nothing more vividly conveys the impression of travel than the great bustling passenger halls and the whining noise of the gas turbine that accompanies the aircrafts' arrivals and departures. The recording of such an atmosphere presents few difficulties, but aviation has now been in existence long enough to have its own history, and when a story is told about past events it is sometimes difficult, if not impossible, to obtain an authentic type of the right vintage when an aeroplane comes into the story. It was to meet the aeronautical needs of the film industry that Captain J. Crewdson formed his company, Film Aviation Services Ltd.

It all started when John Crewdson was flying for a

*See additional note at end of chapter, page 194.

charter company. He was assigned to the then quite novel task of helping in the production of the Alfred Hitchcock film *To Catch a Thief*. On that occasion he was to carry the cameraman in an S-51 helicopter while the latter photographed an exciting car chase through mountain roads and into Monte Carlo. The airborne cameraman is an important part of the business but many would consider the 'taken' to be of more interest than the 'taker'. In *The War Lover* Crewdson used a de Havilland Dove to do the taking, in addition to providing three Boeing B-17s or Flying Fortresses which he eventually located standing in a derelict condition on an airfield in Arizona. They were flown across the Atlantic by Crewdson and his colleagues and then operated during the film sequences. The problem of finding suitable aircraft naturally becomes more acute as the clock is turned back, a typical example being the picture *Lawrence of Arabia*. The producer wanted three World War I aircraft which were unobtainable in flying condition. Film companies are generally believed to operate on a money-no-object basis, so it is perhaps a little surprising that Film Aviation Services were not allowed to produce replicas of the genuine article in their Croydon workshops, although it must be admitted that the solution adopted was a more practical and less wasteful one. Three Tiger Moths were purchased and two of these, G-ANNF and G-ANLC (ex-R.A.F. R5146 and T6945), were radically altered in appearance to resemble Rumpler CIV two-seater fighters. They took an active part in the production which was filmed in Jordan.

A more interesting conversion involved ex-T7438, which became a Fokker D VII. This brilliant transformation involved a number of far-reaching modifications under the supervision of Film Aviation Services' Chief Engineer, Mr. Leslie Hillman. The engine cowling was replaced by the square box so characteristic of this vintage German fighter, and the undercarriage was exchanged for the distinctive wire-braced unit of Fokker design, with its small aerofoil enclosing the axle. The front cockpit was covered in and a machine-gun mounted on the top of the fuselage, which was made flat-sided by removal of the stringers. The fuselage sides were built up giving a deeper appearance, and the fin and rudder were replaced by a replica of the type used on the Fokker D VII. The ailerons were moved from the bottom to the top wing and made to overhang. These various modifications, completed during many months of hard work, so transformed the aeroplane that it seemed impossible that the Tiger Moth had even the remotest connection. But all the ingenuity and effort that went into making the replica Fokker D VII was to no avail for it was never used in the film and made only a brief test flight. Crewdson repurchased it from the film company and it was stored at Croydon until late 1963 when a fire in one of the hangars totally destroyed this remarkable Tiger Moth. The two Rumplers were left in Jordan by the film unit and their fate is unknown.

It is a widely held belief that successful men are endowed with both ability and luck, and few would deny that the former ingredient is rarely instrumental in getting to the top without the latter. The same can be said of most enterprises, and aeroplanes are no exception. Even its biggest supporters would admit that whatever sterling qualities it may possess, the Tiger Moth could not have stayed the course but for certain events which have worked in its favour. Being at the right place at the right time is half the battle, but this is not all for there were sometimes other good aeroplanes ready to compete with the Tiger. Luck has nearly always smiled favourably upon the old biplane in the form of ardent enthusiasts, supporters, friends or call them what you like. The R.A.F. sponsored the type in the early days and the availability of production ensured its wartime propagation. The R.A.F.V.R. kept it to the fore during the early post-war years, as did the flying clubs and various private owners, and in turn it made the top-dressing industry possible at a time when there was nothing else to buy.

It has so often been the case that when a particular national sport or activity of some kind has declined because of official apathy or even disapproval, some private citizen has come forward to salvage the wreckage and create a new interest, often at considerable personal expense.

It is the opinion of many in sporting aviation circles that if anyone should qualify for the title of 'Patron of the Art of Light 'Plane Flying' none is more qualified than Norman Jones. His first interest in flying goes back to the days when he piloted the old World War I DH 9 two-seater biplane which formed the equipment of some of the early Auxiliary Air Force squadrons. Family business commitments prevented a development of this interest until shortly after the resumption of private flying in 1945. Norman Jones amused himself with light aeroplanes but gradually his interest developed and today his activities include the running of several flying schools and ownership of Rollasons, a company already mentioned as having strong Tiger Moth connections. It is another activity with which we are most concerned in this book, one that started as casually as the Tiger itself during a Royal Aero Club Racing Dinner early in 1956.

During the course of the evening someone at Norman Jones's table suggested, 'Why not a club for Tiger Moths?' Those present were Jim Denyer, Jock Lindsay, Chris Wren, Basil Maile, Beverly Snook, the Hon. Peter Vanneck and J. M. Donald. The idea was readily accepted, the Tiger Club was formed and most at the table became Founder Members. C. A. Nepean Bishop was invited to become Hon. Secretary on 30th July 1956 and later held office as Hon. Chief Flying Instructor until his retirement in January 1964.

The first Tiger Club race meeting was held at Elstree on 1st September 1956 during the Association of British Aero Clubs Convention, and Jones, Bailey, Bishop, Ogilvy and Snook raced in five Tiger Moths belonging to Norman Jones. Donald raced his own machine. It was not long before the Tiger Club began to show signs of developing a definite character, and within a few months of its coming into existence the members acquired a taste for formation flying, an activity rarely practised at other clubs. Soon air racing and formation flying were joined by aerobatics and Tiger Club members were doing well at the international events, usually pitting their Tiger Moths against foreign aircraft designed specifically for the purpose. It was largely because the standard Tiger was being outclassed at these meetings that the special Tigers described later came into being. In 1956 Nepean Bishop and Colin Labouchere tied for sixth place in the Lockheed Aerobatic Trophy, and in 1958 Bishop took first place amongst the British contestants, at a time when he was on the wrong side of sixty! The Tiger Club has produced two national Air Racing Champions in Dennis Hartas and Squadron Leader Brian Iles, the latter incidentally an ex-pupil of one of the authors.

The Tiger Club did more than compete in air races and aerobatic championships; it carried on the torch from the pre-war Cobham-inspired air displays by organizing highly entertaining and very well presented air shows which to this day tour the country during the summer season. There are crazy flying shows, aerobatic displays, formation flying, mock dog fights and a thrilling air race around a closed circuit. Although the Tiger Club numbers many different types of aeroplane amongst the twenty or so machines in their hangar at Redhill, the Tiger Moth still makes a very big contribution to these shows and the Club's every-day activities.

With the emphasis on display flying it is not surprising that the Tiger Club should devote so much energy to perfecting new 'acts', and this quest for the unusual has in some instances brought into existence Tiger Moths that have very special talents of their own. Almost as soon as the Tiger became available in 1931 the R.A.F. prepared a small number especially for inverted flying. The attraction of having an engine that will continue giving power when inverted, even for relatively short periods, was explained in one of the early chapters, and with the assistance of the de Havilland company G-ANSH was converted to become the first post-war Tiger capable of sustained inverted flight. The pre-1939 arrangement was incorporated, using a small windmill-driven pump to pressurize an auxiliary tank which was large enough to permit upside-down flying of limited duration. Meanwhile, acting in conjunction with de Havillands, Mr. R. F. Thompson of Rollasons developed an improved system which dispensed with the windmill-driven pump and its associated tank, replacing the pre-war system with one that is both simple in layout and straightforward in operation. Mechanical fuel pumps driven off the camshaft feed petrol to an additional jet inserted into the body of the carburettor. Normally this is inoperative and the engine draws mixture from the usual float chamber and main jet. When the pilot decides to fly inverted a separate control is rotated through ninety degrees, cutting off fuel from the normal carburettor. As the carburettor empties after fifteen seconds or so and the engine begins to stop firing, the pilot takes courage in both hands, disregards his training in engine handling and moves the mixture control into the 'weak' position so that it lies just a fraction behind the throttle. The engine bursts into life again and its power may be controlled by moving both throttle and mixture control together. A half roll and the Tiger is on its back with the engine running perfectly. It will climb inverted, turn inverted and given the right techniques, even loop inverted. An additional oil pump is fitted to the rear cover ensuring a constant supply of oil while all this is going on.

Mr. Thompson's modifications have been carried out on Gipsy Major 1c engines developing 145 h.p. and these have been installed in special Tiger Moths embodying a number of interesting features. The wooden propeller is replaced by a metal one, the wing ribs are stiffened, elevators of 2 in. greater chord are fitted, mainplane incidence is reduced to the minimum allowed by the de Havilland Company, and the entire airframe is covered in a special lightweight fabric giving a worthwhile saving in empty weight—these

special Tigers have averaged 1,126 lbs. as against the usual
1,210 lbs. for the standard aeroplane. The fuel tank is
moved from the top wing to the front cockpit which is
covered by a detachable ply decking. The removal of the
fuel tank from its original position markedly improves the
aerodynamics of the top wing, and drag is still further
reduced by the addition of fillets between the bottom wings
and fuselage. Cleaned up aerodynamically, reduced in
weight and fitted with a higher powered engine capable of
running inverted, these special Tiger Moths perform and
handle magnificently, with take-off and rate of climb
particularly improved. Maximum speed is in excess of
120 m.p.h.

The first machine to receive 'the treatment' by Rollasons was G-APDZ, converted in 1958 and named 'The
Bishop' in honour of C. Nepean Bishop. 'The Archbishop',
G-ANZZ, followed in 1959 and this aeroplane was flown
inverted from Lympne to Le Touquet on 27th June of that
year by E. McAully to mark the fiftieth anniversary of
Bleriot's Channel crossing, twenty-five years after the one
by Geoffrey Tyson in G-ABUL. Two more were modified
in 1960, G-AOAA 'The Deacon' and G-ANMZ. This last
aeroplane, named 'The Canon', had ply-covered leading
edges to the wings. It was while flying this particular Tiger
that Mr. Lewis Benjamin of the Tiger Club had what can
only be described as a miraculous escape. During his
demonstration of low level crazy flying at the 1963 Sywell
air display. 'The Canon' flicked into a spin, digging its
nose into the ground. It bounced back into the air and
landed heavily, spread-eagle fashion, collapsing its undercarriage and shedding its engine. The pilot was lifted from
the wreckage with a broken nose, a bloodshot eye and a
bruised thigh caused when the metal control-stick bent
itself around his leg during the crash. The photograph taken
just before impact (opp. p. 160) describes the incident more
adequately than any number of words. An enlarged version
was pinned to the Tiger Club notice-board and someone,
believed to be John Blake, added this final comment from

the pilot's lips: 'If this doesn't kill me, Norman will!'
Norman Jones had an understandably high regard for 'The
Canon' but the incident was treated with his usual understanding. Benjamin was flying again within two weeks and
the aeroplane despite its ordeal now flies again after an
extensive rebuild.

The very successful Rollason-converted Tiger Moths
owned by the Tiger Club are not alone in the field of
inverted flight. Mr. J. W. Tomkins designed a special
inverted fuel system for his Tiger Moth G-AHRC using
totally different principles to those adopted by Rollasons.
The original fuel tank is retained but is arranged to feed
into a four-gallon flexible tank which is attached to the
cockpit side of the engine bulkhead. The tank, which
incidentally is fireproof, is small enough to allow full use
to be made of the front cockpit. Two S.U. electric fuel
pumps deliver petrol from the auxiliary to an additional
jet in the carburettor, power being supplied by a twelve-
volt accumulator carried in the luggage locker. The
flexible tank may be refilled in flight by transferring fuel
from the main tank in the top wing. The revised fuel
system was installed in G-AHRC by Brooklands Aviation
Ltd., and the principal advantage claimed for the arrangement is that all the fuel is usable, even in inverted flight.

With a view to improving wing efficiency when flying
inverted, Tomkins altered the original aerofoil section by
adding a symmetrical metal-covered portion ahead of the
front spar. This extends along the entire leading edge of
the bottom wing, and between the fuel tank and the slats
on the top wing. Whilst only the front portions of the
wings are of symmetrical sections the aeroplane is said to
handle as well inverted as it does in normal flight.

After the 1959 air display season many of the Tiger Club
members felt that an injection of new ideas was called for.
By that time the antics of the 'Super Tigers' with their
inverted fuel systems and enhanced performances were becoming well known amongst the enthusiasts up and down
the country, although no doubt to many members of the

public these quite exceptional Tigers must have continued to prove highly entertaining. Possibly inspired by memories of the Cobham shows but never expecting to be taken seriously, Lewis Benjamin suggested that someone should stand on the top wing of a Tiger in flight. Response from those members within hearing distance being favourable he sent to the club's Chairman a rough sketch which he describes as '. . . someone crouching wildly above the fuel tank of a Tiger hanging on for grim life to a reins-like arrangement strung back from the leading edge'.

Norman Jones liked the idea and passed it on to Adrian Deverell at Rollasons for translation into practical terms, and from this point onwards the Standing-On-Wing project was known as SOW. A steel tube construction was designed so that it could be fitted to the main spar attachments of the top wing and removed when not required, both procedures taking but a few minutes. The rig was stressed by independent experts, and with the engineering in more or less final form Norman Jones explained the project to the Ministry of Aviation who eventually gave their approval. Meanwhile Deverell had submitted drawings to the Air Registration Board who accepted the matter without raised eyebrows, almost as though they were in the habit of dealing with people standing on wings as a matter of routine. They did however insist that the first trials of SOW should be with a life-size dummy, and 'Brother Ben', an eleven stone, overalled figure with metal feet and a painted face, was produced by Rollasons for the purpose.

With so much to occupy the engineers concerned, it was not until early 1962, one chilly Monday afternoon in February, that the great day arrived for the initial air test before representatives of the A.R.B. One or two Tiger Club members had gathered for the occasion, and since it was his idea Lewis Benjamin had the honour of piloting the first attempt. Tiger Moth G-ARAZ had already received minor modifications—the right hand door to the front cockpit had been removed and a padded edge substituted to enable parachutists to leave the front seat prior to the actual jump from the lower wing. As RAZ taxied out it was indeed a Tiger with a difference, with its man-sized dummy standing on the petrol tank complete with a pair of Deverell's old shoes on its feet. Some preliminary ground manœuvring and a few brief hops preceeded the first uneventful circuit and landing, followed by two more with David Phillips and Dennis Hartas at the controls. All three pilots felt satisfied with the aircraft's controllability and a test report was completed and accepted by the authorities. The way was now clear for a live run.

Benjamin elected to replace 'Brother Ben', and on 4th March a considerable gathering of Tiger Club members waited in anticipation as he donned layer upon layer of clothing. There was some concern at the time about the effect the airflow might have on the passenger's breathing and an oxygen mask was worn as a precaution. Arthur Golding-Barrett, the Tiger Club senior check pilot was there casting an eye on safety in general and another member even suggested a body layer of fat, 'swim-the-Channel' style. If some of these precautions appear over-dramatic it should be explained that in March of that year the ground was covered in snow, and cold air at even Tiger speed assumes a keenness known only to Tiger pilots and those who attempt the ascent of Everest! Hartas flew the Tiger, formed on by David Phillips and Barry Griffiths in a Piper Super Cub and the last named took pictures of Benjamin standing on the top wing.

Within minutes of landing the telephone burst into life. A number of national newspapers had already received reports to the effect that someone was flying around Red-hill standing out on the wing of an aeroplane—was the story true? The Tiger Club had always realized the potential news value of SOW and the story was well exploited by the Club's P.R.O., James Gilbert. Reporters and photo-graphers arrived as if from nowhere, only to be met by a well-organized silence. A leakage of information would have ruined any possibility of selling what amounted to a

The Thruxton Jack-aroo. *Top:* Open crop-dusting version with airspeed indicator mounted in pilot's view outside the cockpit. *Centre:* The standard version, prototype G-AOEX. *Bottom:* Rollason-built example with fuselage of constant taper.

Single passenger air taxi with the front cockpit upholstered and enclosed by a small canopy.

Symmetrical leading edge added to Mr. J. W. Tomkins's Tiger Moth G-AHRC to improve its inverted flying.

valuable exclusive story; SOW had cost quite a lot of money and the time had come for it to show some financial return.

The *Daily Express* took up the story which broke in time to publicize the first Tiger Club air display of the season, the event being presented at Panshangar on Easter Monday. Excellent provincial coverage resulted, but for some reason the story was omitted from the London edition. Then Tiger Club member Ron Jacobs of the *Evening News* handled the story for his paper and copy after copy rolled off the press bringing pictures of SOW before the Londoner. Requests began pouring in for appearances to be made at fêtes; but the general excitement of these early days with SOW probably came to a climax when both the television companies and Pathé Pictorial became interested. Both forms of entertainment made feature films of the act which has probably done more than any other single activity to bring the Tiger Club to the notice of the public —and, of more importance, stimulate interest in sporting flying.

Not that the formulative days of SOW were without excitement. G-ARAZ is not the best of Tiger Moths, and the addition of someone standing bolt upright atop the fuel tank causes a lot of extra drag. During one of the first demonstrations of SOW in the Midlands, the initial rate of climb was so poor that Benjamin to this day feels he has an intimate knowledge of the private gardens surrounding Wolverhampton aerodrome. Possibly it was this experience that persuaded him to move from above the tank to the pilot's seat so that his aerodynamically superior wife Juanita may brave the elements in his place. This she does exceedingly well and by now many thousands of spectators must have seen this husband and wife team, Benjy at the controls and 'Lolita' (to use her air display name) on the top wing, a petite figure waving to the crowd with one hand while a pair of false pigtails trail in the wind (on one occasion one of these blew away to the consternation of the ticket-paying public below).

What a remarkable way to spend one's leisure hours, entertaining the public in this way, for it should be remembered that, unlike those who took part in the Cobham shows of nearly thirty years before, the Tiger Club members are businessmen, solicitors, doctors and, with very few exceptions, only week-end pilots. By any standards the Tiger Club's air displays reach a level of perfection usually associated with professional entertainment. Each member has his function whether on the ground or in the air. The display committee keep the programme running to a strict time-table and something is always in the air to capture the public's attention. The Tiger Club has become the Mecca of flying enthusiasts the world over, and hardly a week-end goes by without a visitor from South African flying circles, or Switzerland, Norway and even some of the Iron Curtain countries. An amazing club with an amazing spirit inspired by an equally amazing aeroplane, for although there are now Jodels and Stampes and Condors at the club, the Tiger is strongly evident and was the inspiration behind it all.

With SOW hitting the headlines and appearing on both silver screen and its little rival it would be reasonable to expect interest to gradually decline, but G-ARAZ and its 'standing-room-only' passenger was to cause something of a sensation in the popular Press yet again. Most of us have ambitions of one kind or another; fairly common is the desire to be first—the first to climb a mountain, the first to play the piano non-stop for forty-eight hours or more, etc. To Barry Griffiths of the Tiger Club must go the distinction of originating a most unusual and decidedly imaginative 'first' when he put forward the proposal that someone should cross the Channel standing on the top of RAZ, since it had never been done before.

Possibly the germ of the idea emanated from the girl who eventually made the trip. Her name is Allanah Campbell and she came to England from Hamilton, Ontario, in 1959. She had not flown when living in her native Canada and the aeroplane never particularly took her interest until a chance meeting with some of the 'aviation set' who introduced her to the Tiger Club. The Benjamins had for some years perfected their very polished SOW demonstration, but Norman Jones felt that there should be an understudy to relieve 'Lolita' on days when she felt that a change was as good as a rest. Allanah so enjoyed the exhilaration of standing on the top wing of RAZ that she expressed a wish to do a longer flight than the usual back and forth over the spectators. When Griffiths suggested a cross-Channel trip the idea was accepted with enthusiasm. Denis Hartas, a B.E.A. Senior First Officer, had been involved in the plan from the beginning and it was decided that he should fly the Tiger. The Ministry of Aviation, so often accused of stifling private and sporting aviation, were approached for permission to carry out the unorthodox venture—they were most co-operative and readily agreed.

The flight was provisionally arranged for Sunday 4th August 1963, but strong winds and heavy rain led to a postponement. The following Sunday was, if not ideal, certainly much better in that visibility was good and although accompanied by scattered showers and gusty winds the general outlook showed little risk of a deterioration in the weather. And so at 1.30 p.m. Sunday 11th August 1963 G-ARAZ left Redhill aerodrome for Lympne, there to clear customs before the flight to France. During this part of the journey Allanah sat in the front cockpit. Mindful of the publicity value of such events, the Tiger was accompanied by the club's Piper Super Cub flown by Ian Trethewey with a camera-laden Barry Griffiths in the back seat. A bumpy thirty minutes and the party landed at Lympne for a quick lunch and customs clearance. Thirty-knot headwinds were reported *en route* and Hartas decided to fill the Tiger's tank; with the added weight of Allanah's protective clothing and all the safety equipment RAZ must have been near its maximum permissible weight.

Allanah Campbell took her place on the top wing and, with the exception of one or two amateur photographers, the send off from Lympne was a dispassionate affair with the airport staff displaying an air of polite indifference. The wind direction precluded use of the longest run and Hartas was confronted with an uphill take-off towards some disturbingly high trees which called for prompt evasive action immediately after leaving the ground. Electric intercom. provided for the trip worked rather intermittently and there was an uncomfortable moment during the climb when 'Allanah seemed to be saying that something had come adrift' although she was later able to explain that the cause of her alarm was a small piece of safety chain not noticed by her on previous flights.

The flight across the Channel at a pre-arranged 1,000 ft. was an uneventful but nevertheless exhilarating experience for Allanah. For no more than five minutes they were out of sight of land although the Super Cub continued to keep company. There were also numerous ships below—good for the morale of a pilot over water with only one engine. At one time they passed some 500 ft. below a Bristol freighter flying in the opposite direction and wonder to this day what its crew must have thought of the Tiger Moth and its upstanding (and outstanding) passenger. The crossing made, Hartas turned starboard and followed the French coast towards his destination. Even at full throttle the addition of a full-length figure on the top wing so damaged the Tiger's performance that an airspeed of 65–70 m.p.h. was all it could attain. Now heading into wind, ground speed dropped to a miserable 35–40 m.p.h. and the thirty odd miles to Berck was to take nearly forty-five minutes. Excited crowds on the beaches kept Allanah busy waving. They were used to the Mad English crossing the Channel in anything from a waterproofed motor-car to a tin bath, but this was really different.

Strong wind and additional drag cut the landing run at Berck to a mere fifteen yards. By now Allanah was tired and cold for she had been out on the wing for an hour and a quarter since leaving Lympne, but the Tiger Club is well known at Berck and both airport officials and local club members gave the little party a rousing welcome. Although RAZ had been at nearly full throttle throughout the flight and poor engine cooling must have resulted from the low airspeed, G-ARAZ never missed a beat and behaved in true Tiger Moth tradition.

If the French airport authorities showed more enthusiasm for the enterprise than their opposite numbers in Britain, it is nevertheless interesting to note that permission for a SOW take-off was refused at Berck and Miss Campbell was made to sit in the front cockpit for the non-stop return journey which terminated at Biggin Hill. Of course the newspapers were there in force and the story was blazoned across the headlines. 'ALLANAH FLIES THE CHANNEL ON A WING,' said the *Daily Mirror* of Monday 12th August. 'GIRL FLIES THE CHANNEL—ON TOP OF A PLANE,' proclaimed the *Daily Sketch* in even bigger type, and the following day the same paper carried on the story, 'When you read about the year's oddest Channel passenger, did you ask . . . IS THE GIRL MAD?'

Whatever readers of the *Daily Sketch* may have asked themselves, readers of *The Tiger Moth Story* can be assured that Allanah Campbell is a quiet, level-headed Canadian and anything but mad. Furthermore the project was organized with much care and a lot of thought. The intercom. between pilot and passenger has already been mentioned; Campbell and Hartas wore life jackets; an emergency drill was practised whereby Allanah could leave the rig and climb down to the front cockpit and a safety rope was attached to her for the purpose. The above-wing position was considered impossible for parachute use and so none was carried.

It was one of the Tiger Moth's more unusual ventures but a genuine 'first' nevertheless.

It is now many years since the flying-boat or seaplane took its place on the air routes of the world and while many quite rightly lament the passing of these exciting aircraft the modern airliners' dependence upon radio aids, particularly when landing under instrument conditions, is but one factor amongst others that have sealed the fate of water-based aircraft as a means of public transport. There are, of course, certain operations which can only be handled by the small float plane and such countries as Canada and Alaska make full use of them on the lakes which form natural landing grounds in places otherwise inaccessible to landplanes.

In 1960 Air Commodore G.J.C. Paul, C.B., D.F.C., R.A.F. (ret.), found that if he wished to obtain a seaplane endorsement on his pilot's licence the nearest place he could go for the necessary experience was Norway, all seaplane flying having stopped in this and many other countries. The matter may well have rested there but it so happens that Air Commodore Paul is Secretary-General of the Air League of The British Empire and a dedicated sporting pilot and private owner. It was not difficult to find others with a feeling of nostalgia for the seaplane and a meeting of the interested parties took place on 18th November 1960 under the chairmanship of J. Lankester Parker, the veteran seaplane and flying-boat pilot who was for many years Chief Test Pilot for Short Bros. The possibility of forming a seaplane club was discussed, a far more complex matter than the setting-up of a land-based flying club. A suitable location for seaplanes is less easy to find than first thoughts may lead one to believe. Eventually the Lee-on-the-Solent area was chosen as providing a stretch of water within reasonable access of potential members. There was also the advantage that the area abounds in sailing activity and the small boat enthusiasts could no doubt be prevailed upon to pass on the benefit of their considerable maritime experience. One of the founders of the Seaplane Club is Dr. Reginald Bennett, Member of Parliament for the district and Commodore of the Lee-on-the-Solent Sailing Club, where members of the Seaplane Club enjoy membership privileges. The Admiralty was most helpful during the formative stages of the new club, support coming from the Commander-in-Chief, Royal Navy, Portsmouth; Flag Officer Air (Home), Lee-on-the-Solent; and Captain, H.M.S. *Ariel* (possibly better known as R.N. Air Station, Lee-on-Solent).

Marshal of the Royal Air Force, Lord Douglas of Kirtleside became President of the club and very soon, largely through his efforts, financial assistance was forthcoming from such famous names as Oswald Short (the pioneer flying-boat and seaplane constructor), Esso Petroleum Co., The British Aircraft Corporation, Short Brothers and Harland Ltd., Rolls-Royce Ltd., Castrol Ltd., The Hawker Siddeley Aircraft Company Ltd., and the then independent de Havilland Aircraft Co. Ltd. The Air League of the British Empire also contributed and there were many other individual donations.

Since no seaplane existed in Britain at that time, arrangements were made to fit an existing landplane with floats. During the early days of the project Norman Jones had with his usual generosity promised to give the infant club a suitable aeroplane, and when the time came he duly presented Tiger Moth G-AIVW. It holds the distinction of being the only one of its breed ever to win the King's Cup Air Race, which it did in the hands of Jim Denyer at an average speed of 118.5 m.p.h. during the 1958 event. It was of course a landplane at the time.

Rollason Aircraft and Engines Ltd. undertook the conversion at Croydon. The Tiger Moth was no stranger to life afloat, for back in 1931 two of the early DH 82 examples had been ordered as seaplanes by the Air Ministry and most of the Queen Bees had been fitted with floats. Nevertheless all this was a long time ago and since, in Britain at any rate, seaplane operation was a lost art the dusty archives had to be consulted. In their search for the long forgotten but very necessary float conversion drawings de Havillands of both Hatfield and Canada proved invaluable.

Mr. J. Rose of Vickers-Armstrongs Ltd. was elected honorary engineer to the Seaplane Club, and Mr. J. P. Hennessy took on the task of producing the float struts that were to replace the Tiger's undercarriage. A pair of floats was obtained from an Aeronca Sedan aircraft that had belonged to Dr. Michael Moore, and soon the conversion was going ahead under the direction of R. F. Thomson, Rollason's General Manager. With the increase in both weight and drag that follows the conversion from wheels to floats, a 145 h.p. Gipsy Major X engine fitted with a fine pitch propeller was substituted for the original 130 h.p. unit. Prop-swinging whilst balancing on one float is not a healthy occupation these days and neither was it considered so during the Queen Bee period, for they were brought to life with the aid of a handle-operated Eclipse mechanical starter. G-AIVW went one better with an electric starter.

Even with the advantages of a free aeroplane costs were beginning to mount up. The floats cost £500 second-hand (£1,500 new!), the conversion £300 while a further £500 went on essential fire and rescue equipment and a speed-boat.

There was the additional difficulty of finding someone to fly G-AIVW since there were no qualified seaplane pilots in the country; this was overcome by the Ministry of Aviation granting special, if restricted, dispensation to a small number of pilots, and in September 1963 Sea Tiger G-AIVW was named 'Oswald Short' and club flying was in progress.

The 'Sea Tiger' is launched down the slipway on a special cradle. Shortly before entering the water the engine is started and the seaplane moves forward gradually submerging the cradle until, fully afloat, she taxis clear and the cradle is drawn back out of the water. The Sea Tiger handles well on the water and the sea rudders positioned at the stern of each float are able to turn the machine through complete circles of no more than 30 ft. radius provided the wind strength is not in excess of twelve knots. A control in the cockpit raises the water rudders—since they are interconnected to the main rudder and cause an unpleasant yaw effect in the air it is usual to take-off with them retracted. In conditions of flat calm water and no wind the Sea Tiger takes fifteen to twenty seconds to leave the surface. An eight-knot wind and small waves is considered ideal, reducing the take-off to twelve seconds. Lift off occurs at forty-two knots. For a seaplane of relatively low power 'Oswald Short' climbs well at a respectable 750 ft./min. The addition of floats has substantially altered the feel of the aeroplane in the air as it cruises along at seventy knots or so.

The Seaplane Club is now under the management of Tom Freer, who replaced the late C. Neapean Bishop, affectionately known as "Bish".

And so the enterprise and initiative shown by the Seaplane Club brings us in an almost full circle to the beginning of the Tiger when more than thirty years before two of its distant predecessors were fitted with floats. It has been a long story embracing many activities quite outside the realm of flying training, the purpose for which it was originally designed. It is a story of contradictions dealing with a little aeroplane that didn't really handle particularly well but was fun to fly, never really broke any records yet outlived all competitors in the field, in many ways led a dull and routine life yet was part and parcel of some of the most colourful aviation activities that occurred before, during and after the war—and in many cases was the inspiration behind these activities. The Tiger Moth has been part of the lives of many people of different nationalities; the engineers and fitters who built them in widely dispersed Australia, Portugal, Canada, England, Norway, New Zealand and Sweden; the legions who kept them airworthy on airfields situated in France, South Africa, Persia, India, China and countries far too numerous to mention; the civil club instructors and their pupils; the countless thousands of war trained pilots whose first attempts to fly were made on the little biplane. The Tiger's friends could populate a city and it is perhaps its biggest success that it made few enemies.

Of the 8,800-odd Tiger Moths built since 1931 probably not more than 250 exist today and these are scattered throughout the world. It is of course inevitable that its numbers will diminish year by year until at some time in the future, and it is hoped the very distant future, the few remaining machines will spend their lives in museums apart from perhaps one or two pampered examples in flying condition. Opportunities to fly the Tiger will, as a matter of course, become few, and many pilots of the younger generation will no doubt ask, 'What was it like to fly?' Different pilots are sensitive to different flying characteristics according to temperament and experience, but to the authors at least the name 'Tiger Moth' will always convey the following impressions:

Flying kit is a must except on the hottest days, so Irving jacket, gloves and flying helmet are donned in preparation for a trip in G-ACDC, the oldest DH 82a Tiger of them all, now completely rebuilt after its last ordeal and looking for all the world like a new aeroplane in its original colour-scheme, red fuselage and silver wings.

Getting in is no trouble, easier in fact than some modern aircraft, but the safety harness can be a nuisance: always helps to drape the two shoulder straps over the cockpit sides before climbing aboard. The wings rock gently to each pull of the propeller as the engine is turned over by the prop. swinger. Wonder if she will start first go? Gipsy Majors are quite easy to start when cold—hot engine can be difficult but not when you know it well. 'Contact'—up with the front switch only. This controls the retarded impulse starter, its 'click, click' audible from the rear cockpit as the willing help pulls the prop. over each compression. Sometimes the vital 'click' is absent and the offending magneto must be hit with a spanner or a loose stone. Click! Click! Click! And with a sudden release of inner power the engine fires—quick, up with the other ignition switch—mustn't let it stop.

Local trip this, so set the altimeter to zero, oil pressure O.K. and Turn and Slip indicator pointing 'North and South'. Controls have full and free movement except the rudder which hardly moves at all while we are stationary because it is linked to the tail skid.

Must lock the slats before taxiing—can't have them hammering in and out as we roll over the rough ground near the signals area.

A wave of the hand and the chocks are whipped away

from before the wheels. Burst of power to start her rolling
—not too fast, remember no brakes and practically no forward vision. What a beautiful undercarriage!—no motor-
car could ride over the field like this. Tail skid steers the
Tiger well on a calm day—not so good in a strong wind. If
she refuses to go round in one direction we must do a 360
the other way. On concrete she can be impossible.

Vital actions before take-off, a recitation learned by every
conscientious pilot:

'Trim for take-off' (move the trimmer half-way along its
quadrant, a curved bar of closely spaced holes).
'Tighten throttle nut'.
'Mixture rich' (some Tigers no longer have the little lever
next to the throttle, others sometimes have it wired back to
stop meddling pupils damaging the engine).
'Pitch, not applicable'.
'Fuel on and sufficient for flight' (the little blob-on-the-
end-of-a-stick is at the top of the fuel gauge—must be full!)
'Free slats' (forward with the lever on the right-hand side
of the rear cockpit only).

All doors are closed, the harness is secured and nothing is
coming in to land, so on to the grass strip without delay.
Let it roll forward a little to straighten the tail skid and
find a distant tree along the left of the nose on which to
keep straight. Seems to be yards of aeroplane in front—how
different to the Bolkow Junior where the engine is almost
in your lap!

All set for take-off, so open the throttle, 'smoothly and
fully'; gets a bit stiff during the last inch or so of movement
as the cold air intake opens. How quickly the tail comes up.
Touch of left rudder and she runs as straight as a train—
funny how pupils over control on the rudder bar: some
try to run it off the ground with their feet. What a marvellous undercarriage this is—speed building up—she wants
to fly—little backward pressure on the stick and off she
comes!

Let the speed build up, 55–60–65 m.p.h., and now into
the climb. Several hundred feet on the clock as the far

boundary of the airfield slips below and the throttle is inched back to take the strain of the engine. 1,000 ft.–1,200–1,500, rate of climb not bad at these heights, 2,000 ft., time to level out so ease the stick forward—85 m.p.h. coming up —reduce power to 1,950 r.p.m. Forward on the tail-trim just a little—now take hands and feet off the controls— flies like a bird—who wants an auto-pilot!

Draughty old brute. Goggles are an absolute must in the back cockpit although you can well manage without them in the front.

Must turn left—all clear behind so give her a little left aileron and a fair amount of rudder, quite a lot by modern standards but the Tiger really needs its rudder. Let's have a look below—little more bank (and more rudder)—getting quite steep now so open the throttle and come back on the stick in case the nose drops into a spiral dive. With one of the centre bracing wires flat on the horizon she pivots on her wing tip like a ballerina. Enough 'g' can be pulled to black out if you really try but there is no fear of breaking the Tiger—what a feeling of rigid security!

All clear below for a stall so close the throttle right back; no carburettor icing because she automatically goes into 'warm air'. Now hold the nose up and let the airspeed decrease (what a hateful expression that is—'airspeed dropping off'). The ailerons really do feel sluggish and the slats are beginning to open, clawing for air as they fight to keep us flying. Sixty–50–45 m.p.h.—there she goes, a gentle nod of the nose and not the slightest attempt to drop a wing. Even with the slats locked most Tigers stall wings level and flying instructors have to cheat a little to demonstrate the full recovery.

What next?—oh yes, a spin, but a bit more height first. Nothing loose in the cockpit, straps good and tight and now lock the slats—must always do this before spins or aerobatics. All clear below so back with the throttle—'pop, pop': the old Gipsy makes the same comment whenever the throttle is shut. Hold up the nose just a little—height 3,250 ft., airspeed 80–75–70–60–50 now—full left rudder and right back with the stick—woosh, down goes the left wing and the nose drops to reveal spinning fields. Looking out towards the horizon it is easy to count the turns as we whisk around at an incredible rate. How the Tiger has changed! No longer a docile little aeroplane, it now lashes its tail as we spin towards the ground—once—twice three turns; must recover—full right rudder in opposition to spin and ease the stick forward until, suddenly, the spinning stops. No time for surprise; centralize the rudder before it spins the other way—now gently back with the stick and pull out of the dive—gently or we may easily black out. The nose on the horizon at last and we have lost more than 1,000 ft., but the Tiger has withdrawn its claws and its tail is still as it purrs along.

Aerobatics are fun in a Tiger with loops, stall turns and barrel rolls well within the capabilities of most pilots; but the slow roll—that's a rather different matter. Strange how few pilots can do a really good slow roll in a Tiger these days—even flying instructors.

It helps keep the nose up while inverted if we trim nose heavy before starting the roll. Now a gentle dive to build up speed, 90–100–110 m.p.h., then back with the stick until the nose is just above the horizon—hold it steady, now roll —stick to the left (those heavy ailerons) and a touch of left rudder—over we go—steeply banked—on our side—wings going past the vertical, so must change to right rudder before the nose swings—start getting the stick forward— we're upside down!—close the throttle but keep her rolling. Round we go nearly on our side again—stick back a bit or we shall do one of those horrible outside steep turns, bags of top rudder as it rolls through the last quarter— power on again and the wings are level once more—phew! hard work but a sense of achievement. No wonder they say 'if you can roll a Tiger, you can roll anything.'

Time for a landing and a well earned cup of tea. The airfield looks inviting as we turn on to the base leg. Pick the right moment—now—close the throttle. speed settled at 65 m.p.h. as we go into the glide with the trimmer practically as far back as it will go. Not much wind today and since the approach may be a little too high, what better than a slipping turn to lose height, with a blast of air on the left cheek as we come down like a lift—'flaps?' asks the Tiger, 'what are flaps?'

Only a few hundred yards to reach the airfield with the engine pop-popping and the wires humming. The ground comes up to meet us, at first a slow moving sea of green, now a deeply piled carpet with blades of grass becoming discernable—must check the descent—now. A small back pressure on the stick and we glide almost silently a few feet from the ground, a silence broken by the ever present 'pop, pop' of the throttled Gipsy and the declining hiss of the airstream as we lose speed. This is the tricky part for Tiger Moth elevators are sensitive to the end; back with the stick, back with the stick—back—back—back, and with a gentle rumble wheels and tailskid run along the ground, wings rocking to each uneven patch of airfield.

The flight is over but others will soon begin. What could be nicer than a Tiger on a hot summer's day?

As we taxi towards the clubhouse and park between a Turbulent and a brightly painted Comanche, a small crowd collects. Some are young people, others not so young, and as they gather round the little biplane with its red fuselage and silver wings, it radiates an unmistakable air of self-assurance, as well it might for G-ACDC was an old hand before many of the onlookers were born.

The events of the past lead into the present, the chance arrival of a Tiger one summer's day at an airfield near London, an arrival which prompted *The Tiger Moth Story*. But it cannot end here for it is a living story, one that continues every day at airfields all over the world, and who knows what the Tiger Moth may do in the future?

*Another cabin version was G-AHVV owned by Mr. and Mrs. C. M. Roberts who made several modifications—canopies over each cockpit, cabin heater, wheel brakes, extra tankage for six hours flying, an anti-collision beacon and a red and silver finish with "Teeny Weeny Airlines" painted on the cowling. They flew some 1,500 hours in "VV", including flights over the Alps at 16,000 feet.

Appendices

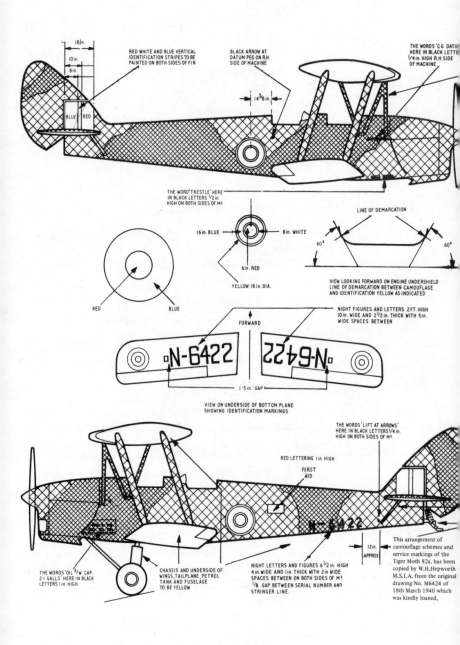

RED WHITE AND BLUE VERTICAL IDENTIFICATION STRIPES TO BE PAINTED ON BOTH SIDES OF FIN

18in.

10in.

8in.

BLUE   RED

BLACK ARROW AT DATUM PEG ON R.H. SIDE OF MACHINE

THE WORDS 'C G DATUM' HERE IN BLACK LETTE 1/4 in. HIGH R.H. SIDE OF MACHINE

14 3/8 in.

THE WORD 'TRESTLE' HERE IN BLACK LETTERS 1/2 in. HIGH ON BOTH SIDES OF Mc

16 in. BLUE   8 in. WHITE

6 in. RED

YELLOW 18 in. DIA.

LINE OF DEMARCATION

60°   60°

VIEW LOOKING FORWARD ON ENGINE UNDERSHIELD LINE OF DEMARCATION BETWEEN CAMOUFLAGE AND IDENTIFICATION YELLOW AS INDICATED

RED   BLUE

FORWARD

NIGHT FIGURES AND LETTERS 2 FT. HIGH 10 in. WIDE AND 2 1/2 in. THICK WITH 5 in. WIDE SPACES BETWEEN

N-6422   ZZ49-N

1·5 in. GAP

VIEW ON UNDERSIDE OF BOTTOM PLANE SHOWING IDENTIFICATION MARKINGS

THE WORDS 'LIFT AT ARROWS' HERE IN BLACK LETTERS 1/4 in. HIGH ON BOTH SIDES OF Mc

RED LETTERING 1 in. HIGH

FIRST AID

N-6422

12 in. APPROX

THE WORDS 'OIL 3/w CAP 2·1 GALLS' HERE IN BLACK LETTERS 1 in. HIGH

CHASSIS AND UNDERSIDE OF WINGS, TAILPLANE, PETROL TANK AND FUSELAGE TO BE YELLOW

NIGHT LETTERS AND FIGURES 6 1/2 in. HIGH 4 in. WIDE AND 1 in. THICK WITH 2 in. WIDE SPACES BETWEEN ON BOTH SIDES OF Mc 1/8 in. GAP BETWEEN SERIAL NUMBER AND STRINGER LINE.

This arrangement of camouflage schemes and service markings of the Tiger Moth 82a, has been copied by W.H.Hepworth M.S.I.A, from the original drawing No. M6424 of 18th March 1940 which was kindly loaned,

And they lived to fly again! The 'Canon' is spinning only two feet from the ground. Lewis Benjamin was flying within two weeks—the Tiger was indisposed rather longer.

Tigers in disguise. Altered by Film Aviation Services Ltd., these very realistic Rumpler CIV replicas were used in the film *Lawrence of Arabia*.

Captain John Crewdson in Jordan with one of the 'Rumplers'.

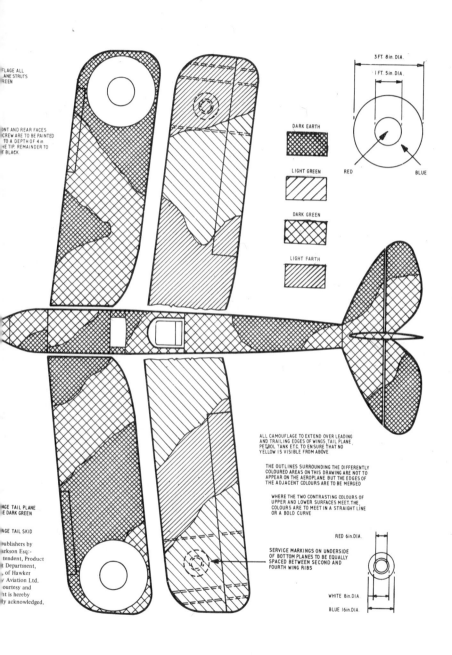

...FLAGE ALL
...ANE STRUTS
...REEN

...NT AND REAR FACES
...CREW ARE TO BE PAINTED
...TO A DEPTH OF 4in
...HE TIP. REMAINDER TO
...BLACK

DARK EARTH

LIGHT GREEN

DARK GREEN

LIGHT EARTH

3 FT. 8in. DIA.

1 FT. 5in. DIA.

RED

BLUE

...AGE TAIL PLANE
...E DARK GREEN

...AGE TAIL SKID

...ublishers by
...arkson Esq:-
...tendent, Product
...t Department,
..., of Hawker
...y Aviation Ltd.
...ourtesy and
...t is hereby
...ly acknowledged,

ALL CAMOUFLAGE TO EXTEND OVER LEADING
AND TRAILING EDGES OF WINGS, TAIL PLANE,
PETROL TANK ETC. TO ENSURE THAT NO
YELLOW IS VISIBLE FROM ABOVE

THE OUTLINES SURROUNDING THE DIFFERENTLY
COLOURED AREAS ON THIS DRAWING ARE NOT TO
APPEAR ON THE AEROPLANE BUT THE EDGES OF
THE ADJACENT COLOURS ARE TO BE MERGED

WHERE THE TWO CONTRASTING COLOURS OF
UPPER AND LOWER SURFACES MEET, THE
COLOURS ARE TO MEET IN A STRAIGHT LINE
OR A BOLD CURVE

RED 6in. DIA.

SERVICE MARKINGS ON UNDERSIDE
OF BOTTOM PLANES TO BE EQUALLY
SPACED BETWEEN SECOND AND
FOURTH WING RIBS

WHITE 8in. DIA.

BLUE 16in. DIA.

DH 82a Tiger Moth to scale

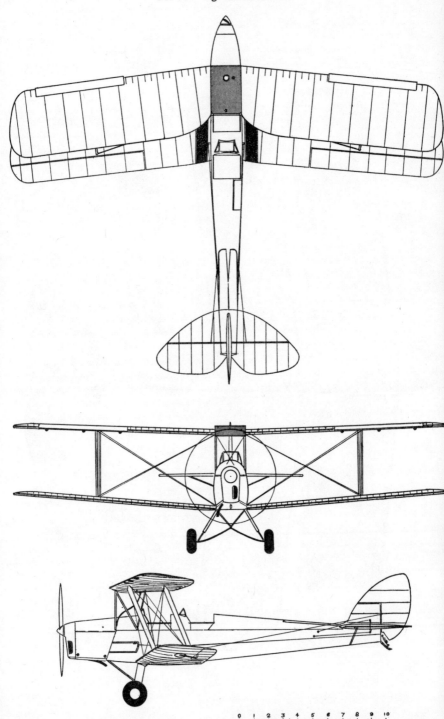

0 1 2 3 4 5 6 7 8 9 10

LEADING PARTICULARS OF DH 82a TIGER MOTH

Principal Dimensions

Span	29 ft. 4 in.
Length overall	23 ft. 11 in.
Height overall	8 ft. 9½ in.

Main Plane

Chord both wings	4 ft. 4⅜ in.
Incidence both wings	4°
Dihedral: Top wing	2° 45′
Bottom wing	4° 30′
Stagger measured at root	1 ft. 10 in.
Stagger measured at interplane strut	1 ft. 8.7 in.
Sweepback at interplane strut: Top wing	11 in.
Bottom wing	9⅛ in.

Tail Plane

Span	9 ft. 10 in.
Incidence	0°

Areas

Mainplanes, including ailerons	239 sq. ft.
Ailerons	22.4 sq. ft.
Tailplane, including elevators	27.2 sq. ft.
Fin and Rudder	12.2 sq. ft.

Undercarriage

Track	5 ft. 3 in.
Shock Absorber legs	Steel Spring
Wheels: Type	A. H. 10022 Dunlop or 833 Palmer
Size	7½ in. × 4·75 in.
Pressure	12–15 lb./sq. in.

Tank Capacities

Fuel	19 galls.
Oil	2·1 galls.

Maximum All-up Weight.

1,825 lbs.

Performance at 1,650 lbs.

Maximum speed at sea level	105–110 m.p.h. (91–95 knots)
Normal cruising speed	85–90 m.p.h. (74–78 knots.)
Climbing and gliding speed	65 m.p.h. (56 knots.)
Stalling speed (indicated)	45 m.p.h.
Rate of climb at sea level	800 ft./min.
Service ceiling (100 ft./min.)	15,800 ft.

TIGER MOTH EQUIPPED SERVICE AND RESERVE FLYING SCHOOLS 1937–54

Pre-war Elementary and Reserve Flying Training Schools at August 1939

Unit	Aerodrome	Contractor
1	Hatfield	de Havilland Aircraft Co. Ltd.
2	Filton	Bristol Aeroplane Co. Ltd.
3	Hamble	Air Service Training Ltd.
4	Brough	Blackburn Aircraft Ltd.
5	Hanworth Park	Flying Training Ltd.
6	Sywell	Brooklands Aviation Ltd.
7	Desford	Reid & Sigrist Ltd.
8*	Woodley	Phillip & Powis Ltd. (later Miles)
9	Ansty	Air Service Training Ltd.
10*	Yatesbury	Bristol Aeroplane Co. Ltd.
11	Perth	Airwork Ltd.
12	Prestwick	Scottish Aviation Ltd.
13*	White Waltham	de Havilland Aircraft Co. Ltd.
14	Castle Bromwich	Airwork Ltd.
15	Redhill	British Air Transport Ltd.
16	Shoreham	Martin's School of Air Navigation
17*	Manchester (Barton)	Airwork Ltd.
18	Fair Oaks	Universal Flying Services Ltd.
19*	Gatwick	Airwork Ltd.
20*	Gravesend	Airports Ltd.
21*	Stapleford Abbots	Reid & Sigrist Ltd.
22	Cambridge	Marshalls Ltd.
23*	Rochester	Short Bros. Ltd.
24	Belfast (Sydenham)	Short Bros. Ltd.
25*	Grimsby	Herts & Essex Aero Club Ltd.
26*	Oxford	Marshalls Ltd.
27*	Nottingham (Tollerton)	Nottingham Airports Ltd.
28*	Stoke-on-Trent (Meir)	Reid & Sigrist Ltd.
29*	Luton	Birkett Air Service Ltd.
30*	Derby	Air Schools Ltd.
31*	Gloucester & Cheltenham	Airwork Ltd.
32*	West Hartlepool	Portsmouth, Southsea and Isle of Wight Aviation Ltd.
33*	Bristol (Whitchurch)	Chamier Gilbert Lodge & Co. Ltd.
34*	Southend-on-Sea	Air Hire Ltd.
35*	Grangemouth	Airwork Ltd.
43*	Newcastle	Newcastle-on-Tyne Aero Club.
44*	Birmingham (Elmdon)	Airwork Ltd.

* Schools closed on outbreak of war.

Wartime Elementary Flying Training Schools within the Empire Training Scheme

GREAT BRITAIN

Name of Unit and Location	Formation, Disbandment	Remarks
1 E.F.T.S. Stag Lane Hatfield 1930 Panshangar 7.9.42	1. 5.23 ———	Trained Army Pilots.
2 E.F.T.S. Filton Staverton 3.8.40	28. 5.23 1.11.41	Renamed 6(S)F.I.S. Nov. '41
Re-formed Worcester Yatesbury 9.7.45	22. 7.42 ———	
3 E.F.T.S. Hamble Watchfield 20.7.40 Shellingford 17.12.41	31. 7.23 ———	
4 E.F.T.S. Brough	21. 5.24 ———	
5 E.F.T.S. Hanworth Meir 17.6.40	10. 6.35 23.12.41	
6 E.F.T.S. Sywell	10. 6.35 ———	
7 E.F.T.S. Desford	25.11.35 ———	
8 E.F.T.S. Woodley	25. 1.35 15.10.42	Became 10 F.I.S.(E)
9 E.F.T.S. Ansty	6. 1.36 31. 3.44	
10 E.F.T.S. Yatesbury Weston-super-Mare 7.9.40 Stoke Orchard 20.7.41	6. 1.36 21. 7.42	
11 E.F.T.S. Perth	27. 1.36 18. 3.47	
12 E.F.T.S. Prestwick	17. 2.36 22. 3.41	

201

Name of Unit and Location	Formation, Disbandment	Remarks
13 E.F.T.S. White Waltham Peterborough Dec. 40	18.11.35 1. 6.41	Became 21 E.F.T.S. at Booker.
14 E.F.T.S. Castle Bromwich Elmdon 9.9.39	1. 7.37 1. 5.42	
15 E.F.T.S. Redhill Carlisle 2.6.40	1. 7.37 ———	Trained Poles.
16 E.F.T.S. Shoreham	1. 7.37 1. 9.39	
Re-formed Derby	10. 4.40 ———	Formerly 30 E.F.T.S.
17 E.F.T.S. Barton	1.10.37 1. 9.39	
Re-formed North Luffenham Peterborough 15.7.41	18. 1.41 1. 6.42	
18 E.F.T.S. Fair Oaks	1.10.37 ———	
19 E.F.T.S. Gatwick	1.10.37 1. 9.39	
Re-formed Sealand	10. 2.41 27.12.41	
20 E.F.T.S. Gravesend	1.10.37 1. 9.39	
Re-formed Yeadon	17. 3.41 3. 1.42	
21 E.F.T.S. Stapleford Tawney	1. 1.38 1. 9.39	
Re-formed Booker	1. 6.41 ———	Formerly 13 E.F.T.S. Trained Army Pilots.
22 E.F.T.S. Cambridge	1. 2.38 ———	Also F.I.S.(E)

Name of Unit and Location	Formation, Disbandment	Remarks
24 E.F.T.S. Belfast Luton 22.7.40 Sealand 7.2.42	1. 1.39	
25 E.F.T.S. Grimsby	24. 6.38 1. 9.39	
Re-formed Peterborough Hucknall 14.7.41	9. 6.41	Formerly 1 F.T.S. (Polish)
26 E.F.T.S. Oxford	24. 6.38 1. 9.39	
Re-formed Theale	20. 8.41 9. 7.45	Later pre-F.I.S.
28 E.F.T.S. Meir	1. 8.38 1. 9.39	
Re-formed Wolverhampton	15. 9.41	Trained Turks.
29 E.F.T.S. Luton	1. 8.38 1. 9.39	
Re-formed Cliffe Pypard	15. 9.41	Trained Fleet Air Arm Pilots.
30 E.F.T.S. Derby	20. 9.28 10. 4.40	Renumbered 16 E.F.T.S.

CANADA

No. of School and Location	Formation, Disbandment	Remarks
1 E.F.T.S. Malton, Ont.	—— 3. 7.42	Tiger Moths replaced Fleet Finches 20.3.41.
2 E.F.T.S. Fort William, Ont.	24. 6.40 31. 5.44	Used Tiger Moths only.
4 E.F.T.S. Windsor Mills, P.Q.	—— 25. 8.44	Tiger Moths replaced Fleet Finches 7.6.42.
5 E.F.T.S. Lethbridge, Alta. High River, Alta.	22. 7.40 30.11.40	Moved to High River June 1941. Converted to Cornells Nov. 1942.
6 E.F.T.S. Prince Albert, Sask.	22. 7.40 15.11.44	Converted to Cornells April 1944. Last Tiger Moth left June 1944.
7 E.F.T.S. Windsor, Ont.	—— 31.10.44	Tiger Moths replaced Fleet Finches May 1942. Converted to Cornells Oct. 1943.
8 E.F.T.S. Vancouver	23. 7.40 2. 1.42	Used Tiger Moths until airfield required for operational purposes.
9 E.F.T.S. St. Catherines, Ont.	—— 14. 1.44	Tiger Moths replaced Fleet Finches March, 1942
10 E.F.T.S. Mount Hope & Pendleton, Ont.	—— 15. 9.45	Tiger Moths replaced Fleet Finches Nov. 1941. Moved to Pendleton Aug. 1942. Converted to Cornells June 1944.
12 E.F.T.S. Goderich, Ont.	—— 14. 7.44	Tiger Moths replaced Fleet Finches Mar. 1942.
14 E.F.T.S. Winnipeg & Portage la Prairie, Man.	17.10.40 30. 6.42	Used Tiger Moths throughout.
15 E.F.T.S. Regina, Sask.	11.11.40 11. 8.44	Opened with Tiger Moths. Converted to Cornells June 1943.
16 E.F.T.S. Edmonton, Alta.	1.12.40 17. 7.42	Used Tiger Moths only.
17 E.F.T.S. Stanley, N.S.	—— 14. 1.44	Tiger Moths replaced Fleet Finches Aug. 1943.
18 E.F.T.S. Boundary Bay, B.C.	10. 4.41 6. 6.42	Used Tiger Moths only. Later absorbed 8 E.F.T.S.

No. of School and Location	Formation, Disbandment	Remarks
19 E.F.T.S. Vinden, Man.	16. 5.41 15.11.44	Opened with Tiger Moths. Converted to Cornells Oct. 1943 but kept one Tiger until Oct. 1944.
20 E.F.T.S. Oshawa, Ont.	1. 6.41 15.12.44	Opened with Finches and Tiger Moths but by 31 Oct. only 2 Finches left as against 64 Tigers. Converted to Cornells May 1944.
25 E.F.T.S. (R.A.F.) Assiniboia, Sask.	1. 2.44 21. 8.44	See 34 E.F.T.S.
26 E.F.T.S. (R.A.F.) Neepawa, Man.	1. 2.44 26. 8.44	See 35 E.F.T.S.
31 E.F.T.S. (R.A.F.) Calgary & DeWinton, Alta.	10. 5.41 25. 9.44	Moved to DeWinton 16 Oct. 1941. Flew Tiger Moths and P.T.-27's until March 1943 when latter retired. Converted to Cornells April 1943.
32 E.F.T.S. (R.A.F.) Swift Current, Sask. & Bowden, Alta.	2. 6.41 15. 9.44	Opened with Tiger Moths. Moved to Bowden 27 Nov. 1941. Converted to Cornells April 1943.
33 E.F.T.S. (R.A.F.) Coron, Sask.	9. 1.42 14. 1.44	Opened with Tiger Moths. Converted to Cornells Jan. 1943.
34 E.F.T.S. (R.A.F.) Assiniboia, Sask.	2. 2.42 21. 8.44	Opened with Tiger Moths. Converted to Cornells Feb. 1943. Redesignated 25 E.F.T.S. 1 Feb. 1944.
35 E.F.T.S. (R.A.F.) Neepawa, Sask.	Mar. 1942 26. 8.44	Used Tiger Moths throughout but received 2 Cornells Dec. 1943. Redesignated 26 E.F.T.S. 1 Feb. 1944.
36 E.F.T.S. (R.A.F.) Pearce, Alta.	17. 3.42 14. 8.42	Operated Tiger Moths and P.T.-27's.

Canadian Wireless Schools Equipped with Tiger Moths

1 W.S. St. Hubert, P.Q.
2 W.S. Calgary, Alta.
3 W.S. Winnipeg, Man.
4 W.S. Guelph, Ont.

AUSTRALIA

No. of School and Location	Formation	Disbandment
2 F.T.S.		
Melbourne, Vic.	6.11.39	4.12.39
Parafield, S.A.	5.12.39	28. 5.44
Tamworth, N.S.W.	29. 5.44	12.12.44
(Renamed 1 E.F.T.S.)	2. 1.40	——
3 F.T.S.		
Archerfield, Qld.	6.11.39	24. 4.42
(Renamed 2 E.F.T.S)	2. 1.40	——
3 E.F.T.S.		
Essendon, Vic.	2. 1.40	1. 5.42
4 E.F.T.S.		
Mascot, N.S.W.	2. 1.40	24. 4.42
5 E.F.T.S.		
Narromine, N.S.W.	24. 5.40	14. 8.44
6 E.F.T.S.		
Tamworth, N.S.W.	22. 8.40	5. 5.42
7 E.F.T.S.		
Western Junction, Tas.	29. 8.40	31. 8.45
8 E.F.T.S.		
Narrandera, N.S.W.	19. 9.40	15. 6.45
9 E.F.T.S.		
Cunderdin, W.A.	11.12.40	17.10.45
10 E.F.T.S.		
Temora, N.S.W.	1. 5.41	12. 3.46
11 E.F.T.S.		
Benalla, Vic.	26. 6.41	1. 3.46
12 E.F.T.S.		
Bundaberg, Qld.	16.10.41	12. 1.42

NEW ZEALAND

No. of School and Location	Formation, Disbandment	Remarks
1 E.F.T.S. Taieri, Dunedin	20.10.39 Oct. 1944	Continued as Grading School until 1955.
2 E.F.T.S. Bell Block, New Plymouth	Nov. 1939 Oct. 1942	Commenced with variety of light aircraft, later equipped with Tiger Moths.
Ashburton, South Island	Oct. 1942 Oct. 1944	
3 E.F.T.S. Harewood, Christchurch	Aug. 1940 Jul. 1945	——
4 E.F.T.S. Whenuapai, Auckland	Dec. 1940 Mar. 1942	Absorbed into other flying schools.

Note: Tiger Moths continued at R.N.Z.A.F. training schools until July 1955.

RHODESIAN AIR TRAINING GROUP

No. of School and Location	Formation	Remarks
25 E.F.T.S. Belvedere, Salisbury	May, 1940	1st C.O. W/Cdr. David.
26 E.F.T.S. Guinea Fowl, Gwelo	Aug. 1940	1st C.O. W/Cdr. Marlow.
27 E.F.T.S. Induna, Bulawayo	Nov. 1940	——
28 E.F.T.S. Mount Hampden, Salisbury	April, 1941	1st C.O. W/Cdr. Hendrikz.
33 F.I.S. Norton	1943	Flying Instructor's School formed from Rhodesian Central Flying School. C.O. G/Capt. Craig.

SOUTH AFRICA

No. of School	Location
1 E.F.T.S.	Baragweneth
2 E.F.T.S.	Randfontein
3 E.F.T.S.	Wonderboom
4 E.F.T.S.	Benoni
5 E.F.T.S.	Witbank
6 E.F.T.S.	Potchefstroom
7 E.F.T.S.	Kroonstaad

INDIA

No. of School	Location	
1 E.F.T.S.	Begumet	(227 Group)
2 E.F.T.S.	Jodhpur	(226 ,,)

Note: At their peak these two flying schools accommodated 142 pupils on a 12-week flying course.

Post-War Reserve Flying Schools

No. of School and Location	Formation, Disbandment	Remarks
1 R.F.S. Panshangar	Apr. 1947 Feb. 1953	Re-equipped with Chipmunks Apr. 1950.
2 R.F.S. Manchester (Barton)	Oct. 1948 Feb. 1953	Re-equipped with Chipmunks Jan. 1951—reverted to Tiger Moths Dec. 1951.
3 R.F.S. Cardiff	Aug. 1948 Aug. 1953	Re-equipped with Chipmunks Feb. 1950.
4 R.F.S. Brough	Mar. 1947 Feb. 1948	Tiger Moths only.
5 R.F.S. Castle Bromwich	Oct. 1947 May 1954	Re-equipped with Chipmunks July 1951.
6 R.F.S. Sywell	Apr. 1947 Feb. 1953	Re-equipped with Chipmunks Dec. 1950.

No. of School and Location	Formation, Disbandment	Remarks
7 R.F.S. Desford	Apr. 1947 Aug. 1953	Tiger Moths only.
8 R.F.S. Woodley	Mar. 1947 Feb. 1953	Re-equipped with Chipmunks Apr. 1950 continued to operate Tiger Moths as well.
9 R.F.S. Doncaster	Oct. 1947 May 1954	Re-equipped with Chipmunks Aug. 1953.
10 R.F.S. Exeter	Apr. 1949 May 1954	Re-equipped with Chipmunks July 1953.
11 R.F.S. Perth	Mar. 1947 May 1954	Re-equipped with Chipmunks Apr. 1950.
12 R.F.S. Filton	Mar. 1948 Feb. 1953	Re-equipped with Chipmunks Apr. 1951.
14 R.F.S. Hamble	Aug. 1947 Aug. 1953	Re-equipped with Chipmunks Dec. 1950.
15 R.F.S. Redhill	Feb. 1948 May 1954	Re-equipped with Chipmunks Mar. 1951.
16 R.F.S. Derby	Mar. 1947 Aug. 1953	Re-equipped with Prentices Dec. 1951.
17 R.F.S. Hornchurch	June 1948 Aug. 1953	Re-equipped with Chipmunks Aug. 1952.
18 R.F.S. Fair Oaks	Apr. 1947 July 1953	Re-equipped with Chipmunks Apr. 1950.
19 R.F.S. Hooton Park	July 1950 May 1954	Re-equipped with Chipmunks Feb. 1951. Moved to Woodvale late 1951.
22 R.F.S. Cambridge	Mar. 1947 May 1954	Re-equipped with Chipmunks Apr. 1950 continued to operate Tiger Moths.
23 R.F.S. Usworth	Dec. 1948 Aug. 1953	Re-equipped with Chipmunks Feb. 1951.
24 R.F.S. Rochester	Apr. 1947 Feb. 1953	Re-equipped with Chipmunks Aug. 1952.
25 R.F.S. Wolverhampton	Apr. 1947 Feb. 1953	Tiger Moths only.

University Air Squadrons

No. of School	Location of University
1 U.A.S.	Aberdeen
2 U.A.S.	Belfast
3 U.A.S.	Birmingham
4 U.A.S.	Bristol
5 U.A.S.	Cambridge
6 U.A.S.	Durham
7 U.A.S.	Edinburgh
8 U.A.S.	Glasgow
9 U.A.S.	Hull
10 U.A.S.	Leeds
11 U.A.S.	Liverpool
12 U.A.S.	London
13 U.A.S.	Manchester
14 U.A.S.	Nottingham
15 U.A.S.	Oxford
16 U.A.S.	St. Andrews
17 U.A.S.	Southampton
18 U.A.S.	Wales

APPENDIX III

SUMMARY OF PRODUCTION OF NEW TIGER MOTHS*

1931 to Aug. 1939

DH 82 Tiger Moths

De Havilland Stag Lane	114	
Norway	17	
Sweden	3	
	134	134

DH 82a and DH 82c Tiger Moths

De Havilland Stag Lane and Hatfield	1063	
De Havilland Technical School	3	
De Havilland Aircraft of Canada	227	
Norway	20	
Sweden	20	
Portugal	91	
	1424	1424

Sept. 1939 to Aug. 1945

De Havilland Hatfield	795	
De Havilland Aircraft of Canada	1520	
De Havilland Aircraft of New Zealand	345	
De Havilland Aircraft Pty. Australia	1085	
Morris Motors Ltd.	3508	
	7253	7253

TOTAL TIGER MOTH PRODUCTION 8811

* With the passage of time records have been destroyed and memories have become dimmed so that it has been difficult to obtain accurate production figures in some cases. The information presented in this Appendix and in Appendix IV is the result of recent inquiries from the manufacturers and the air forces concerned.

DH 82b Queen Bee

1935 to Aug. 1939
De Havilland, Hatfield   210   210

Sept. 1939–July 1944
De Havilland, Hatfield	110	
Scottish Aviation	100	
	210	210

TOTAL QUEEN BEE PRODUCTION   420

A sheep in wolf's clothing! It is hard to credit that this Fokker DVII is in fact a Tiger Moth, so convincingly is it transformed by Film Aviation Services Ltd. The 'German officer' in the cockpit is Captain Crewdson.

Lolita on the wing. Juanita Benjamin during one of her celebrated
performances with the Tiger Club air displays.

APPENDIX IV

LIST OF REGISTRATIONS

DH 82 TIGER MOTHS CONSTRUCTED BY THE DE HAVILLAND COMPANY IN GREAT BRITAIN

Works Number	Registration	Remarks	Works Number	Registration	Remarks	Works Number	Registration	Remarks
1733	G-ABRC	1st DH 82 TIGER MOTH (Sir A. Cobham)	1766	K2594		3117	101	
1739	K2567		67	K2595		18	102	
40	K2568		68	K2596		19	103	
41	K2569		69	K2597	AIR MINISTRY CONTRACT 120255/31	3120	104	
42	K2570		1770	K2598		21	105	
43	K2571		71	K2599		22	106	
44	K2572		72	K2600		23	107	
45	K2573		73	K2601		24	108	
46	K2574		74	S1675	AIR MINISTRY CONTRACT 113208/31 SEAPLANES	25	109	
47	K2575		75	S1676		26	110	PERSIAN AIR FORCE
48	K2576		76	G-ABSK		27	111	
49	K2577		3100	VR-HAR	HONG KONG	28	112	
1750	K2578		01	G-ABTB	Std. Telephones	29	113	
51	K2579	AIR MINISTRY CONTRACT 120255/31	02	G-ABSW		3130	114	
52	K2580		03	G-ABSX		31	115	
53	K2581		04	G-ABSY		32	116	
54	K2582		05	G-ABSZ		33	117	
55	K2583		06	G-ABTA		34	118	
56	K2584		07	G-ABUL	Sir A. Cobham	35	119	
57	K2585		08	–		36	120	
58	K2586		09	–	SWEDISH AIR FORCE	37	G-ABYJ	
59	K2587		3110	–		38	–	
1760	K2588		11	–		39	–	SWEDISH AIR FORCE
61	K2589		12	SE-ADE	SWEDEN	3140	–	
62	K2590		13	SE-ADF		41	–	
63	K2591		14	SE-ADG		42	D-2357	
64	K2592		15	SE-ADH		43	–	BRAZIL
65	K2593		16	–	Nosawa Co. JAPAN	44	–	

Wks. No.	Registration	Remarks	Wks. No.	Registration	Remarks	Wks. No.	Registration	Remarks
3145	–	} BRAZIL	3155	G–ACBD		3165	–	}
46	–		56	G–ACBE		66	–	
47	–		57	G–ACBF		67	–	PORTUGUESE AIR FORCE
48	G–ACBN		58	G–ACBG		68	–	
49	–	} SHANGHAI	59	–	}	69	–	}
3150	–		3160	–		3170	S1	}
51	–		61	–	} PORTUGUESE AIR FORCE	71	S2	
52	G–ACBA		62	–		72	S3	DANISH AIR FORCE
53	G–ACBB		63	–		73	S4	
54	G–ACBC		64	–	}	3174	S5	}

DH 82 TIGER MOTHS BUILT ABROAD UNDER LICENCE

NORWAY (Total 17)

Wks. No.	Registration	Remarks	Wks. No.	Registration	Remarks	Wks. No.	Registration	Remarks
149	127	}	155	139	}	161	151	}
150	129		156	141		162	153	
151	131	ROYAL NORWEGIAN AIR FORCE	157	143	ROYAL NORWEGIAN AIR FORCE	163	155	ROYAL NORWEGIAN AIR FORCE
152	133		158	145		164	157	
153	135		159	147		165	159	}
154	137	}	160	149	}			

SWEDEN (Total 3)

Wks. No.	Registration	Remarks
38	FV597	} SWEDISH AIR FORCE
39	FV598	
40	FV599	}

DH 82A TIGER MOTHS CONSTRUCTED BY THE DE HAVILLAND COMPANY IN GREAT BRITAIN

Wks. No.	Registration	Remarks	Wks. No.	Registration	Remarks	Wks. No.	Registration	Remarks
3175	G-ACDA		3205	126	PERSIAN AIR FORCE	3235	137	PERSIAN AIR FORCE
76	G-ACDB		06	127		36	138	
77	G-ACDC	Now Tiger Club	07	128		37	139	
78	G-ACDE		08	129		38	K4242	
79	G-ACDF		09	S10	DANISH AIR FORCE	39	K4243	
3180	G-ACDG		3210	S11		3240	K4244	
81	G-ACDH		11	S12		41	K4245	
82	G-ACDI		12	–	PORTUGUESE AIR FORCE	42	K4246	
83	G-ACDJ		13	–		43	K4247	
84	G-ACDK		14	–		44	K4248	
85	G-ACEH		15	–		45	K4249	
86	G-ACEZ	Sir A. Cobham	16	–		46	K4250	
87	G-ACFA	Sir A. Cobham	17	–		47	K4251	
88	G-ACGE		18	–		48	K4252	
89	G-ACDY	S.M.T.Co. Ltd.	19	–		49	K4253	AIR MINISTRY CONTRACT 307396/34
3190	PH-AJG	HOLLAND	3220	–		3250	K4254	
91	G-ACJA		21	–		51	K4255	
92	33-2	SPANISH AIR FORCE	22	A78	AUSTRIA	52	K4256	
93	33-3		23	G-ACKS		53	K4257	
94	33-4		24	G-ACVK		54	K4258	
95	33-5		25	G-ACVL		55	K4259	
96	S6	DANISH AIR FORCE	26	G-ACWB		56	K4260	
97	S7		27	–	AUSTRALIA	57	K4261	
98	S8		28	130	PERSIAN AIR FORCE	58	K4262	
99	S9		29	131		59	K4263	
3200	121	PERSIAN AIR FORCE	3230	132		3260	K4264	
01	122		31	133		61	K4265	
02	123		32	134		62	K4266	
03	124		33	135		63	K4267	
04	125		34	136		64	K4268	

Wks. No.	Regis- tration	Remarks	Wks. No.	Regis- tration	Remarks	Wks. No.	Regis- tration	Remarks
3265	K4269		3295	145		3325	2-1-6	
66	K4270		96	146		26	2-1-7	
67	K4271		97	147		27	2-1-8	
68	K4272		98	148		28	2-1-9	
69	K4273		99	149		29	2-1-10	BRAZILIAN AIR FORCE
3270	K4274		3300	150		3330	2-1-11	
71	K4275		01	151		31	2-1-12	
72	K4276		02	152		32	2-1-13	
73	K4277		03	153	PERSIAN AIR FORCE	33	2-1-14	
74	K4278		04	154		34	2-1-15	
75	K4279	AIR MINISTRY CONTRACT 307396/34	05	155		35	2-1-16	
76	K4280		06	156		36	OY-DOK	DENMARK
77	K4281		07	157		37	G-ADGS	
78	K4282		08	158		38	G-ADGT	
79	K4283		09	159		39	G-ADGU	
3280	K4284		3310	2		3340	G-ADGV	
81	K4285		11	3		41	G-ADGW	
82	K4286		12	4	URUGUAY	42	G-ADGX	
83	K4287		13	5		43	G-ADGY	
84	K4288		14	G-ACYN		44	G-ADGZ	
85	K4289		15	G-ACZY		45	G-ADGF	
86	K4290		16	G-ACZZ		46	G-ADGG	
87	K4291		17	S13	DANISH AIR FORCE	47	G-ADGH	
88	1	URUGUAY	18	G-ADCG		48	238	ROYAL CANADIAN AIR FORCE
89	OA-CCH		19	G-ADCH		49	G-ADIH	
3290	140		3320	VH-UTD	AUSTRALIA	3350	G-ADII	
91	141	PERSIAN AIR FORCE	21	40	IRAQI AIR FORCE	51	G-ADIJ	
92	142		22	41		52	G-ADIW	
93	143		23	42		53	G-ADIX	
94	144		24	2-1-5	BRAZILIAN AIR FORCE	54	G-ADIY	

Wks. No.	Registration	Remarks	Wks. No.	Registration	Remarks	Wks. No.	Registration	Remarks
3355	G-ADIZ		3385	G-ADJI		3415	G-ADNU	
56	G-ADJA		86	G-ADJJ		16	G-ADNV	
57	G-ADLU		87	G-ADOW		17	G-ADNW	
58	VT-AGQ	INDIA	88	G-ADOX		18	G-ADNX	
59	VT-AGR		89	G-ADOY		19	G-ADNY	
3360	G-ADLX		3390	G-ADOZ		3420	G-ADNZ	
61	G-ADKG		91	G-ADPA		21	G-ADOA	
62	G-ADLZ		92	G-ADPB		22	G-ADOB	
63	G-ADMA		93	G-ADPC		23	G-ADSI	
64	G-ADLV		94	G-ADPD		24	G-ADSH	
65	G-ADLW		95	G-ADPE		25	G-ADUC	
66	G-ADHY		96	G-ADPF		26	G-ADUK	
67	G-ADHZ		97	G-ADPG		27	G-ADVN	
68	G-ADIA		98	G-ADPH		28	G-ADVO	
69	G-ADIB		99	G-ADOF		29	G-ADVP	
3370	G-ADIC		3400	G-ADOG		3430	G-ADXB	
71	G-ADHR		01	G-ADOH		31	G-ADXC	
72	G-ADHS		01	G-ADOI		32	G-ADXD	
73	G-ADHT		03	G-ADOJ		33	G-ADXE	
74	G-ADHU		04	G-ADOK		34	G-ADXI	
75	G-ADHV		05	G-ADOL		35	G-ADXJ	
76	G-ADHW		06	G-ADOM		36	G-ADXT	
77	G-ADHX		07	G-ADON		37	G-ADXU	
78	G-ADJB		08	G-ADOO		38	G-ADXV	
79	G-ADJC		09	G-ADOP		39	G-ADXW	
3380	G-ADJD		3410	G-ADOR		3440	G-ADXX	
81	G-ADJE		11	G-ADNP		41	G-ADVX	
82	G-ADJF		12	G-ADNR		42	G-ADVY	
83	G-ADJG		13	G-ADNS		43	G-ADVZ	
84	G-ADJH		14	G-ADNT		44	G-ADWA	

Wks. No.	Registration	Remarks	Wks. No.	Registration	Remarks	Wks. No.	Registration	Remarks
3445	G-ADWB		3475	G-ADXZ		3505	9	URUGUAY
46	G-ADWC		76	G-ADYA		06	–	S. AFRICA
47	G-ADWD		77	G-ADYB		07	VP-YBG	CENTRAL AFRICA
48	G-ADWE		78	CF-CBR ⎫		08	VH-UYZ	AUSTRALIA
49	G-ADWF		79	CF-CBT ⎬ CANADA		09	G-AELA	
3450	G-ADWJ		3480	CF-CBU ⎪		3510	G-AELB	
51	G-ADWK		81	CF-CBS ⎭		11	G-AELC	
52	G-ADWL		82	43 ⎫		12	G-AELD	
53	G-ADWM		83	44 ⎬ IRAQI AIR FORCE		13	G-AELP	
54	G-ADWN		84	45 ⎭		14	G-AEMF	
55	G-ADWO		85	G-AEBY		15	VH-UXC	AUSTRALIA
56	G-ADWP		86	G-AEBZ		16	G-AEMU	
57	G-ADXK		87	46	IRAQI AIR FORCE	17	G-AENK	
58	G-ADXN		88	G-AECG		18	–	S. AFRICA
59	G-ADXO		89	G-AECH		19	VP-YBH	CENTRAL AFRICA
3460	G-ADXP		3490	G-AECI		3520	VT-AIF	INDIA
61	G-ADXR		91	G-AECJ		21	G-AE0E	
62	VT-AHD ⎫ INDIA		92	G-ADWG	C.W.A. Scott's Air Display	22	ZS-AIN ⎫ S. AFRICA	
63	VT-AHE ⎭		93	LY-LAT	LITHUANIA	23	ZS-AIO ⎭	
64	160		94	0E-DAX	AUSTRIA	24	0E-DIK	AUSTRIA
65	161		95	G-AEEA		25	ZS-AIL ⎫ S. AFRICA	
66	162		96	– ⎫ S. AFRICA		26	ZS-AIM ⎭	
67	163		97	– ⎭		27	0E-DAF	AUSTRIA
68	164	PERSIAN AIR FORCE	98	G-AEID		28	ZS-AIP ⎫ S. AFRICA	
69	165		99	6	URUGUAY	29	ZS-AIR ⎭	
3470	166		3500	K8336 ⎫ SEAPLANES A.M. Contract 419031/35.		3530	– ⎫ S. AFRICA	
71	167		01	K8337 ⎭		31	– ⎭	
72	168		02	VT-AHL	INDIA	32	VP-CAB	CEYLON
73	169		03	7 ⎫ URUGUAY		33	– ⎫ S. AFRICA	
74	G-ADHN		04	8 ⎭		34	– ⎭	

APPENDIX IV

Wks. No.	Registration	Remarks	Wks. No.	Registration	Remarks	Wks. No.	Registration	Remarks
3535	–	S. AFRICA	3565	L6942	R.A.F.	3595	G-AFDD	
36	–		66	L6943		96	–	S. AFRICA
37	VR-RAM	FED. MALAY STATES	67	L6927		97	SU-ABX	EGYPT
38	–		68	L6928		98	VH-UYK	AUSTRALIA
39	–		69	L6924	R.A.F.	99	G-AEUV	
3540	–	IRAQI AIR FORCE	3570	L6925		3600	VH-UYL	AUSTRALIA
41	–		71	L6936		01	VT-AIS	INDIA
42	LY-LAM	LITHUANIA	72	L6937		02	G-AFAI	
43	G-AERW		73	L6941		03	VP-YBO	CENTRAL AFRICA
44	G-AESA		74	G-AETP		04	ZS-AJA	S. AFRICA
45	G-AESC		75	L6949		05	–	
46	–		76	L6947		06	–	S. AFRICA
47	–		77	L6929		07	–	
48	–	IRAQI AIR FORCE	78	L6930	R.A.F.	08	SU-ABY	EGYPT
49	–		79	L6944		09	–	
3550	–		3580	L6945		3610	–	S. AFRICA
51	–		81	L6926		11	S15	DANISH AIR FORCE
52	G-AESD		82	G-AESM		12	10	
53	L6920		83	L6938	R.A.F.	13	11	
54	L6921		84	G-AEXG		14	12	
55	L6932		85	L6931	R.A.F.	15	13	
56	L6933	R.A.F.	86	G-AESN		16	14	URUGUAY
57	L6922		87	G-AESO		17	15	
58	L6923		88	L6948	R.A.F.	18	16	
59	L6934		89	G-AEWG		19	17	
3560	L6935		3590	–	S. AFRICA	3620	18	
61	G-AETO		91	VR-RAN		21	VH-UYR	
62	L6939		92	VR-RAO	FED. MALAY STATES	22	VH-UYP	AUSTRALIA
63	L6940	R.A.F.	93	VH-AYJ	AUSTRALIA	23	VH-UYQ	
64	L6946		94	G-AFDC		24	G-AEZC	

219

Wks No.	Regis-tration	Remarks	Wks. No.	Regis-tration	Remarks	Wks. No.	Regis-tration	Remarks
3625	–	S. AFRICA	'3655	F-AQJU		3685	F-AQOZ	
26	ZS-AMN	S. AFRICA	56	F-AQJV		86	F-AQ0Q	FRANCE
27	G-AFAR		57	F-AQJX	FRANCE	87	F-AQ0V	
28	G-AFAS		58	F-AQJY		88	F-AQ0X	
29	ZK-AFN	NEW ZEALAND	59	F-AQJZ		89	VH-AAI	AUSTRALIA
3630	ZK-AFO		3660	–	S. AFRICA	3690	VH-AAJ	
31	–	S. AFRICA	61	VT-AJV	INDIA	91	F-AQ0Y	FRANCE
32	VH-UZT	AUSTRALIA	62	–	S. AFRICA	92	F-ARAR	
33	–	S. AFRICA	63	ZS-ANU	S. AFRICA	93	ZK-AGG	NEW ZEALAND
34	ZS-AMZ	S. AFRICA	64	G-AFEJ		94	–	S. AFRICA
35	VH-UZV	AUSTRALIA	65	F-AQNF		95	G-AFHT	
36	–	S. AFRICA	66	F-AQNG		96	ZK-AGH	NEW ZEALAND
37	G-AFCA		67	F-AQNH	FRANCE	97	ZK-AGI	
38	ZK-AFY		68	F-AQNI		98	–	S. AFRICA
39	ZK-AFZ		69	F-AQNJ		99	F-AFGY	
3640	ZK-AGA		3670	VH-AAE	AUSTRALIA	3700	G-AFGZ	
41	ZK-AFU	NEW ZEALAND	71	ZK-AGF	NEW ZEALAND	01	VP-YBW	CENTRAL AFRICA
42	ZK-AFV		72	ZS-ANV	S. AFRICA	02	HB-OKU	SWITZERLAND
43	ZK-AFW		73	–	S. AFRICA	03	VH-ABM	AUSTRALIA
44	ZK-AFX		74	G-AFFO		04	VH-AAR	
45	–		75	–	S. AFRICA	05	ZK-AGL	NEW ZEALAND
46	–		76	–		06	G-AFFA	
47	–		77	F-AQOS	FRANCE	07	N5444	R.A.F.
48	–	PORTUGUESE AIR FORCE	78	VP-RAG	N. RHODESIA	08	N5445	
49	–		79	G-AFGJ		09	N5446	
3650	–		3680	ZK-AFP	NEW ZEALAND	3710	N5447	
51	–		81	G-AFGT		11	N5448	
52	–		82	G-AFHI		12	N5449	
53	–		83	–	MOZAMBIQUE	13	N5450	
54	ZK-AGE	NEW ZEALAND	84	G-AFGW		14	N5451	

Wks. No.	Registration	Remarks	Wks. No.	Registration	Remarks	Wks. No.	Registration	Remarks
3715	N5452		3745	N5477	R.A.F.	3775	N6445	
16	N5433		46	VH-AAK	AUSTRALIA	76	N6446	
17	N5454		47	G-AFJI		77	N6447	
18	N5455	R.A.F.	48	G-AFJK		78	N6448	
19	N5456		49	G-AFJL		79	N6449	
3720	N5457		3750	VP-CAE	CEYLON	3780	N6450	
21	SX-AAK	GREECE	51	N5478		81	N6451	
22	G-AFJF		52	N5479		82	N6452	R.A.F.
23	VH-AAP	AUSTRALIA	53	N5480		83	N6453	
24	G-AFJG		54	N5481		84	N6454	
25	G-AFJH		55	N5482		85	N6455	
26	N5458		56	N5483		86	N6456	
27	N5459		57	N5484		87	N6457	
28	N5460		58	N5485	R.A.F.	88	N6458	
29	N5461		59	N5486		89	ZK-AHA	NEW ZEALAND
3730	N5462		3760	N5487		3790	G-AFLX	
31	N5463		61	N5488		91	-	S. AFRICA
32	N5464		62	N5489		92	VT-AKS	INDIA
33	N5465		63	N5490		93	G-AFMC	
34	N5466		64	N5491		94	G-AFMD	
35	N5467	R.A.F.	65	N5492		95	ZK-AGZ	NEW ZEALAND
36	N5468		66	G-AFJM		96	N6459	
37	N5469		67	G-AFJN		97	N6460	
38	N5470		68	-	S. AFRICA	98	N6461	
39	N5471		69	ZS-APF	S. AFRICA	99	N6462	
3740	N5472		3770	-	S. AFRICA	3800	N6463	AIR MINISTRY CONTRACT 778402/38
41	N5473		71	ZS-APE	S. AFRICA	01	N6464	
42	N5474		72	N5493		02	N6465	
43	N5475		73	N6443	R.A.F.	03	N6466	
44	N5476		74	N6444		04	N6467	

Wks. No.	Registration	Remarks	Wks. No.	Registration	Remarks	Wks. No.	Registration	Remarks
3805	N6468		3735	ZK-AGY	NEW ZEALAND	3865	N6552	
06	N6469		36	N6523		66	N6553	
07	N6470		37	N6524		67	N6554	
08	N6471		38	N6525		68	N6555	
09	N6472		39	N6526		69	N6556	
3810	N6473		3840	N6527		3870	N6576	
11	N6474		41	N6528		71	N6577	
12	N6475		42	N6529		72	N6578	R.A.F.
13	N6476		43	N6530		73	N6579	
14	N6477		44	N6531		74	N6580	
15	N6478		45	N6532		75	N6581	
16	N6479	AIR MINISTRY CONTRACT 778402/38	46	N6533		76	N6582	
17	N6480		47	N6534		77	N6583	
18	N6481		48	N6535		78	N6584	
19	N6482		49	N6536		79	N6585	
3820	N6483		3850	N6537	R.A.F.	3880	VT-AKW	INDIA
21	N6484		51	N6538		81	G-AFNP	
22	N6485		52	N6539		82	G-AFNR	
23	N6486		53	N6540		83	G-AFNS	
24	N6487		54	N6541		84	G-AFNT	
25	N6488		55	N6542		85	G-AFNU	
26	N6489		56	N6543		86	G-AFNV	
27	N6490		57	N6544		87	N6586	
28	N6519		58	N6545		88	N6587	
29	N6520		59	N6546		89	N6588	
3830	N6521	R.A.F.	3860	N6547		3890	N6589	
31	N6522		61	N6548		91	N6590	R.A.F.
32	ZK-AHB		62	N6549		92	N6591	
33	ZK-AGW	NEW ZEALAND	63	N6550		93	N6592	
34	ZK-AGX		64	N6551		94	N6593	

Wks. No.	Registration	Remarks	Wks. No.	Registration	Remarks	Wks. No.	Registration	Remarks
3895	N6594		3925	N6624		3955	N6651	
96	N6595		26	N6625		56	N6652	
97	N6596		27	N6630	R.A.F.	57	N6653	
98	N6597		28	N6631		58	N6654	
99	N6598		29	N6632		59	N6655	
3900	N6599		3930	-		3960	N6656	
01	N6600		31	-		61	N6657	
02	N6601		32	-	PERSIAN AIR FORCE	62	N6658	
03	N6602		33	-		63	N6659	
04	N6603		34	-		64	N6660	
05	N6604		35	ZK-AHF	NEW ZEALAND	65	N6661	
06	N6605		36	ZK-AHG		66	N6662	
07	N6606		37	N6633		67	N6663	
08	N6607		38	N6634		68	N6664	
09	N6608	R.A.F.	39	N6635		69	N6665	R.A.F.
3910	N6609		3940	N6636		3970	N6666	
11	N6610		41	N6637		71	N6667	
12	N6611		42	N6638		72	N6668	
13	N6612		43	N6639		73	N6669	
14	N6613		44	N6640		74	N6670	
15	N6614		45	N6641	R.A.F.	75	N6671	
16	N6615		46	N6642		76	N6672	
17	N6616		47	N6643		77	N6673	
18	N6617		48	N6644		78	N6674	
19	N6618		49	N6645		79	N6706	
3920	N6619		3950	N6646		3980	N6707	
21	N6620		51	N6647		81	N6708	
22	N6621		52	N6648		82	N6709	
23	N6622		53	N6649		83	N6710	
24	N6623		54	N6650		84	N6711	

Wks. No.	Registration	Remarks	Wks. No.	Registration	Remarks	Wks. No.	Registration	Remarks
3895	N6712		82015	N6737		82045	N6781	R.A.F.
86	N6713		16	N6738		46	N6782	
87	N6714		17	N6739		47	–	
88	N6715		18	N6740		48	–	
89	N6716		19	N6741		49	–	PERSIAN AIR FORCE
3990	N6717		82020	N6742		82050	–	
91	N6718		21	N6743		51	–	
92	N6719		22	N6744		52	ZK-AHH	NEW ZEALAND
93	N6720		23	N6745		53	N6783	
94	N6721	R.A.F.	24	N6746		54	N6784	
95	N6722		25	N6747		55	N6785	
96	N6723		26	N6748		56	N6786	
97	N6724		27	N6749		57	N6787	
98	N6725		28	N6750		58	N6788	
99	N6726		29	N6751	R.A.F.	59	N6789	
82000	N6727		82030	N6752		82060	N6790	
01	N6728		31	N6753		61	N6791	
02	N6729		32	N6754		62	N6792	
03	N6730		33	N6755		63	N6793	R.A.F.
04	G-AFSX		34	N6770		64	N6794	
05	–		35	N6771		65	N6795	
06	–		36	N6772		66	N6796	
07	–	PERSIAN AIR FORCE	37	N6773		67	N6797	
08	–		38	N6774		68	N6798	
09	–		39	N6775		69	N6799	
82010	N6732		82040	N6776		82070	N6800	
11	N6733		41	N6777		71	N6801	
12	N6734	R.A.F.	42	N6778		72	N6802	
13	N6735		43	N6779		73	N6803	
14	N6736		44	N6780		74	N6804	

Wks. No.	Registration	Remarks	Wks. No.	Registration	Remarks	Wks. No.	Registration	Remarks
82075	N6805		82105	N6850		82135	N6880	
76	N6806		06	N6851		36	N6881	R.A.F.
77	N6807		07	N6852		37	N6882	
78	N6808		08	N6853		38	N6900	
79	N6809		09	N6854		39	G-AFSH	
82080	N6810		82110	N6855		82140	G-AFSK	
81	N6811		11	N6856		41	G-AFSL	
82	N6812		12	N6857		42	G-AFSI	
83	N6834	R.A.F.	13	N6858		43	ZS-API	S. AFRICA
84	N6835		14	N6859		44	ZS-ARG	
85	N6836		15	N6860		45	N6901	
86	N6837		16	N6861		46	N6902	
87	N6838		17	N6862		47	N6903	
88	N6839		18	N6863		48	N6904	
89	N6840		19	N6864	R.A.F.	49	N6905	
82090	N6841		82120	N6865		82150	N6906	
91	N6842		21	N6866		51	N6907	
92	"	PERSIAN AIR FORCE	22	N6867		52	N6908	R.A.F.
93	"		23	N6868		53	N6909	
94	"		24	N6869		54	N6910	
95	"		25	N6870		55	N6911	
96	"		26	N6871		56	N6912	
97	G-AFSG		27	N6872		57	N6913	
98	N6843		28	N6873		58	N6914	
99	N6844		29	N6874		59	N6915	
82100	N6845		82130	N6875		82160	N6916	
01	N6846	R.A.F.	31	N6876		61	N6917	
02	N6847		32	N6877		62	N6918	
03	N6848		33	N6878		63	N6919	
04	N6849		34	N6879		64	N6920	

Wks. No.	Registration	Remarks	Wks. No.	Registration	Remarks	Wks. No.	Registration	Remarks
82165	N6921		82195	N6945		82225	N6987	
66	N6922		96	N6946		26	N6988	
67	N6923		97	N6947		27	N9114	R.A.F.
68	N6924		98	N6948		28	N9115	
69	N6925		99	N6949		29	N9116	
82170	N6926		82200	N6962		82230	ZK-AHO	
71	N6927		01	N6963		31	ZK-AHM	NEW ZEALAND
72	N6928		02	N6964		32	ZK-AHR	
73	N6929	R.A.F.	03	N6965		33	G-AFTI	
74	N6930		04	N6966		34	G-AFXZ	
75	N6931		05	N6967		35	G-AFYA	
76	N6932		06	N6968		36	N9117	
77	N6933		07	N6969		37	N9118	
78	N6934		08	N6970		38	N9119	
79	N6935		09	N6971	R.A.F.	39	N9120	
82180	N6936		82210	N6972		82240	N9121	
81	N6937		11	N6973		41	N9122	
82	G-AFSJ		12	N6974		42	N9123	
83	G-AFSM		13	N6975		43	N9124	
84	G-AFSN		14	N6976		44	N9125	
85	G-AFNL		15	N6977		45	N9126	R.A.F.
86	G-AFNM		16	N6978		46	N9127	
87	G-AFWI		17	N6979		47	N9128	
88	N6938		18	N6980		48	N9129	
89	N6939		19	N6981		49	N9130	
82190	N6940		82220	N6982		82250	N9131	
91	N6941	R.A.F.	21	N6983		51	N9132	
92	N6942		22	N6984		52	N9133	
93	N6943		23	N6985		53	N9134	
94	N6944		24	N6986		54	N9135	

Wks. No.	Registration	Remarks	Wks. No.	Registration	Remarks	Wks. No.	Registration	Remarks
82255	N9136	⎫	82285	N9174	⎫	82315	N9198	⎫
56	N9137		86	N9175		16	N9199	
57	N9138		87	N9176		17	N9200	
58	N9139		88	N9177		18	N9201	
59	N9140		89	N9178	R.A.F.	19	N9202	
82260	N9141		82290	N9179		82320	N9203	
61	N9142		91	N9180		21	N9204	
62	N9143		92	N9181	⎭	22	N9205	
63	N9144		93	G-AFZC		23	N9206	
64	N9145		94	–	R.N.Z.A.F.	24	N9207	
65	N9146		95	G-AFZF		25	N9208	
66	N9147		96	–	⎫	26	N9209	
67	N9148		97	–	R.N.Z.A.F.	27	N9210	
68	N9149		98	–	⎭	28	N9211	
69	N9150	R.A.F.	99	N9182	⎫	29	N9212	R.A.F.
82270	N9151		82300	N9183		82330	N9213	
71	N9152		01	N9184		31	N9214	
72	N9153		02	N9185		32	N9215	
73	N9154		03	N9186		33	N9238	
74	N9155		04	N9187		34	N9239	
75	N9156		05	N9188		35	N9240	
76	N9157		06	N9189	R.A.F.	36	N9241	
77	N9158		07	N9190		37	N9242	
78	N9159		08	N9191		38	N9243	
79	N9160		09	N9192		39	N9244	
82280	N9161		82310	N9193		82340	N9245	
81	N9162		11	N9194		41	N9246	
82	N9171		12	N9195		42	N9247	
83	N9172		13	N9196		43	N9248	⎭
84	N9173	⎭	14	N9197	⎭	44		R.N.Z.A.F.

Wks. No.	Registration	Remarks	Wks. No.	Registration	Remarks	Wks. No.	Registration	Remarks
82345	–		82375	N9274		82405	N9318	
46	–	R.N.Z.A.F.	76	N9275		06	N9319	
47	–		77	N9276		07	N9320	
48	VH-ADH	AUSTRALIA	78	N9277		08	N9321	
49	VH-ADI		79	N9278		09	N9322	
82350	N9249		82380	N9279		82410	N9323	
51	N9250		81	N9300		11	N9324	
52	N9351		82	N9301		12	N9325	
53	N9252		83	N9302	R.A.F.	13	N9326	
54	N9253		84	N9303		14	N9327	
55	N9254		85	N9304		15	N9328	
56	N9255		86	N9305		16	N9329	
57	N9256		87	N9306		17	N9330	
58	N9257		88	N9307		18	N9331	
59	N9258		89	N9308		19	N9332	R.A.F.
82360	N9259		82390	N9309		82420	N9333	
61	N9260		91	N9310		21	N9334	
62	N9261	R.A.F.	92	NZ746		22	N9335	
63	N9262		93	NZ747		23	N9336	
64	N9263		94	NZ748	R.N.Z.A.F.	24	N9337	
65	N9264		95	NZ749		25	N9338	
66	N9265		96	NZ750		26	N9339	
67	N9266		97	NZ751		27	N9340	
68	N9267		98	N9311		28	N9341	
69	N9268		99	N9312		29	N9342	
82370	N9269		82400	N9313		82430	N9343	
71	N9270		01	N9314	R.A.F.	31	N9344	
72	N9271		02	N9315		32	N9345	
73	N9272		03	N9316		33	N9346	
74	N9273		04	N9317		34	N9347	

First Channel crossing made standing on a wing. Allanah Campbell and Dennis Hartas approach the French coast.

Sea Tiger G-AIVW of the Seaplane Club.

C. Nepean Bishop wades in to help beach the Sea Tiger.

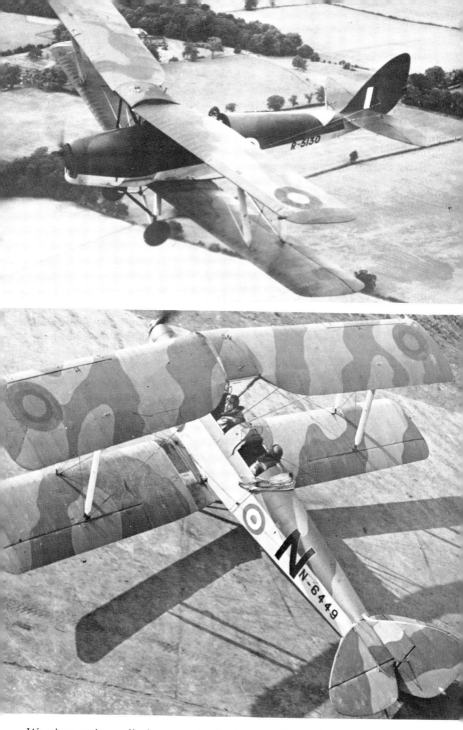

Wartime trainers display non-standard camouflage schemes. The upper (R5130) carries a mustard gas detector panel on the rear fuselage; the lower (N6449) is a naval aircraft.

Top: Flying-Club Tiger in New Zealand; *centre*: two aircraft of the Royal Singapore Flying Club fleet; *bottom*: Bankstown-based Tiger on beach landing-strip in Australia.

Wks. No.	Registration	Remarks	Wks. No.	Registration	Remarks	Wks. No.	Registration	Remarks
82435	N9348	⎫	82465	N9395	⎫	82495	N9441	⎫
36	N9349		66	N9396		96	N9442	
37	N9367		67	N9397		97	N9443	
38	N9368		68	N9398		98	N9444	
39	N9369		69	N9399		99	N9445	
82440	N9370		82470	N9400		82500	N9446	
41	N9371		71	N9401		01	N9447	
42	N9372		72	N9402		02	N9448	
43	N9373		73	N9403		03	N9449	
44	N9374		74	N9404		04	N9450	
45	N9375		75	N9405		05	N9451	
46	N9376		76	N9406		06	N9452	
47	N9377		77	N9407		07	N9453	
48	N9378		78	N9408		08	N9454	
49	N9379	R.A.F.	79	N9409	R.A.F.	09	N9455	R.A.F.
82450	N9380		82480	N9410		82510	N9456	
51	N9381		81	N9427		11	N9457	
52	N9382		82	N9428		12	N9458	
53	N9383		83	N9429		13	N9459	
54	N9384		84	N9430		14	N9460	
55	N9385		85	N9431		15	N9461	
56	N9386		86	N9432		16	N9462	
57	N9387		87	N9433		17	N9463	
58	N9388		88	N9434		18	N9464	
59	N9389		89	N9435		19	N9492	
82460	N9390		82490	N9436		82520	N9493	
61	N9391		91	N9437		21	N9494	
62	N9392		92	N9438		22	N9495	
63	N9393		93	N9439		23	N9496	
64	N9394	⎭	94	N9440	⎭	24	N9497	⎭

Wks. No.	Regis-tration	Remarks	Wks. No.	Regis-tration	Remarks	Wks. No.	Regis-tration	Remarks
82525	N9498		82555	A17-1		82585	G-AFSR	
26	N9499		56	A17-2		86	G-AFSS	
27	N9500		57	A17-3		87	G-AFST	
28	N9501		58	A17-4		88	G-AFSU	
29	N9502		59	A17-5		89	G-AFWC	
82530	N9503		82560	A17-6		82590	G-AFWD	Canadian built Fuselages
31	N9504		61	A17-7		91	G-AFWE	
32	N9505		62	A17-8		92	G-AFWF	
33	N9506		63	A17-9		93	G-AFYB	
34	N9507		64	A17-10	ROYAL AUSTRALIAN AIR FORCE	94	G-AFYC	
35	N9508		65	A17-11		95	G-AFZD	
36	N9509		66	A17-12		96	VP-KCT	
37	N9510		67	A17-13		97	VP-KCU	KENYA
38	N9511		68	A17-14		98	VP-KCV	
39	N9512	R.A.F.	69	A17-15		99		
82540	N9513		82570	A17-16		82600		
41	N9514		71	A17-17		01		
42	N9515		72	A17-18		02		
43	N9516		73	A17-19		03		
44	N9517		74	A17-20		04		
45	N9518		75	G-AFTJ		05		Reserved for Canadian Fuselages
46	N9519		76	VT-ALL		06		
47	N9520		77	VT-ALB		07		
48	N9521		78	VT-ALC		08		
49	N9522		79	VT-ALD	INDIA	09		
82550	N9523		82580	VT-ALE		82610		
51	R4748		81	VT-ALF		11		
52	R4749		82	VT-ALG		12		
53	R4750		83	VT-ALH		13		
54	R4751		84	G-AFSP	Canadian built Fuselage	14		

Wks. No.	Regis-tration	Remarks	Wks. No.	Regis-tration	Remarks	Wks. No.	Regis-tration	Remarks
82615			82645			82675		
16			46			76		
17			47			77		
18			48			78		
19			49			79		
82620			82650			82680		
21			51			81		
22			52			82		Reserved for Canadian Fuselages
23			53			83		
24			54			84		
25			55			85		
26			56			86		
27			57			87		
28			58			88		
29		Reserved for Canadian Fuselages	59		Reserved for Canadian Fuselages	89		
82630			82660			82690		
31			61			91	R4750	
32			62			92	R4751	
33			63			93	R4752	
34			64			94	R4753	
35			65			95	R4754	
36			66			96	R4755	
37			67			97	R4756	
38			68			98	R4757	R.A.F.
39			69			99	R4758	
82640			82670			82700	R4759	
41			71			01	R4760	
42			72			02	R4761	
43			73			03	R4762	
44			74			04	R4763	

Wks. No.	Registration	Remarks	Wks. No.	Registration	Remarks	Wks. No.	Registration	Remarks
82705	R4764		82735	R4791		82765	R4833	
06	R4765		36	R4792		66	R4834	
07	R4766		37	R4793		67	R4835	
08	R4767		38	R4794		68	R4836	
09	R4768	R.A.F.	39	R4795		69	R4837	
82710	R4769		82740	R4796		82770	R4838	
11	R4770		41	R4797		71	R4839	
12	R4771		42	R4810		72	R4840	
13	NZ752		43	R4811		73	R4841	
14	NZ753	R.N.Z.A.F.	44	R4812		74	R4842	
15	NZ754		45	R4813		75	R4843	
16	R4772		46	R4814		76	R4844	
17	R4773		47	R4815		77	R4845	
18	R4774		48	R4816		78	R4846	
19	R4775		49	R4817	R.A.F.	79	R4847	R.A.F.
82720	R4776		82750	R4818		82780	R4848	
21	R4777		51	R4819		81	R4849	
22	R4778		52	R4820		82	R4850	
23	R4779		53	R4821		83	R4851	
24	R4780		54	R4822		84	R4852	
25	R4781	R.A.F.	55	R4823		85	R4853	
26	R4782		56	R4824		86	R4854	
27	R4783		57	R4825		87	R4855	
28	R4784		58	R4826		88	R4856	
29	R4785		59	R4827		89	R4857	
82730	R4786		82760	R4828		82790	R4858	
31	R4787		61	R4829		91	R4859	
32	R4788		62	R4830		92	R4875	
33	R4789		63	R4831		93	R4876	
34	R4790		64	R4832		94	R4877	

Wks. No.	Registration	Remarks	Wks. No.	Registration	Remarks	Wks. No.	Registration	Remarks
82795	R4878		82825	R4908		82855	R4947	
96	R4879		26	R4909		56	R4948	
97	R4880		27	R4910		57	R4949	
98	R4881		28	R4911		58	R4950	
99	R4882		29	R4912		59	R4951	
82800	R4883		82830	R4913	R.A.F.	82860	R4952	
01	R4884		31	R4914		61	R4953	
02	R4885		32	R4915		62	R4954	
03	R4886		33	R4916		63	R4955	
04	R4887		34	R4917		64	R4956	R.A.F.
05	R4888		35	R4918		65	R4957	
06	R4889		36	NZ755		66	R4958	
07	R4890		37	NZ756		67	R4959	
08	R4891		38	NZ757		68	R4960	
09	R4892	R.A.F.	39	NZ758	R.N.Z.A.F.	69	R4961	
82810	R4893		82840	NZ759		82870	R4962	
11	R4894		41	NZ760		71	R4963	
12	R4895		42	R4919		72	R4964	
13	R4896		43	R4920		73	R4965	
14	R4897		44	R4921		74	XY-AAB	BURMA
15	R4898		45	R4922		75	XY-AAC	
16	R4899		46	R4923		76	R4966	
17	R4900		47	R4924		77	R4967	
18	R4901		48	R4940	R.A.F.	78	R4968	
19	R4902		49	R4941		79	R4969	
82820	R4903		82850	R4942		82880	R4970	R.A.F.
21	R4904		51	R4943		81	R4971	
22	R4905		52	R4944		82	R4972	
23	R4906		53	R4945		83	R4973	
24	R4907		54	R4946		84	R4974	

233

Wks. No.	Registration	Remarks	Wks. No.	Registration	Remarks	Wks. No.	Registration	Remarks
82585	R4975		82915	R5020		82945	NZ764	
86	R4976		16	R5021		46	NZ765	
87	R4977		17	R5022		47	NZ766	R.N.Z.A.F.
88	R4978		18	R5023		48	NZ767	
89	R4979		19	R5024		49	NZ768	
82890	R4980		82920	R5025		82950	R5043	
91	R4981		21	R5026		51	R5044	
92	R4982		22	R5027		52	R5057	
93	R4983		23	R5028	R.A.F.	53	R5058	
94	R4984		24	R5029		54	R5059	
95	R4985		25	R5030		55	R5060	
96	R4986		26	R5031		56	R5061	
97	R4987		27	R5032		57	R5062	
98	R4988		28	R5033		58	R5063	
99	R4989		29	R5034		59	R5064	
82900	R5005	R.A.F.	82930	R5035		82960	R5065	
01	R5006		31	R5036		61	R5066	
02	R5007		32	–		62	R5067	R.A.F.
03	R5008		33	–		63	R5068	
04	R5009		34	–	S. AFRICAN AIR FORCE	64	R5069	
05	R5010		35	–		65	R5070	
06	R5011		36	–		66	R5071	
07	R5012		37	–		67	R5072	
08	R5013		38	R5037		68	R5073	
09	R5014		39	R5038		69	R5074	
82910	R5015		82940	R5039	R.A.F.	82970	R5075	
11	R5016		41	R5040		71	R5076	
12	R5017		42	R5041		72	R5077	
13	R5018		43	R5042		73	R5078	
14	R5019		44	NZ763	R.N.Z.A.F.	74	R5079	

Wks. No.	Registration	Remarks	Wks. No.	Registration	Remarks	Wks. No.	Registration	Remarks
82975	R5080		83005	R5123		83035	R5173	
76	R5081		06	R5124		36	R5174	
77	R5082		07	R5125		37	R5175	
78	R5083		08	R5126		38	R5176	
79	R5084		09	R5127		39	R5177	
82980	R5085		83010	R5128		83040	R5178	
81	R5086		11	R5129		41	R5179	
82	R5100		12	R5130		42	R5180	
83	R5101		13	R5131		43	R5181	
84	R5102		14	R5132		44	R5182	
85	R5103		15	R5133		45	R5183	
86	R5104		16	R5134		46	R5184	
87	R5105		17	R5135		47	R5185	
88	R5106		18	R5136		48	R5186	
89	R5107	R.A.F.	19	R5137	R.A.F.	49	R5187	R.A.F.
82990	R5108		83020	R5138		83050	R5188	
91	R5109		21	R5139		51	R5189	
92	R5110		22	R5140		52	R5190	
93	R5111		23	R5141		53	R5191	
94	R5112		24	R5142		54	R5192	
95	R5113		25	R5143		55	R5193	
96	R5114		26	R5144		56	R5194	
97	R5115		27	R5145		57	R5195	
98	R5116		28	R5146		58	R5196	
99	R5117		29	R5147		59	R5197	
83000	R5118		83030	R5148		83060	R5198	
01	R5119		31	R5149		61	R5199	
02	R5120		32	R5170		62	R5200	
03	R5121		33	R5171		63	R5201	
04	R5122		34	R5172		64	R5202	

Wks. No.	Registration	Remarks	Wks. No.	Registration	Remarks	Wks. No.	Registration	Remarks
83065	R5203		83085	3		83105	R5246	
66	R5204		86	4		06	R5247	
67	R5205		87	5	FRANCE	07	R5248	
68	R5206		88	6		08	R5249	
69	R5207		89	7		09	R5250	
83070	R5208		83090	R5215		83110	R5251	
71	R5209	R.A.F.	91	R5216		11	R5252	
72	R5210		92	R5217		12	R5253	
73	R5211		93	R5218		13	R5254	
74	R5212		94	R5219		14	R5255	R.A.F.
75	R5213		95	R5236		15	R5256	
76	R5214		96	R5237		16	R5257	
77	NZ769		97	R5238	R.A.F.	17	R5258	
78	NZ770		98	R5239		18	R5259	
79	NZ771	R.N.Z.A.F.	99	R5240		19	R5260	
83080	NZ772		83100	R5241		83120	R5261	
81	NZ773		01	R5242		21	R5262	
82	NZ774		02	R5243		22	R5263	
83	1	FRANCE	03	R5244		23	R5264	
84	2		04	R5245		24	R5265	

DH 82A TIGER MOTHS CONSTRUCTED 1934-6 AT THE DE HAVILLAND TECHNICAL SCHOOL

Constructors No.	Registration	Remarks
1993	G–ACPS	Used by the
2262	G–ADGO	London Aeroplane
2264	G–AEVB	Club

DH 82A TIGER MOTHS CONSTRUCTED BY MORRIS MOTORS LTD., AT COWLEY

T5360–5384	T6734–6778	T8022–8066	DF111–159
T5409–5433	T6797–6831	T8096–8145	DF173–214
T5454–5503	T6854–6878	T8166–8210	EM720–756
T5520–5564	T6897–6921	T8230–8264	EM771–819
T5595–5639	T6942–6991	DE131–178	EM835–884
T5669–5718	T7011–7055	DE192–224	EM893–931
T5749–5788	T7085–7129	DE236–284	EM943–989
T5807–5856	T7142–7191	DE297–323	NL690–735
T5877–5921	T7208–7247	DE336–379	NL748–789
T5952–5986	T7259–7308	DE394–432	NL802–847
T6020–6069	T7325–7369	DE445–490	NL859–898
T6094–6138	T7384–7418	DE507–535	NL903–948
T6158–6202	T7436–7485	DE549–589	NL960–999
T6225–6274	T7509–7553	DE603–640	NM112–158
T6286–6320	T7583–7627	DE654–697	NM171–214
T6362–6406	T7651–7700	DE709–747	PG614–658
T6427–6471	T7723–7757	DE764–791	PG671–716
T6485–6534	T7777–7821	DE808–856	PG728–746
T6547–6596	T7840–7884	DE870–904	
T6612–6656	T7899–7948	DE919–957	
T6671–6720	T7960–8009	DE969–999	

Note: Constructor's Numbers believed to start 83125, sequence irregular.

DH 82A TIGER MOTHS BUILT BY MORRIS MOTORS LTD. AGAINST OVERSEAS ORDERS

Wks. No.	Registration	Remarks	Wks. No.	Registration	Remarks	Wks. No.	Registration	Remarks
83202	NZ775	R.N.Z.A.F. Assembled by D.H. New Zealand. Their works numbers DHNZ 25–30	83389	NZ791	R.N.Z.A.F. Assembled by D.H. New Zealand. Their works numbers DHNZ 41–48	83633	VT-AMV	INDIA
03	NZ776		83390	NZ792		83654	VT-AMW	
04	NZ777		91	NZ793		55	VT-AMX	
05	NZ778		92	NZ794		56	VT-AMY	
06	NZ779		93	NZ795		57	VT-AMZ	
07	NZ780		94	NZ796		58	VT-ANA	
83352	-	PERSIAN AIR FORCE	95	NZ797		59	VT-ANB	
53	-		96	NZ798		83660	VT-ANC	
55	-		83515	-	SOUTH AFRICAN AIR FORCE	83701	VT-AND	
57	-		16	-		02	VT-ANE	
58	-		17	-		03	VT-ANF	
59	-		18	-		04	VT-ANG	
83360	-		19	-		05	VT-ANH	
61	-		83571	VT-AMI		83746	VT-ANI	
62	-		72	VT-AMJ		83774	-	NOT TRACED
63	-		83587	VT-AMK		75	-	
83379	NZ781	R.N.Z.A.F. Assembled by D.H. New Zealand. Their works numbers DHNZ 31–40	88	VT-AML		76	-	
83380	NZ782		83599	VT-AMM		77	-	
81	NZ783		83600	VT-AMN		78	-	
82	NZ784		01	VT-AMO	INDIA	79	-	
83	NZ785		83627	VT-AMP		83780	-	
84	NZ786		28	VT-AMQ		81	-	
85	NZ787		29	VT-AMR		82	-	
86	NZ788		83630	VT-AMS		83	-	
87	NZ789		31	VT-AMT				
88	NZ790		32	VT-AMU				

DH 82A TIGER MOTHS BUILT ABROAD UNDER LICENCE

NORWAY (Total 20)

Wks. No.	Regis-tration	Remarks	Wks. No.	Regis-tration	Remarks	Wks. No.	Regis-tration	Remarks
-	161	ROYAL NORWEGIAN AIR FORCE	-	175	ROYAL NORWEGIAN AIR FORCE	-	189	ROYAL NORWEGIAN AIR FORCE
-	163		-	177		-	191	
-	165		-	179		-	-	
-	167		-	181		-	-	
-	169		-	183		-	-	
-	171		-	185		-	-	
-	173		-	187				

SWEDEN (Total 20)

Wks. No.	Registration	Remarks	Wks. No.	Registration	Remarks	Wks. No.	Registration	Remarks
41	FV519	SWEDISH AIR FORCE	48	FV516	SWEDISH AIR FORCE	70	FV548	SWEDISH AIR FORCE
42	FV520		49	FV517		71	FV549	
43	FV521		50	FV518		72	FV550	
44	FV522		66	FV509		73	FV553	
45	FV523		67	FV510		74	FV589	
46	FV524		68	FV546		75	FV590	
47	FV515		69	FV547				

PORTUGAL (Total 91)

WORKS NUMBERS P1 to P91

REGISTRATIONS UNCERTAIN.

DH 82A AND C TIGER MOTHS CONSTRUCTED BY
DE HAVILLAND AIRCRAFT OF CANADA LTD*

Known Works Numbers	Known Registrations	Tiger Moth Type	Remarks
DHC301	239 – 258	DH82a	ROYAL CANADIAN AIR FORCE
	CF – CFJ	DH82a	
	275 – 279	DH82a	ROYAL CANADIAN AIR FORCE
	CF – BNF	DH82a	
	CF – BNC	DH82a	
	Unknown	DH82a	199 Civil untraced. Some possibly to U.K.
	1100 – 1299	DH82c	200 made for U.S.A.A.F. (Their designation P.T.24) Given U.S. Serials FEIOO – 266 and FH618 – 50. Diverted to R.C.A.F.
	3842 – 3991	DH82c	ROYAL CANADIAN AIR FORCE
	4001 – 4404	DH82c	ROYAL CANADIAN AIR FORCE
	4810 – 4945	DH82c	136 fitted with 120 H.P. Menasco Engines for R.C.A.F.
	4946 – 5175	DH82c	ROYAL CANADIAN AIR FORCE
	5800 – 5999	DH82c	ROYAL CANADIAN AIR FORCE
	8851 – 8999	DH82c	ROYAL CANADIAN AIR FORCE
DHC1087	9645 – 9695	DH82c	ROYAL CANADIAN AIR FORCE

	TOTALS:	DH82a	227
		DH82c	1,520

DH 82A TIGER MOTHS CONSTRUCTED BY
DE HAVILLAND AIRCRAFT OF NEW ZEALAND*

Known Works Numbers	Registrations	Remarks
DHNZ 31 to DHNZ 181 and others	NZ 650 to NZ 900 NZ 1401 to NZ 1494	ROYAL NEW ZEALAND AIR FORCE

NOTE. Some of the 345 Tiger Moths listed in this table are believed to have been part manufactured in England and Australia.

* Details incomplete

DH 82A TIGER MOTHS CONSTRUCTED BY
DE HAVILLAND AUSTRALIA PTY, LTD

Date Delivered	Registrations	Remarks
June 24, 1940 to Dec. 18, 1940	A17-24-30, 32-46, 31, 47-70; 73, 74, 71, 72, 75-88, 90, 89, 91-6, 98, 97, 99-103, 105, 107, 104, 106, 108, 109, 113, 115-117, 110-112, 118-27, 114, 129-33, 135, 137, 138, 140, 141, 134, 139, 142, 147, 143, 145, 136, 144, 148, 149, 150, 152, 153, 155, 151, 128, 146, 154, 156, 158, 163, 159-61, 165, 166, 168, 170, 171, 173, 162, 167, 174, 175, 178, 179, 157, 164-9, 172, 181, 183, 185, 176, 177, 180, 182, 184, 186, 187-9, 191, 193, 196, 190, 192, 194, 195, 197-205, 207, 223.	Royal Australian Air Force
Dec. 1940	3 machines (Reg. unknown)	Madras Flying Club
Dec. 1940	2 machines (Reg. unknown)	Government of Burma
Dec. 23, 1940 Apr. 10, 1941	A17-206, 208-11, 212-22, 224, 226, 225, 227-32, 233-8, 245, 239-44, 246-9, 255, 253, 254, 251, 252, 256, 258, 260, 261, 250, 257, 262, 268, 259, 263-7, 269-74, 276, 277, 279-83, 275, 287, 289, 294, 278, 284-6, 288, 290-3, 295-303, 305, 304, 307, 310, 319, 308, 323, 314.	Royal Australian Air Force
Apr. 1941	1 machine (Reg. unknown)	Broken Hill Aero Club
Apr. 14, 1941 to June 28, 1941	A17-306, 309, 311-13, 315, 316, 318, 320-2, 324-31, 333-40, 317, 341, 332, 342-59, 361, 364, 366, 360, 362, 365, 367-70, 372, 373, 363, 371, 374-77, 382, 379-81, 384-6, 388, 389, 378, 383, 390-404, 387.	Royal Australian Air Force
June. 1941 to Sept. 1941	60 machines (Reg. unknown) 20 machines (Reg. unknown) 18 machines NZ 1402-19 5 machines (Reg. unknown)	Dutch East Indies Government of India R. N. Z. A. F. Government of India

Date Delivered	Registrations	Remarks
Sept. 15, 1941 ↓ to Nov. 21, 1941	A17-407, 409, 411, 414, 406, 410, 412, 405, 413, 416, 418, 419, 408, 415, 417, 420-5, 426-35, 438, 436, 437, 441, 439, 440, 442-54.	Royal Australian Air Force
Nov. 1941 Apr. 1942 to	DX437-61, DX 474-512, DX526-557, DX569-612, DX627-65, DX679-716, DX750-835 *	R.A.F. orders for Rhodesia and South Africa
Apr.13, 1942 ↓ do July 25, 1942	A17-455-464, 466, 465, 467-88, 490, 492, 489, 491, 495, 497, 496, 498-500, 502, 504, 493, 494, 503, 505, 506, 507, 501, 509, 508, 510-23, 525, 526, 524, 527-32, 537, 534, 533, 536, 538-40, 549, 535, 541-47, 551, 550, 552-60, 548, 562, 561, 563, 564, 566, 567, 569, 570, 590, 568, 571, 573, 572, 574-88.	Royal Australian Air Force
July 29, 1942 to Aug.21, 1942	A17-565, 591, 592, 589, 593-6, 600, 597, 598, 599, 601-8, 610, 609, 611-16, 618, 617, 619, 620.	R.A.F. A17-565 was 1,000th Tiger Moth to be made in Australia
July 16, 1943 to Nov.24, 1943	A17-627, 628, 630, 631, 629, 632, 633, 636, 634, 637-40, 635, 641-73, 692-724.	Royal Australian Air Force
Sept.20, 1944 to Feb. 5, 1945	A17-725-727, 729, 728, 730-42, 744, 743, 745, 747, 746, 748, 749, 751, 750, 753, 754, 752, 755-60.	

NOTE: Australian Constructors numbers are believed to commence T.021. No complete records exist, but details of the aircraft made for the Royal Australian Air Force are authentic and listed in order of delivery. Although de Havilland Australia are usually quoted as having built 1,085 Tiger Moths, 1,125 are evident on these pages.

* Additional machines were sent from Australia to Rhodesia without the prefix DX, e.g. 527, 529, 541-5, 576, 578, 680, 683, 686 and 691.

Index

Top: G-ANFM at Booker in gaudy colouring for film-making; *centre*: scene at Leinster Aero Club Display in August 1958; *bottom*: Morris-built EM960 undergoing three-man movement in India.

Top: Recent photograph of Australian aircraft with modified crew seating; *centre*: American N12731 in pre-war colour scheme; *bottom*: Free-French officer aboard AX856 in 1942.

Top: A17-161, preserved at Perth, Australia; *centre*: two Tiger Moths and a Harvard of the Royal Naval College; *bottom*: T5823, sole R.A.F. representative at 1955 '21st birthday' Tiger Rally.

Top: Ex-Croydon aircraft now registered in France as F-BGCZ; *centre*: Tiger as engine test rig in India—note extra fuel tank; *bottom*: VH-FAS in smart lining at Jandacot, Australia.

De Havilland Co.—*Cont.*
65-6; founder-members of, 65; moves to Hatfield, 66; and 'Queen Bees', 81; buys fuselages from De H. (Canada), 85; and mosquito production, 110; its post-war enterprises, 147; and Doran-Webb's conversion plan, 166; and float-conversion drawings, 187

De Havilland Aircraft of Canada, Ltd.: 30, 82, 84, 131; its production of T.M.'s, 84; committed to DH 82c, 85; and float-conversion drawings, 187

De Havilland Aircraft of New Zealand, Ltd.: 135

De Havilland Aircraft Proprietary, Ltd. (Australia): 133-6; *passim*, 140

De Havilland Aircraft Since 1915 (Jackson): 113

De Havilland Gazette: quoted, 16-17

De Havilland, Sir Geoffrey: 2-3, 32 *n*; his first aircraft, 3; his grandfather's confidence, 3, 4; his second aircraft, 4; designer of aircraft, 4; forms Company, 4; and 'everyman's aeroplane', 4, 6, 7, 9-10, 11; entomologist, 13; tests DH 60, 13; on flying a 'Moth', 18-20; and 'Cirrus' engines, 21; and T.M. prototype, 32; and Alan Cobham, 49; and military and civil contracts, 64-5; his choice of men, 65; and the light bomber, 110

De Havilland, Hereward: 97, 100
De Havilland Technical School: 81
Denyer, Jim: 187
Derby Flying School: 148
Desford Flying School: 68-70, 94
Deverell, Adrian: 179
Display's, Air: Cobham's (2), 50-3; Hendon, 14; Rochester, 144;

Sywell, 177-8; techniques of, 53-4. *See also* Tiger Club

Doran-Webb, Squadron Leader J. E.: 163-4, 165 & *passim*

Douglas of Kirtleside, M.R.A.F. Lord: 186

'Dove', de Havilland: 147, 172
'Dragon', de Havilland (DH 84): 82, 96
Dunkirk: 88, 96
Dutch East Indies (*now* Indonesia): 134, 135 *n*
Dyce: 101

E.F.T.S.: *see* Flying Training Schools, Elementary
Edgware: 4. *See also* Stag Lane
Elstree: 174
Empire Air Training Scheme: 114-17, 131-41; in Great Britain, 200-2; in Canada, 203; in Australia, 205; in New Zealand, 206; in Rhodesia (RATG), 206; in South Africa, 207; in India, 207
Engine, the: importance of, 3
Engines (*see also under names and numbers*): power-weight ratio, 7; for light aeroplanes, 10; inverted, 28; for 'Moths' (*names and details*), 29
Esso Petroleum Co., Ltd.: 187
European countries: 27
Evaluation trials, Air Ministry: 34, 41-3
Evening News: 181
Exhaust fumes poisoning: 132

F.I.S. (Flying Instructors' School): 120
F.T.S.: *see* Flying Training School
Fairoaks Aero Club *and* Aerodrome: 161. *See also* Fairoaks
Fairey Aviation, Ltd.: 167
'Fairey IIIF' (seaplane, auto-controlled): 80
'Fairey' Monoplane: 49-50

Top: G-AMLF in a wartime storage hangar; *centre*: DP262 in India during the war; *bottom*: Belgian Air Force T15 flanked by Morane and Hurricane at Brussels Air Salon, August 1939.

Top: G-AOIO, Jackaroo conversion from Tiger Moth; *centre and bottom*: recent photographs of G-ANDE and G-AXXE—the former at Stapleford and the latter being serviced at Doncaster.

UNITED KINGDOM

G–ACDC	N. H. Jones, The White House, Church Road, Claygate, Surrey	DH No. 3177 of 1933
G–ACDJ	Agricultural Aviation and Engineering, Wood Farm, Denton, Harleston, Norfolk	DH No. 3183 of 1933
G–ADAI	J. Beaty, Drayton House Farm, Lowick, Kettering, Northants	DH No. 3368 of 1935
G–ADJJ	L. B. Jefferies, Ash Tree Cottage, Fuller's Hill, Little Gransden, Sandy, Beds	DH No. 3386 of 1935
G–AGYU	J. F. Thurlow, 2 Richardson Walk, Lexden, Colchester, Essex (The Essex-Suffolk Gliding Club)	DH No. 8301
G–AHIZ	D. Jackson, 128 Hinton Way, Gt Shelford, Cambridge and W. F. Ison, 39 Windsor Road, Cambridge (Cambridge Private Flying Group)	DH No. 4610 of 1944
G–AHMN	Scottish Gliding Union Ltd, Portmoak, Scotlandwell, by Kinross	Ex-RAF N6985
G–AHRC	C. Boddington, 16 Townwell Lane, Irchester, Wellingborough, Northant	Ex-RAF T6064
G–AHUE	W. C. Hutchinson & Partners, 13 Poplar Way, Stafford (Staffordshire Gliding Club)	Ex-RAF T7868
G–AHUV	W. G. Gordon, Lude, Blair Atholl, Perthshire	Ex-RAF N6593
G–AHVV	D. R. Wilcox, 63a Queen's Park Parade, Northampton and F. D. Ruddington, 232 Kimbolton Road, Bedford	Ex-RAF EM929
G–AIIZ	F. J. Lock, London Transport (Central Road Services) Sports Association Flying Club, 301 Camberwell New Road, London SE8	Ex-RAF
G–AIRI		DH No. 3761 of 1940
G–AIRK	C. R. Boreham & Partners, 146 Swan Street, Sible Hedingham, Halstead, Essex	DH No. 82336
G–AIVW	(As G–ACDC above)	Floatplane
G–AIXD	D. L. Lloyd, Pipewell Hall, nr Kettering, Northants	DH No. 82224 of 1938
G–AJHS	R.A.E. Aero Club Ltd, Royal Airrcaft Establishment, Farnborough, Hants	Ex-RAF N6866
G–AJHII	F. P. le Coyte, 50 Roundway Road, Swindon, Wilts (Calleva Flying Group)	Ex-RAF T7471
G–AJOA	(As G–ACDC above)	Ex-RAF T5424
G–AKXS	D. A. Smith, 53 Baronsmede, Ealing, London W5	Ex-RAF T7105
G–ALBD	Drive Lease Ltd, 42 St Stephens Street, Aston, Birmingham 6	Ex-RAF T7748
G–ALNA	W. J. Fairbairn & Partners, 'Clairville', Ashurst Bridge, Totton, Southampton, Hants (Wessex Flying Group)	Ex-RAF T6774
G–ALND	Bustard Flying Club, A&AEE, Boscombe Down, Salisbury, Wilts	Ex-RAF N9191

G–ALTW	W. R. Calway, The Gables, Hertingfordbury Rd, Hertford	Ex-RAF T7799
G–ALWW	(As G–ALBD above)	Ex-RAF NL932
G–AMIU		Ex-RAF T5495
G–AMLF	I. M. Peschcha-Koedt, 47 Ladygate Lane, Ruislip, Middx	Ex-RAF PG675
G–ANCX	D. R. Wood, Owlsnest Wood, Tonbridge Road, Pembury, Tunbridge Wells, Kent	Ex-RAF T7229
G–ANDE	R. Sanders, 126 Hertford Road, London N9	Ex-RAF E726
G–ANDI	P. J. Benest, 10 Edinburgh Gardens, Windsor, Bucks	Ex-RAF N6642
G–ANDP	W. J. Ogle & Partners, 72 Beveley Gardens, Bangor, County Down, N. Ireland (Ards Tiger Group)	Ex-RAF R4960
G–ANEF	Royal Air Force College Flying Club, RAF College, Cranwell, nr Sleaford, Lincs	Ex-RAF T5493
G–ANEY	W. P. Maynell, Ravensworth, Richmond, Yorks	Ex-RAF N9238
G–ANEZ	Isle of Wight Gliding Club Ltd, Lea Aerodrome, Sandown, Isle of Wight	Ex-RAF T7849
G–ANFC	London Gliding Club Ltd, The Club House, Dunstable Downs, Beds	Ex-RAF DE363
G–ANFI	Cambridge University Gliding Trust Ltd, 10 Peas Hill, Cambridge	Ex-RAF DE623
G–ANFM	J. H. Hassard-Short, 10 Mayfield Drive, Caversham, Reading, Berks (Reading Flying Group)	Ex-RAF T5888
G–ANFW	K. A. Norman, Rosedon, Stoike Road, Kelly Bay, Callington, Cornwall and G. L. Morel, Fairview, Florence Road, Valley Bay, Callington, Cornwall	DH No. 3737
G–ANFY	M. F. Ogilvie-Forbes, Esseborne Manor, Hurstbourne Tarrant, Andover, Hants	Jackaroo Ex-NL906
G–ANJA	H. G. Craik, 6 Harrington Avenue, Lowestoft, Suffolk and W. T. Wix, Kondinin, Church Road, Blunderston, Lowestoft, Suffolk (Waveney Flying Group)	Ex-FAR N9389
G–ANJD		Ex-RAF T6226
G–ANJK	C. D. Millington & Partners, Green Acre, Salop Road, Welshpool, Montgomery (Montgomery Ultra Light Flying Club)	Ex-RAF T6066
G–ANKB	I. D. Hay, 7 Foxgrove Avenue, Beckenham, Kent	Ex-RAF N6911
G–ANKK	R. V. Guck, 15 Elmbank Grove, Wansworth Wood, Birmingham 21 and J. Spring, 165 Lichfield Road, Birmingham 6 (Birmingham Tiger Group)	Ex-RAF T5854
G–ANKT	Quislats Ltd, Ryland House, Newell Road, Redditch, Worcs	Ex-RAF T6818
G–ANLS	Rollason Aircraft & Engines Ltd, Croydon Airport, Croydon, Surrey	Ex-RAF DF113

G–ANMO	C. Goodman, Sywell	DH No. 3255
G–ANMV	The Norfolk & Norwich Aero Club Ltd, The Clubhouse, Swanton Morley, Dereham, Norfolk	Ex-RAF T7404
G–ANMZ	N. H. Jones, The White House, Church Road, Claygate, Surrey	Ex-RAF DE634
G–ANNG	P. F. Walter, Heather Cottage, Hazeley Heath, Hartley, Wintney, Hants	Ex-RAF DE524
G–ANON	R. Corry & D. Harrison, Ardvara, Cultra, Holywood, N. Ireland	Ex-RAF T7909
G–ANOO	M. F. Caiger & Partners, Flat 1, Bromham Rd, Bedford (National Aeronautical Establishment Aero Club)	Ex-RAF DE401
G–ANOR	A. J. Cheshire, 43 Park Hill Road, Croydon, Surrey	Ex-RAF DE694
G–ANPK		Ex-RAF L6936
G–ANRF	B. Tempest & Partners, 4 Clarence Court, Rushden, Northants	Ex-RAF T5850
G–ANRN	G. J. & R. G. Adans, Adamix Refactories, Hall Yard Works, King's Cliffe, Northants	Ex-RAF T5368
G–ANSM	T. R. Davey, 'Little Court', Golden Valley Road, Bitton, Glos	Ex-RAF R5014
G–ANSP	Mrs. E. M. Bianchi, Le Vallon, Seymour Court Road, Marlow, Bucks	Ex-RAF DE877
G–ANTE	R. Jones, 7 Penrhyn, Cheshire View, Marchwell, Wrexham, Denbighshire and T. I. Sutton 'Monofran', Chester Road East, Shotton, Chester (Hawker Siddeley Aviation (Chester) Sports & Social Club)	Ex-RAF T6562
G–ANZT	(As G–ANFY above)	Jackaroo Ex-T7798
G–ANZU		DH No. 3583 of 1939
G–ANZZ	(As G–ACDC above)	Ex-RAF DE974
G–AOAA	(As G–ACDC above)	Ex-RAF DF159
G–AOAC	(As G–ACDC above)	Ex-RAF N6978
G–AOBO	D. J. Ronayne, 86 Sunnyhill Avenue, Biggin Hill, Kent and A. J. Cheshire, 43 Park Hill Road, Croydon, Surrey	Ex-RAF N6473
G–AOBX	(As G–ACDC above)	Ex-RAF T7187
G–AOCV	S. H. Potter, 13 Lakeside, Earley, Reading, Berks	Ex-RAF N6670
G–AODS	(As G–ACDC above)	Ex-RAF R5041
G–AODT	N. A. Brett, Crome Cottage, Old Catton, Norwich and A. H. Warminger, 8 Bracondale, Norwich	Ex-RAF R5250
G–AODX	Bristol Gliding Club Ltd, Nympsfield, Stonehouse, Glos	Ex-RAF T5716
G–AOEG	D. E. Leatherland & Partners, 8 Southey Street, Nottingham (Midland Tiger Flying Group)	Ex-RAF T7124

G–AOEI	D. Jackson & Partners ,128 Hinton Way, Gt Shelford. Cambridge (Cambridge Private Flying Group)	Ex-RAF N6946
G–AOEL	(As G–ANFC above)	Ex-RAF N9510
G–AOES	(As G–AOBO above)	Ex-RAF T6056
G–AOGS	R. B. Newton, 11 Lismore Road, Whistable, Kent	DH No. 3815
G–AOIM	M. J. Fallon, 23 Heron Court, Harrow-on-the-Hill, Middx	Ex-RAF T7019
G–AOIO	P. R. Harris, 11 The Horseshoe, Leverstock Green, Hemel Hempstead, Herts	Jackaroo Ex-N6907
G–AOIR	P. Martin, The Old Rectory, Claughton, Lancs	Jackaroo Ex-R4972
G–AOIS	V. B. Wheele, 19 Mill Hill, Shoreham-by-Sea, Sussex and R. G. Wheele, Tobago, 37 Withdean Road, Brighton, Sussex	Ex-RAF R5172
G–AOXN	D. W. Mickleburgh, 14 Sedgefield Drive, Thurnby, Leicester	Ex-RAF EM727
G–AOYU	(As G–ALBD above)	Ex-RAF N9151
G–AOZB	M. H. Reid, Coopers Farm, Stonegate, Wadhurst, Sussex	Ex-RAF N6616
G–AOZH	(As G–AOIS above)	Ex-RAF NM129
G–APAJ	R. V. Snook, Lodge Farm, Milsham, Kings Lynn, Norfolk	Jackaroo Ex-T5616
G–APAL	M. J. Brett, 5 Ashwell Road, Bygrave, Baldock, Herts (Stevenage Flying Club)	Jackaroo Ex-N6847
G–APAM	R. Jones, Southern Sailplanes, Thruxton Aerodrome, nr Andover, Hants	Jackaroo Ex-N6850
G–APAO	R. W. Biggs, 'Wild Harvest', 8 Micheldever Road, Whitchurch, Hants	Jackaroo Ex-R4922
G–APAP	H. D. Leach, 27 St Stephens Road, Weeke, Winchester, Hants	Jackaroo Ex-R5136
G–APBI	P. G. Bell & Partners, 8 Heather Lane Avenue, Dore, Sheffield	Ex-RAF EM903
G–APCC	R. J. Moody, Henbury Farm, Each Orchard, Shaftesbury, Dorset	Ex-RAF PG640
G–APCU	J. C. Hoyland, Lennerton Lodge, Sherburn-in-Elmet, Leeds, Yorks	DH No. 82535
G–APFU	(As G–ANOR above)	Ex-RAF EM879
G–APHZ	D. Hughes, Avondale, Hackthorne Corner, Durrington, Salisbury, Wilts	Jackaroo Ex-N6924
G–APMX	Mrs. M. Harriott & Partners, 41 Euston Road, Croydon, Surrey (Rollason Flying Group)	Ex-RAF DE715
G–APVT	E. A. Gilbert, Pymans Farm House, Scarning, Dereham, Norfolk	Ex-RAF K4245
G–ARAZ	C. F. Hall, 55 Goldsmith Road, London N11 and W. S. Green, Cedar Cottage, Hendon Wood Lane, London NW7	Ex-RAF R4959

Top: Recently restored G-ANMO in glossy camouflage finish; *centre*: G-ANDI at Esso Tiger Trophy contest in September 1969; *bottom*: G-AMIU at Booker, 1969, showing unusual rudder decoration.

Top: 'Tiger-shark' ZK-AIA of the Auckland Gliding Club; *centre*: G-AXAN photographed in flight from Denham; *bottom*: Nepean Bishop flying G-ANZZ in the National Air Races, 1959.

Top: A contrast in sizes between a Beverly aircraft of No. 47 Sqdn., R.A.F., and the unit's own Tiger; *bottom*: Royal Indian Air Force Tigers lined up for a graduation parade.

IN RETIREMENT

Discarded 1969 at Grimbergen, near Brussels, are these Tiger Moths once of the Belgium State Flying School.

The late C. A. Nepean Bishop, a famed "Tiger" enthusiast, who instructed on the type in Britain and Rhodesia, and after whom the racing "Tiger" was named "The Bishop"

Wg. Cdr Cyril Arthur, a pilot since 1917, who commanded the Fairoaks Reserve Flying School in 1937 and continued instructing on Tiger Moths at Fairoaks until retirement in 1969.

G–AREH	Sunderland Flying Club Ltd, Sunderland Airport, Washington Road, Sunderland, Co. Durham	Ex-RAF DE241
G–ARTL	Defford Aero Club (Worcestershire) Ltd, R.R.E., Air Station, Pershore, Worcs	Ex-RAF T7281
G–ASET	J. V. Johnston, The Surgery, Park Street, Thaxted, Essex	Ex-RAF NL775
G–ASKP	(As G–ACDC above)	DH No. 3889
G–ASSC	J. D. Menzies, 'Eden Roc', Florida Road, Ferring, Sussex	Ex-RAF R4776
G–ASXB	W. Verling, 75 Grant Road, Farlington, Portsmouth, Hants and D. O. Wallis, 23 Broadclyst Gardens, Thorpe Bay, Essex	Ex-RAF N6539
G–AVPJ		Ex-RAF NL879
G–AXAN	(As G–ANOR above)	Ex-RAF EM720

ADEN

| VR–AAY | | Ex-RAF T6825 |

AUSTRALIA

VH–ARW		Ex-A17-84
VH–CCE	Nevill Parnell, Bankstown, NSW	
VH–FAS	Mervyn Prime, Jandacot, WA	
A17–161	Perth (preserved)	

CANADA

| CF–COU Can. DH 82C | Red River Tiger Moth Club, Tuxedo, Manitoba T. Dow, 327 N. Vickers St, Ft. William, Ontario | Ex-RCAF |

FIJI

| VQ–FAG | Nausori Flying Group, c/o Fiji Airways, Nausori Airport, Fiji | DH No. 83502 |

NEW ZEALAND

| ZK–AIA | |
| ZK–BDH | |

SINGAPORE

| VR–SCY | Royal Singapore Flying Club |

FRANCE

F–BDOB	Aero Club de Moulins, Moulins-Avermes	Ex-RAF DF130
F–BDOC	Aero Club du Finistere, Brest-Guipavas	Ex-RAF NM136
F–BDOK	Aero Club des Deux-Sevres, Niort-Souche	Ex-RAF PG621
F–BDOQ	Aero Club de Belfort, Belfort-Chaux	Ex-RAF PG651
F–BDOS	Aero Club St. Vauclusien, Avignon-Montfavet	Ex-RAF PG671
F–BFDO	Max Simeoni, 71 Avenue O. Butin, Margny-Les-Compiegne, Compiegne	Ex-RAF T7290
F–BFVU	Aero Club de Picardie, Amiens	Ex-RAF PG706
F–BGCF	Aero Club de Bourgogne-les-Bains, Damblain	Ex-RAF NM181
F–BGCJ	Aero Club de Saintonge et d'Aunis, Saintes-les-Gonds	Ex-RAF NM192
F–BGCK	Aero Club de l'Aisne, St Quentin	Ex-RAF NM193
F–BGCL	Association Aero d'Aquitaine, Bordeaux-Saucats	Ex-RAF DF195
F–BGCQ	Union Aero du Centre, Issoudun	Ex-RAF NM206
F–BGCS	Aero Club de Champagne, Reims-St Leanard	Ex-RAF DF210
F–BGCZ	Aero Club du Languedoc, Toulouse-Lasbordes	Ex-RAF PG617
F–BGDD	Aero Club de Dinan, Dinan	Ex-RAF PG626
F–BGDE	(As F–BGCQ above)	Ex-RAF PG636
F–BGDG	Aero Club d'Haguenau, Haguenau	Ex-RAF PG644
F–BGDH	Aero Club de Villefranche, Villefranche-Anse	Ex-RAF PG647
F–BGDL	Aero Club de Bearn and Charles Mace, Pau-Idron	Ex-RAF PG655
F–BGDN	Aero Club du Blanc, Le Blanc	Ex-RAF PG657
F–BGDS	S.F.A., Dijon-Darois	Ex-RAF PG680
F–BGDT	Aero Club Charentais, Rochefort-sur-Mer	Ex-RAF PG687
F–BGED	Clun Air Touraine, Bois-le-Breuil	Ex-RAF EM731
F–BGEE	(As F–BDOQ above)	Ex-RAF PG732
F–BGEG	Aero Club de Sarreguemines, Sarreguemines	Ex-RAF PG735
F–BGEL	Union Aero du Cambresis, Cambrai-Niergnies	Ex-RAF EM778
F–BGEO	Aero Club d'Annenay, St Rambert-d'Albon	Ex-RAF DE831
F–BGEP	(As F–BBGEG above)	Ex-RAF NL838
F–BGEV	Aero Club de la Basse Moselle, Thionville-Basse-Yutz	Ex-RAF NL877
F–BGEZ	Aero Club de l'Oise, Compiegne	Ex-RAF NL896
F–BGJE	Aero Club de Brive, Biarritz-Parme	Ex-RAF NL864
F–BGJH	Aero Club d'Alsace, Strasbourg-Neuhof	Ex-RAF DE991
F–BGJI	Association Aero Provence, Cote d'Azur, Fayence	Ex-RAF DE992
F–BGJJ	Association of Aeroclubs de la Cote d'Emeraude, St Servan	Ex-RAF NL935
F–BHAT	(As F–BDOC above)	Ex-RAF T7397

262

ITALY

I–APLI	Luciano Alberti, Via degli Etruschi, Milan	Ex-RAF PG653
I–BANG	Aero Club Bologna, Via Panigale 52, Bologna	Ex-RAF DE486
I–CEDE	Aero Club Sarzana, Aeroporto di Sarzana, (La Spezia), Sarzana	Ex-RAF DE352
I–GATO	Claudio Balzarotti, Corso Porta Nuova 48, Milan	Ex-RAF DE193
I–GIVI	Vittorio Grimaldi, Viale Italia 373, La Spezia, Sarzana	Ex-RAF T6068
I–JENA	Giovanni Castaldi, Via Dondini 3, Rome	Ex-RAF T6256
I–NONO	Pietro Marzotto, Valgagno (Vicenza), Trissino	Ex-RAF N6739

FEDERAL REPUBLIC OF GERMANY

D–EBIG	Aero-Club (Kreisverband) Geinhausen e.V. Geinhausen, Herzbachweg 29	Ex-E16
D–ECEF	Fliegergruppe Offenburg e.V. 1 Gustav-Ree-Anlage, Offenburg	DH No. 83172
D–EDEM	Aero-Club Geinhausen e.V. 15 Stettiner Str, Geinhausen	Ex-E14
D–EDES	Luftwerbedienst Westfalen, 14 Nehelm-Husten, Kolpingstr 14	Ex-RAF T5823
D–EDIL	Luftsportvereinigung Grenzland e.V., Flugplatz, Grefrath	Ex-RAF R4789
D–EDIS	(As D–EDEM above)	Ex-RAF DE526
D–EFPH	Segelfluggruppe Nordstern e.V., 33 Bruckner Str, Alsdorf	Ex-RAF T7410
D–EFYZ	August Kemmerer, 21 Theodor-Heuss-Allee, Trier	DH No. 82814
D–EGIT	Luftsportverein Aachen e.V., Postfach 932, Bad Aachen	Ex-RAF T7129
D–EGXY	Wolfgang Scherpf, 8–10 Brunckstr, Speyer am Rhein	
D–EGYN	Carl-Heinz Schafer, Flugplatz, Eudenbach uber Siegburg	Ex-RAF T6037

NORWAY

LN–BDM	Oslo Flyklubb Seilflygruppen	DH No. 85294
LN–VYG	T. Naess, Ørland	Ex-RAF DE282

DENMARK

OY–DET	K. L. Houggard, Kastrup	Ex-RAF T6122
OY–DGH	J. T. Toft, Stauning	Ex-RAF DF203
OY–DGJ	L. Jensen and V. Christensen, Herning	Ex-RAF R5086

OY–DYJ	M. Dam, Herning	Ex-RAF DE153
OY–BAK	Egeskov Castle Museum	Ex-RAF NL913
D–EDON	Helsinge/Trafikhistorisk Museum	Ex-RAF N6779

ICELAND

| TF–KBD | J. Erlendsson, Kopavogi | DH No. 1407 |

SPAIN

EC–AFM	Subsecretaria de Aviacion Civil, Ministerio del Aire, Madrid	
EC–AHY		
EC–AMF	R.A.C. de Baleares, Palma de Mal	Ex-RAF T6022

PORTUGAL

CS–AAA	Aero Clube de Portugal, Sintra	DH No. 3650
CS–AEF	Aero Clube do Porto, Porto	
CS–AEL	C.A.A.A.C., Coimbra	
CS–AEO	Aero Clube da Costa Verde, Espinho	
CS–AEQ	Aero Clube de Portugal, Sintra	
CS–AEV	Aero Clube de Portugal, Sintra	
CS–AFC	Aero Clube de Portugal, Sintra	
CS–AFF	Aero Clube da Costa Verde, Espinho	
CS–AFX	Aero Clube de Portugal, Sintra	
CS–AFZ	Aero Clube de Braga, Braga	

BELGIUM

OO–BYL	Vormezeele Herent, Bierset	Ex-RAF T7952
OO–DJU	Schepens, Antwerp (based at Brasschaat)	Ex-712
OO–DLA	Aeroclub du Hainaut Mons, Maubray	Ex-164
OO–EVA	C.N.V.A.V., Brussels (based at Schaffen)	Ex-124
OO–EVE	(As OO–EVA above)	Ex-722
OO–EVH	(As OO–EVA above but based at Wevelgem)	Ex-972
OO–EVM	(As OO–EVA above but based at St Hubert)	Ex-3963
OO–EVO	(As OO–EVH above)	Ex-4623
OO–EVP	(As OO–EVA above but based at Gossoncourt)	Ex-4592
OO–EVS	(As OO–EVM above)	Ex-4276
OO–EVT	(As OO–EVM above)	
OO–JEU	Aeroclub de Brasschaat, Brasschaat	Ex-RAF R5063
OO–MOS	P. peeraer, Wilryk, nr Antwerp	Ex-41
OO–MOT	Limburgse Vieugels, Genk	Ex-677

OO–NCN	E. Jacobs, Retie	Ex-744
OO–SOA	Etat Belge, Brussels	Ex-RAF DF186
OO–SOB	(As OO–SOA above)	Ex-RAF T7025
OO–SOE	(As OO–SOA above)	Ex-857
OO–SOG	(As OO–SOA above)	Ex-5238
OO–SOI	(As OO–SOA above)	Ex-7238
OO–SOM	(As OO–SOA above)	Ex-6102
OO–SOW	(As OO–SOA above)	Ex-6100
OO–SOY	(As OO–SOA above)	Ex-7110

FINLAND

OH–ELC	Rovaniemen Ilmailukerho r.y., Koskikatu 24, Rovaniemi	Ex-RAF N9215

IRELAND (EIRE)

EI–AGP	P. W. Kennedy, Weston Park, Leixlip, Co Kildare	Ex-RAF N9240

NETHERLANDS

PH–ALG	M. J. Duijvesstijn, Witte de Withstraat 46, Twello	
PH–NLC	(As PH–ALG above)	
PH–UAI	N.V. Luchtvaart Maatschappij General Aviation, Luchthaven, Rotterdam	Ex-4520
PH–UAO	N.V. Nationale Luftvaart School, Vliegveldweg 30, Luchthaven, Rotterdam	DH No. 85959
PH–UAT	(As PH–UAI above)	Ex-RAF T7452
PH–UDB	(As PH–ALG above)	DH No. 84734
PH–UDZ	C. Wakker and S. J. Dijkstra Jr, Rosariumlaan, 43, Driebergen	Ex-RAF DE941

SWEDEN

SE–ALM	Kgl Svenska Aeroklubben, Skeppsbron 40, 111 30 Stockholm	Ex-172
SE–ANL	Angermanlands Flygklubb, Vallmovagen 11, 890 30 Hoglandssjon	Ex-161
SE–BYL	(As SE–ALM above)	Ex-Fv 553
SE–CGI	(As SE–ANL above)	DH No. 84661
SE–ATI	Kgl Svenska Aeroklubben, Stockholm	DH No. 3113
SE–CHG	Ake G. Backman, Havstenavagen 42B, 541 00 Skovde and P. C. Hollander, Harpsundsvagen, 10, 124 40 Bandhagen	DH No. 85867
SE–COG	S. I. Andersson, Skolvagen 13D, 184 00 Akerberga	DH No. 85593

SE–COO	Eskilstuna Flygklubb, Box 53, 631 02 Eskilstuna	Ex-RAF NL929
SE–COY	B. Lindstrom, Nyhamm, Sundsvall	DH No. 85882
SE–CPW	Bo Modee, Stellan Kristoffersson, Kurt Nilsson, and Bo Rex, c/o Bo Rex, Box 4007, 305 90 Halmstad	Ex-RAF T7219
SE–CWG	E. Svensson, 290 72 Asarum and Blekinge Flygklubb, Box 2000, 373 00 Kallinge	Ex-RAF BB750

SWITZERLAND

| HB–UBB | Allenbach Hans und Miteigentumer, Fasanenweg 7, Steffisburg-Station | Ex-RAF T7340 |
| HB–UBC | Werner Ulmer, 2723 Marly-le-Petit | Ex-RAF N6652 |

U.S.A.

The Antique Aircraft Association Moth Club, chaired by Ralph M. Wefel, of 8400 Fullbright Avenue, Canoga Park, California 91306, is organised and maintained by persons interested in all de Havilland Moth aircraft, and is devoted to the preservation of these machines. The following list of Tiger Moth owners in the U.S.A. (not claimed to be complete) has been compiled from Club files and presented to the publishers by Dr J. D. Hay, of 7 Foxgrove Avenue, Beckenham, Kent, to whom they are indebted.

DH 82A	Jim Ap Roberts, 4603 Orange Knoll, La Canada, Calif. 91011
DH 82A	Bill Barnes, 44434 3rd St, Lancaster, Calif.
DH 82A	Dave and Ginny Davidson, 1651 Lyndhurst St, Camarillo, Calif. 93010
DH 82C	Robert C. Freeman, 1300 S. Burdick St, Kalamazoo, Michigan 49001
Tiger Moth	Hans A. L. Gerstl, 2208 Fontaine Avenue, Charlotsville, Va.
DH 82A	Clay Henley, Box 66, Kellog, Idaho
DH 82A	Bill and Chris Huerth, 20903 Amie St, Apt. 17, Torrance, Calif. 90503
DH 82C	Walt MacDonald, 15770 E. Alta Vista Way, San Jose, Calif. 95127
DH 82A	Robert N. Kirby, 114 Wm Moffet Pl., Goleta, Calif. 93071
DH 82A	Capt. Michael V. Love, 17 Kellie Court, Edwards AFB, Calif. 93523
DH 82A	Earl F. Nelson, 467 S. 93rd East Avenue, Tulsa, Oklahoma 74112
DH 82A	Stanley Nowak Vintage Car Store Inc., 93–95 S. Broadway, Nyack, NY
DH 82C	Bill Orbeck, 2152 S.W. 322nd St, Federal Way, Washington 98002
DH 82C	H. R. Pass, 806 N.E. 92nd Avenue, Vancouver, Washington 98664
DH 82A	Ace G. Powers MD, Suite 25, Medical Arts Sq., Albuquerque, N.M.
DH 82A	Cliff Robertson, 14920 Ramos Pl., Pacific Palisades, Calif.
DH 82A	Robert E. Rust, RFD 3, Fayetteville, Georgia 30214
Tiger Moth	John Schildberg, Greenfield, Iowa
DH 82A	Bill Shaw, 22126 Providencia St, Woodland Hills, Calif.
DH 82A	Ralph M. Wefel, 8400 Fullbrights Avenue, Canoga Park, Calif. 91306
DH 82C	Buck Wheat, Box 639, Richland, Washington
DH 82A	Col. Harry E. Williams, 5 N.W. Road, Randolph AFB, Texas 78148
DH 82A	Col. Harry E. Williams, 5 N.W. Road, Randolph AFB, Texas 78148
DH 82A	J. F. McNulty, Rockford, Illinois

GUIDE FOR TIGER MOTH ENTHUSIASTS

SCALE PLANS

"Aeromodeller" Plans Service, 13/35 Bridge Street, Hemel Hempstead, Herts

MARKINGS

Harleyford's "Aircraft Camouflage & Markings 1907–1954", available direct from Harleyford Publications Ltd, Letchworth, Herts

CLUBS

The Tiger Club, Redhill Aerodrome, Surrey (Michael Jones, Secretary)
The American Tiger Club, International Sport Aviation Centre, Municipal Airport, Waco, Texas (Frank A. Price, Secretary)

FACTORY HELP (ENGINES)

Rolls-Royce Ltd, Small Engine Division
de Havilland Engines, c/o Mr C. Downs, Support Office, Service Depo ,
Leavesden, Watford, Herts
Hawker de Havilland Australia Pty Ltd, Engine Division, P.O. Box 78,
Lidcombe, NSW 2141, c/o R. J. Moppett, Engineering Manager

FLIGHT WEAR

American Sport Aviation Society Inc., c/o Chuck Gupton, 2938 Eckleson Street, Lakewood, Calif. 90712
British Goggles: D. Lewis Ltd, P.O. Box 2DL, 124 Great Portland Street, London W1

MODELS

1/72nd scale plastic kit: Airfix Products Ltd, Haldane Place, London SW18

MANUALS

Factory: Rolls-Royce Ltd, Small Engine Division
Factory: de Havilland Engines, Leavesden, Watford
Stag Lane Flight (Australia) (see address below)
Various: Air Service Caravan, Municipal Airport, New Bedford, Mass. 02747
Various: Air Navigation Service, 1837 East D. St, Bellville, Illinois 62221
(C. A. Woodford, Manager)

AIRCRAFT

The Stag Lane Flight, 121 Plateau Road, Bilgola, NSW 2107, Australia
(Mr M. Whittington, Hon. Secretary)
Stag Lane USA representative: Leo Gay, 2511 Allenjay Street, Glendale,
Calif. 91208
Rollason Aircraft & Engines Ltd, Croydon, Surrey

PARTS

Rollason Aircraft & Engines Ltd
Provincial Airmotive Corporation, R.R.1, Port Severn, Honey Harbor,
Ontario, Canada
Flying wires: Leaven Bros, c/o Doug Leaven, 3200 Dufferin Street, Toronto, Canada
Brake sets: (Bellanca, with Scott heel brakes), Leo Gay (address above)

FAA AIRCRAFT TYPE CERTIFICATES (ATC) ON TIGER MOTHS

English: ATC A8EU – DH 82A, 7th Feb., 1966
Australian: ATC A5PC – DH 82A, 15th Aug. 1968

ADDITIONAL MANUALS & LITERATURE

Wing Commander F. E. F. Prince, Fidlers Hall, Eashing, Godalming, Surrey

SOUTH AFRICA

ZSBXB	Mr. I. W. Hosford, 2 Quest Road, Milnerton, Capetown, S. Africa	Ex-SAAF 4636